HOLLYWOOD
ON THE
VELD

WHEN MOVIE MAYHEM GRIPPED
THE CITY OF GOLD

◆ TED BOTHA ◆

JONATHAN BALL PUBLISHERS
JOHANNESBURG · CAPE TOWN

© Text: Ted Botha 2025
© Photos: *Stage & Cinema*
© Published edition: Jonathan Ball Publishers 2025

Published in South Africa in 2025 by
JONATHAN BALL PUBLISHERS
A division of Media24 (Pty) Ltd
PO Box 33977
Jeppestown
2043

ISBN 978-1-77619-468-1
ebook ISBN 978-1-77619-469-8

jonathanball.co.za
x.com/JonathanBallPub
facebook.com/JonathanBallPublishers

Cover by Sean Robertson
Cover images: 'In the Johannesburg Zoo' postcard, c. 1918,
and *Stage & Cinema*
Design and typesetting by Martine Barker
Maps by Roland Metcalfe
Set in Iowan Old Style

Ex Africa semper aliquid novi.

– Pliny the Elder

*South Africa! South Africa! How often people talk
of it to me! And yet, somehow, one never sees any but the
old spots – New York, London, Paris, Monte Carlo.*

– Gloria Swanson,
one of the biggest movie stars
of the Hollywood silent era

CONTENTS

JOHANNESBURG

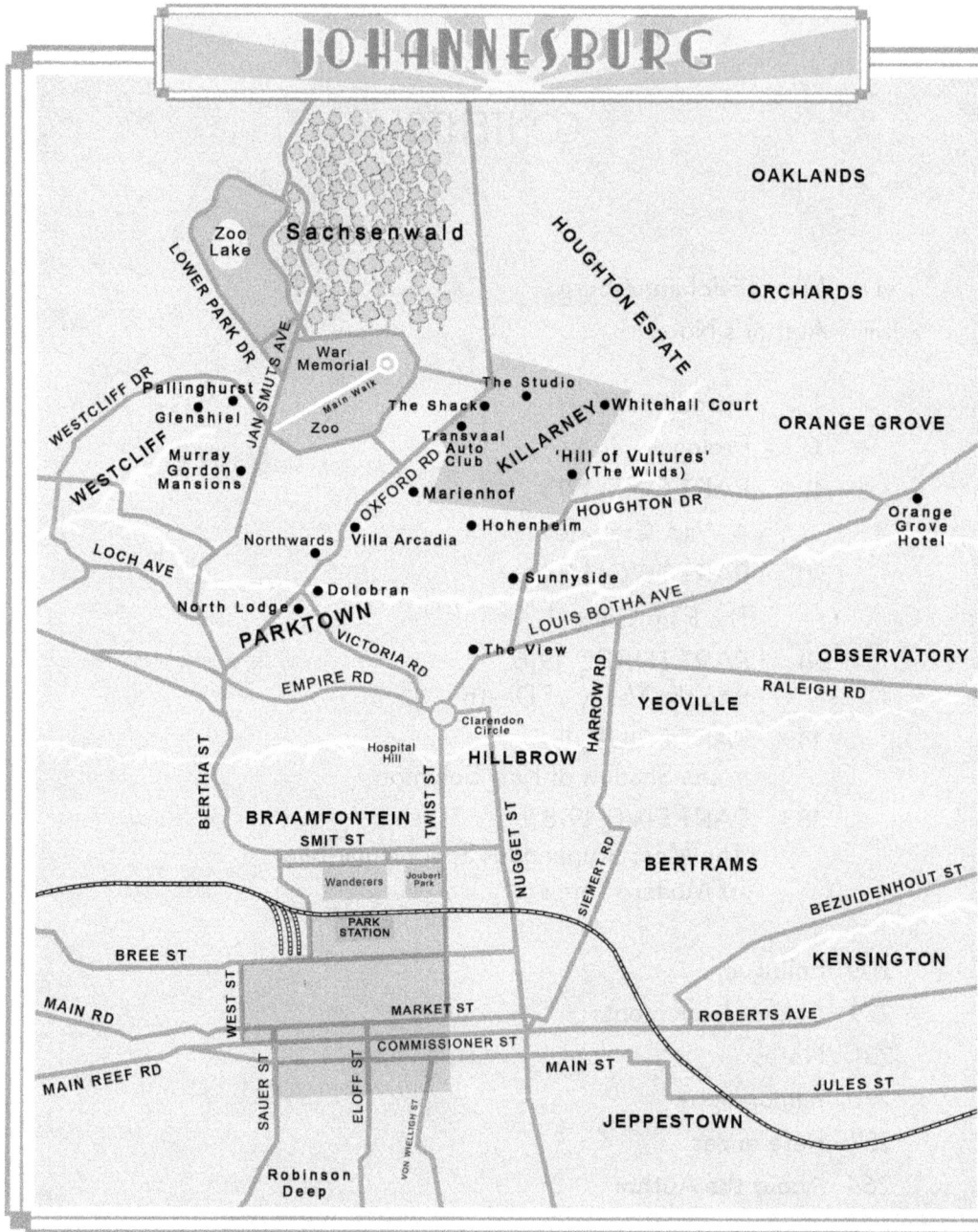

OAKLANDS

ORCHARDS

Zoo Lake

Sachsenwald

HOUGHTON ESTATE

ORANGE GROVE

LOWER PARK DR

JAN SMUTS AVE

War Memorial

Main Walk

The Studio

Zoo

The Shack●

●Whitehall Court

WESTCLIFF DR

Pallinghurst●

Glenshiel●

Transvaal Auto Club

KILLARNEY

'Hill of Vultures' (The Wilds)

WESTCLIFF

Murray Gordon● Mansions

OXFORD RD

●Marienhof

HOUGHTON DR

Orange Grove Hotel

LOCH AVE

Northwards● Villa Arcadia

●Hohenheim

●Dolobran

●Sunnyside

North Lodge●

PARKTOWN

VICTORIA RD

LOUIS BOTHA AVE

OBSERVATORY

●The View

EMPIRE RD

HARROW RD

RALEIGH RD

YEOVILLE

Clarendon Circle

BERTHA ST

Hospital Hill

TWIST ST

HILLBROW

BRAAMFONTEIN

SMIT ST

NUGGET ST

BERTRAMS

Wanderers

Joubert Park

SIEMERT RD

BEZUIDENHOUT ST

PARK STATION

BREE ST

KENSINGTON

MAIN RD

WEST ST

MARKET ST

ROBERTS AVE

COMMISSIONER ST

MAIN REEF RD

SAUER ST

ELOFF ST

VON WELLIGH ST

MAIN ST

JULES ST

JEPPESTOWN

Robinson Deep

CENTRAL JOHANNESBURG

JOUBERT PARK

JOHANNESBURG ART GALLERY

WANDERERS

NOORD ST
NOORD ST
TWIST ST

PARK STATION

DE VILLIERS ST

UNION GROUND

JOUBERT ST

HOEK ST

PLEIN ST

RISSIK HOTEL

JB BROADCASTING STUDIO

METRO

BREE ST

BIJOU

FILLIS'S CIRCUS

BRISTOL HOTEL

JEPPE ST

SAUER ST

FRASER ST

SIMMONDS ST

HARRISON ST

LOVEDAY ST

ORPHEUM THEATRE

PLAZA

PHONE EXCHANGE

KERK ST

GRAND NATIONAL HOTEL

SUPREME COURT

LUTJE'S LABONAR HOTEL

VAUDETTE THEATRE

PRITCHARD ST

THE STAR NEWSPAPER

HEATH'S HOTEL

OXFORD THEATRE

PRESIDENT ST

DIAGONAL ST

MARKET SQUARE

TRAM TERMINUS

CITY HALL

POST OFFICE

STANDARD THEATRE

TIVOLI

MARKET ST

KORT ST

COLONIAL & BANKING TRUST

NATIONAL BANK

BARCLAYS BANK

CARLTON THEATRE

THE EMPIRE

GLADSTONE HOTEL

LIBRARY HOTEL

PALLADIUM

CORNER HOUSE

CARLTON HOTEL

GRAND THEATRE

COMMISSIONER ST

GAIETY

CONSOLIDATED GOLDFIELDS

RAND CLUB

HIS MAJESTY'S

COLOSSEUM

GLOBE

THEATRE ROYAL

FOX ST

WEST ST

FERREIRA ST

MCLAREN ST

HOLLARD ST

MAIN ST

GOLDFIELDS HOTEL

LOVEDAY ST

RISSIK ST

GOVERNMENT SQUARE

ELOFF ST

VON BRANDIS ST

KRUIS ST

SMALL ST

VON WIELLIGH ST

DELVERS ST

TROYE ST

MARSHALL SQUARE

CHAMBER OF MINES

MARSHALL ST

GANDHI'S OFFICE

ANDERSON ST

vii

AUTHOR'S NOTE

In the early days of movies, when things were often in chaos, the words 'produce' and 'direct' were used interchangeably. As the big studios started taking shape, producers were the money men – with names like Mayer, Zukor and Goldwyn – and they became famous. Only a few directors – whose place was on set and behind the camera, such as DW Griffith and Cecil B DeMille – were well known.

Very few people filled both roles, producer and director. IW Schlesinger was one of them.

Movies in the silent era of the early 20th century were very short, maybe one reel or 1 000 feet, running for 15 minutes. In about 1913, 'features' arrived, lasting for six reels or more, which meant more than an hour.

That changed everything.

INTRODUCTION

In 1913 – near the height of Johannesburg's rich, violent and intoxicating golden age – an American millionaire living in a penthouse at the top of the Carlton Hotel suddenly had a mad idea. He would go into competition with a brand-new industry that had the entire world entranced – the movies. His name was Isidore William Schlesinger, better known by his initials, IW.

More than 110 years later, it's hard to believe any of this ever happened. The dusty mining town was booming, to be sure, but it was thousands of miles away from the major movie centres, London, Paris, Berlin, New York and especially Los Angeles, where a dirt-tracked piece of farmland was still to become famous around the world as 'Hollywood'.

Movies were in their infancy. Countless small companies were manoeuvring their way through a jungle of constantly changing technology and public tastes, and in global terms South Africa was just a blip on the screen. Yet within several years IW Schlesinger had not only joined the international melee but triggered some of the most important events in early motion pictures.

With no experience in entertainment, he started buying theatres, and then produced movies to show in them. He sent his crews on location, to film in the bushveld and at historic battle sites, at Victoria Falls, and in Zululand and the forests of Portuguese East Africa, when the norm almost everywhere else in the world was to shoot close to home on confined stages, often inside buildings, with painted canvases serving as backdrops.

He employed extras in record-breaking numbers – up to 25 000, by some accounts – and was one of the first moviemakers to use African actors in leading roles. In 1916, he started shooting the first of two huge, very costly and unprecedented historical spectacles, which themselves would make news at home and abroad.

All of this happened at a time of turbulence and upheaval in Johannesburg. IW started his movie company the very same month that the devastating miners' strike of 1913 erupted, and he ended production just after the 1922 Red Revolt. His cameramen captured both disastrous events on film.

By 1919, the American had produced some of the biggest, most expensive and most innovative feature movies the world had ever seen, not only the two historical spectacles but also the adventure stories *King Solomon's Mines* and *Allan Quatermain*. After these came a romance between two teenage castaways on a tropical island, *The Blue Lagoon*.

Few people today realise that IW made the first versions of these now famous and often remade movies, or that he built a studio in the shadow of the Parktown ridge. Indeed, little physical evidence remains that any of his empire ever existed.

His vision for his movies was breathtaking, not only in scale but also in the array of people from around the world who were associated with his empire.

Through his doors, over two decades, came Englishmen and Russians, Americans and Germans, Australians and Indians, dancers, novelists, inventors, broadcasters, politicians, talent agents, actors, directors. From a little-known new filmmaker in London named Alfred Hitchcock to the novelist Olive Schreiner; from Hollywood producers like Carl Laemmle and Adolph Zukor to the Russian dancer George Balanchine; from the statesman Jan Smuts to the novelist Sir Henry Rider Haggard; from Mahatma Gandhi to George Bernard Shaw; from PL Travers, the author of *Mary Poppins*, to Sir Percy Fitzpatrick; from Sol Plaatje, the African nationalist and himself a movie lover, to the Russo-German actress Olga Tschechowa, who was later wooed by Adolf Hitler – the list goes on.

In both physical appearance and work ethic, IW bore an uncanny resemblance to the titans of Hollywood, and he followed much the same path that they did. Sometimes, quite remarkably, he was also far ahead of them. In the turbulent 1920s, when the American studios were floundering around in the uncertain new age of sound movies, IW had already bought an American company that would help him become one of the first to make a 'talkie' picture.

Like the US media tycoon William Randolph Hearst, IW married a movie starlet (Hearst wed Marion Davies; IW a young British actress named Mabel May) and each one built a mansion for himself. Hearst had a castle overlooking San Simeon in central California, which he started building in 1919; four years later, IW dug the foundations for Whitehall Court, his architectural confection that was a strange amalgam of an apartment block and a mansion, between the Parktown and Houghton ridges.

When IW died, in 1949, a story in *The New York Times* suggested that if he had lived in his home country, the US, 'he would be a world figure like Henry Ford or JP Morgan.' Even though he never gave up his American passport, and he often travelled back there, home remained Johannesburg, and IW's passion for South Africa, both its landscape and its potential, was almost fanatical. Paraphrasing the American journalist Horace Greeley's famous dictum, 'Go West, young man,' IW exhorted people to 'Go South, young man, where Nature invites you and where health, happiness and prosperity await you.'

His demise in the world of movies came in the early 1930s during a perfect storm: the Great Depression; a devastating fire at the new studio he had built in London; and a protracted legal battle with the major American studios over several important patents for talking pictures. In the end, he was brought to his knees by the very entertainment Mecca that he had meticulously tried to copy – Hollywood.

Much of the story of those early moviemaking days in Johannesburg – like the rest of IW's life – died with him. His studio under the Parktown ridge eventually made way for a shopping mall, the apartment buildings of Killarney and a golf course, his own name all but forgotten.

Secretive in the extreme, IW never granted interviews, kept his affairs private, almost obsessively so, and always had a small coterie of front men to do his bidding for him. In an industry as public as entertainment, he was a master at staying almost entirely out of the spotlight.

Even the burial place that he chose for himself – in the middle of some nondescript veld and thorn trees on the farm Zebediela – ensured that he carried his desire for privacy to the grave.

The journey to unearth IW's story has been as long and frustrating as it has been fascinating. It took me to libraries and archives in Johannesburg, New York, Cambridge, Cape Town and London, where I riffled through the pages of many a forgotten publication and dusty newspaper. I eventually found a long-lost manuscript that, I hoped, would disclose many secrets about his life. In the end, it didn't.

But by connecting all the dots, a line here, a paragraph there, a mention in someone's biography, comments by people who had worked with him, errant reports that had slipped through the cracks, court cases that, much to IW's chagrin, had mentioned his name, an image of the man has gradually emerged.

He was a visionary as much as a gambler; a micromanager and a globalist; a workaholic who expected nothing less of his employees; a fastidious dresser; headstrong, fiery and single-minded; someone who didn't suffer fools and followed his own course, regardless of what people thought of him; someone who was able to spot a con artist a mile away and was dedicated to those few people whom he trusted.

He left the Lower East Side of New York in 1894 with almost nothing except a fob his mother had given him – and which he had to pawn on arrival in Cape Town. Soon he was trekking thousands of miles along the back roads of southern Africa selling insurance to anyone – from Afrikaner farmer to railway worker to Swazi chief. Within a year or two he had broken all the records, and over the next decade he invested in numerous businesses, insurance and real estate mostly.

In 1913, IW purchased a theatre in downtown Johannesburg, and a business that he didn't care much for, entertainment, suddenly became a passion. A man usually very careful with his money was suddenly beguiled by an enterprise whose existence couldn't financially be justified. Within two years he was planning to shoot a spectacular historical movie (*Winning a Continent*) and then follow it up with an even bigger one (*The Symbol of Sacrifice*).

On both sets there was as much drama on the ground during filming as there would be on screen: political intrigue; clashes of oversized personalities; public outbursts; lots of money being spent and wasted; big risks taken; plenty of madness and disasters; incendiary judicial inquiries; and several tragic deaths. And behind it all, mostly standing in the shadows but always in total control, was a man with a dream and a crazy idea.

This is the strange, never-told-before story of how Hollywood on the Veld began and, quite magnificently, reached for the stars.

PROLOGUE

Early on the morning of Sunday 15 October 1916, the ominous rumbling could be heard long before the chanting, stomping crowds appeared over the horizon. On the hillside to the east, like an audience gathering for an open-air spectacle, people kept arriving, a few by car but most by wagon, by Cape cart, on horseback and on foot.

A tall, handsome young man stood on the ridge, checking the positions where he had stationed the other cameramen. There were six of them in all, each one waiting behind a heavy wooden box with a crank handle fixed to a tripod, the strange equipment standing out like small sentinels. Besides the four cameras on the ridge, there were two in the valley below.

About each cameraman, as he stood waiting, there was a sense of excitement and apprehension. They understood how much was riding on this single event: thousands of pounds spent on costumes and equipment, thousands of extras organised, months of preparation, intricate battle formations planned, and even an entire waterway created. There would be a single chance to capture it on film – just one.

Luckily for the tall man in charge of the camera team, his men were all experienced and had covered hard news before – strikes, wars, rebellions, even expeditions to the Antarctic – so they would hopefully be ready for whatever came their way.

And come their way it did.

At six o'clock the sun slipped over the jagged koppies behind them, quickly spreading its glow between the rocks and across the veld. The almost treeless terrain fell away to the valley floor, a narrow stream cutting it in half. Several dozen ox-wagons were drawn up in a half-moon formation, a laager, behind them a dam big enough to form a natural barrier.

Around the laager were several hundred people dressed in old-fashioned outfits. The men wore waistcoats, neckcloths and straw hats, and some of them sat on the backs of the wagons, casually smoking crooked old ceramic pipes, while women moved haphazardly between them, their dresses full and big-sleeved, the ensemble finished off with shawls and oddly shaped poke bonnets.

Nearby, several dozen horses were tied up, occasionally pulling anxiously at their tethers when they heard a sudden noise, which was usually a shot from one of the old rifles that were being handed out by a military man at a nearby tent.

Striding across the veld from the pair of cameras in the valley, maybe a hundred yards away, were several men, two of them dressed in suits, as if they were on their way to the office, and a police officer. From his movements it was clear that the stockier of the two suited men, with sandy-coloured hair and lively eyes behind metal-rimmed glasses, was in command. In his hand he held a bullhorn.

After conferring with the men at the wagons, he pointed to the southern end of the dam, where there was a sluice, and below it the narrow stream that would play a crucial role in the day's events.

Up on the ridge, in the meantime, the crowd behind the cameramen had grown in number, people from nearby towns and gold mines – both white and black – who had heard the news: *Something was happening at Elsburg!* In no time, hundreds became thousands.

In the open space between them and the cameras patrolled scores of policemen, some on horseback, while other men in uniform stood at positions along the eastern ridge and down its side.

Several minutes before seven o'clock, the threatening rumbling began, a sound both in the air and on the ground, like an approaching stampede. It grew louder until the first group of 500 men breeched the ridge, the air filled with a chilling sound. Then came another squadron, then a third, until they were several thousand strong. To a man they were dressed in *moochis* made of animal skins, as well as armlets and leg pieces, each one carrying a shield and an assegai.

Once they had all come to a stop, the dust churned up by their stomping feet hung menacingly over them. In the valley, the men in waistcoats had by now taken up their positions under and behind the crescent of wagons, their rifles at the ready. Unlike the carefully arranged warriors on the ridge, however, there was a distinct sense of disorder about them.

A rushing sound of water came from near the wagons, as the sluice was opened to flood the stream. At that moment, the man with the sandy hair, who had once again taken his place behind the camera on the valley floor, raised a hand to the ridge and shouted into his bullhorn. The African warriors came streaming down the hill, chanting and waving their assegais as they ran.

The cameramen had barely begun filming the warriors charge the wagons when something strange happened. They heard gunfire, erratic yet persistent. And then, from their right-hand side, the direction of the wagons, came a dozen men on horseback, charging straight for the oncoming horde. The guns kept blazing.

In almost no time, the two sides confronted each other, and the men were clashing and falling. Africans were being shot at, unable to cover themselves from the stampeding men around them, and whites were being pulled off their horses and attacked. The man with the bullhorn ran towards them and started waving and shouting, but whatever he said was drowned out by the noise and gunfire around him.

Dozens of policemen raced down the hill and were quickly in

the midst of the fighting. By this stage, the warriors had reached the wagons and were in hand-to-hand combat with the men there. More rifle shots rang out, even from between the rocks, and people were running in all directions. Numerous men from both sides fell to the ground and didn't get up.

The cameramen on the hill had a choice: to keep filming, with dozens of policemen and technicians running haphazardly between the fighters and trying to break them up, or to miss their single opportunity to capture the production's biggest and most important scene. It didn't seem like any choice at all.

As the fighting raged on in front of them, the greatest movie in the world lay on the brink of collapse.

PART ONE
1913

A Wild, Crazy Idea

'The handsomest theatre in the subcontinent', the Empire Palace.

THE FALL OF THE EMPIRE

It all began, quite fittingly, with a death.

One wintry Monday morning three years earlier, on 19 May 1913, a flurry of people made their way to Commissioner Street on the east side of Marshalltown. Snaking around the corner into Kruis Street was a line beginning under a marquee that sparkled brightly at night. Even in daytime, two large words identified the building, 'Empire Palace', but to everyone it was more familiarly known as 'The Empire'.

With ornate turrets at each corner, the two-storey gabled building had become a landmark. 'A spectacle of Edwardian luxury with 18 boxes, plus upholstery and drapes in green and gold – the handsomest theatre in the subcontinent,' a newspaper bragged when it opened in 1906, although there was surely nothing as splendid between Commissioner Street and Leicester Square. With its 1 200 seats, the Empire was as big as the Aldwych Theatre in Covent Garden, and bigger than the Liberty Theatre on 42nd Street in New York.

Inside the foyer, usually full of gaily dressed people bustling into a performance of a play or a musical, the outfits were now sombre work clothes or plain dresses. The theatre was already full, so new arrivals stood in the aisles and at the back or peered from the boxes above.

No one was calling it a funeral exactly, but that's what it felt like. The death of the Empire, and they the mourners who had come to pay their last respects. Many of them, whether housewife, miner, salesman or receptionist, carried a cherished memory, a performance they'd seen on this very stage: Marie Lloyd singing favourites like 'Wink the Other Eye' and 'Twiggy-Vous'; the Spanish dancer La Tortajada clattering across the floorboards; Paul Cinquevalli, 'the king of jugglers'; the opera singer Signor Foli from Ireland; the Flying Jordan acrobats; the French tightrope walker Blondin.

From across the world, artists had come to Johannesburg, as if to some kind of El Dorado, a place of fantastic wealth and possible fame. Even though it was almost 400 miles inland from the nearest port, Durban, it had earned a place on most global tours – South Africa, Batavia, India, China, Australia – not just for solo artists but for major productions fresh off the stages of New York and London. 'Recently on Broadway!' read the banners, and 'Just off the West End!' They made the city feel just a little bit closer to the outside world.

It had been like that almost from the very moment that gold was discovered in 1886. A troupe of Australian actors and opera singers, with several tons of costumes and scenery, made the excruciating trip to the City of Gold, first by train and then, when the tracks ran out, by ox-wagon. In the lead was a man previously known as Isaac Israel, who, with his black beard and retroussé nose, renamed himself to sound as magnificent as he was, Luscombe Searelle. On the mining camp he set up a shed that he called the Theatre Royal.

After that, things were never the same. Musicals, boxing tourneys, betting parlours, penny arcades, roller-skating rinks, bars, peep shows, a racing track, motorcycle events – anything and everything was tried that could entertain the fast-growing town, of men mostly to start with, looking for places to spend their money. The number of brothels exploded.

And oh, the circuses!

Feeley competed with Cooke, Wirth and, of course, the German

Pagel and his wife, who 'swore like a trooper', sold tickets but never gave change and 'secured unprecedented publicity by driving in an open car accompanied by a large-maned lion which went with her on foot on a leash'.

Out of them all, however, theatres were the fulcrum, regularly bending and shaping themselves to offer whatever was needed: vaudeville, music hall artistes, Shakespeare, magic lanterns, Gilbert & Sullivan, dance troupes, opera, tightrope walkers, magicians and prestidigitators like The Great Carter and Horace Goldin. They took to the stages of the Empire, His Majesty's, the Grand and the Gaiety, the Standard, the German Turnhalle and the Wanderers, where Mark Twain, during his world tour of 1895, held his one-man show.

For showmanship, few could outdo the circus master Frank Fillis. In 1888, four years before an actual train steamed into town, he brought his own train, a caravan of wagons that travelled all the way from Ladysmith, in Natal, preceded by a 'Ceylon elephant', five lions, five tigers, four jackals, two hyenas, two four-horned sheep, zebra, and so it went on. With them were tumblers, gymnasts, pigeon charmers, clowns and horses. The tent he set up was 130 feet in diameter, and later his property was big enough to stretch between Loveday and Harrison streets. Even the dour and serious president of the Transvaal, Paul Kruger, travelled from Pretoria to see Fillis perform stupefying acts, such as recreating Niagara Falls using thousands of gallons of precious water that the dry mining town seriously lacked.

Entertainment was a balm, an elixir, an aphrodisiac, for those who needed to forget their isolation and regular adversity. If it wasn't violent strikes, it was rampant phthisis among miners and unfair taxes foisted on the foreign-born residents called Uitlanders by Kruger's government. A pervasive feeling of inequality and discontent pitted miner against magnate. Then came the war between the British and the Boers, in 1899, when almost everyone escaped, bought a one-way ticket out of town, to anywhere they could. Three years later, with the signing of a peace treaty in 1902, they returned in their thousands, and entertainment in the City of Gold was soon bigger than ever.

Excess kept breaking boundaries. More and more money was spent to bring out shows, no matter how big, sometimes with entire orchestras, and to sail them, and tons of equipment, across the Atlantic and then put them on a train for another two days to reach the highveld. Visiting artists were booked for months in hotels like Luthje's Langham and the Grand, sometimes even at the most famous of them all, the Carlton, which took up almost an entire block, provided air conditioning and a central vacuum cleaning system, and in its Turkish baths in the basement mining magnates were said to clinch their deals.

WC Fields, Lillie Langtry, Owen Nares, Zena Dare – they all headlined here. And their salaries kept going up. At the Palladium, 'only open for a few months, it came to light that the management was paying £650 a week for artists, including Daisy Wood, a vaudeville star. (It was an exorbitant sum, equivalent to more than £14 000 today.)

The spending spree just couldn't last, and by 1912 things started falling apart – rapidly. Actors were left stranded, and auctions and charity drives had to be held to pay for their tickets home, and for lodgings until then. Quite suddenly, it wasn't just the Empire that was facing liquidation. It was almost every big theatre in the country.

The way things were going, there would be many funerals.

As the auctioneer Richard Currie stood on the bare stage of the Empire in May 1913, he was straight-faced. It didn't take him long to see that the people in front of him had no interest in what he was selling off. They were mostly curious spectators.

He had a long list of items to go through, most of them a tougher sell than usual, laden as they were with incredible debt, and their liabilities understated. There were leases, shares and 'furniture and appurtenances' of the Empire and several other theatres around the country, all of them called the Grand, except for one, the Hall on the Sea in Durban. Included in one of the leases was an account for £20 000 spent on actors.

Who in their right mind would buy any of this?

Two men sat in the front, directly below Currie. One of them was Leonard Rayne, well known to audiences, friendly and respected. His theatre, the Standard, was almost the only one to have survived the ravaging storm tearing through his competitors.

Next to him was a smaller man who was impeccably dressed, as if he had been put together by his own personal dresser that morning. He wore a starched collar, bow tie and colourful shirt, and not a hair on his head was out of place.

Most people at the Empire would have known who he was, would have already seen his unusual Talbot touring car, which was famous for its speed, parked outside. He was the American Isidore William Schlesinger. His reason for being at the Empire was less clear, however, for his business was in real estate and insurance.

When Currie opened the floor, the auditorium was as silent as a church. Only two offers were made, for one of the Grands, and both offers were paltry. 'For the rest there were no bids.'

As the crowd trickled out into the glaring white winter light and headed back to work or to Eloff or Twist streets for the tram, it was a sad day indeed. It felt like the end not only of a once-great theatre but also of an exciting world of showmanship for which the city had been famous for almost three decades.

Little did they know that it was nothing of the kind. It was not a funeral at all, but the birth of something incredible, something they couldn't have imagined in their wildest dreams. Like a phoenix rising, a whole new era of entertainment was upon them, and it would be led by the man being chauffeured away from the Empire in his shiny Talbot sedan.

MAKING THINGS HUM

For several months already, from early 1913, things had been happening behind closed doors.

Inside a number of offices close to Market Square – at Barclays Bank and the imposing ten-storey National Bank, but most importantly at an ornate building directly opposite it on Harrison Street, the Colonial & Banking Trust – deals had been cut, voices raised, heavy sighs of resignation exhaled and contracts drawn up and signed.

On the one side of the table were the desperate owners of the Empire, the Palladium, the Orpheum, the Alhambra and several other theatres around the country – the number was growing all the time – along with their creditors, the banks.

On the other side was a man flush with cash and a well-known taste for investing in businesses that were struggling and cheap, despite knowing nothing about them. Besides being able to 'sell hot potatoes in Hell', he was 'always on the *qui vive*', as a friend put it, sniffing around for a new venture, and his ability to step in and turn around a failing business had earned him the reputation for being a kind of Mr Fixit with a Midas touch.

It was IW Schlesinger.

As much as he told people he wasn't a gambler, Schlesinger clearly loved a risk, especially if he was the only person betting and he had complete control over the odds. His mining magnate friend Solly Joel, who had a passion for race horses, once invited him to the Turffontein track. IW declined, but added, 'I will go with you only when I own the race track, the jockeys and the horses.'

And that was exactly what he had in mind for the country's theatres: buy as many as possible, for as little as possible, and then restructure and control them all. He believed in the power of the trust, a kinder word for a cartel or a monopoly. He would cut costs, merge businesses, put them all under one administration.

Men who were once known for owning theatres were suddenly demoted and offered jobs managing them. There was the young Australian Rufe Naylor, '(c)olourful to a fault,' a man who 'alternated between "turf accountancy", as he called it, otherwise bookmaking, theatre ownership (the Amalgamated chain) and newspaper production'; the Vaudette chain's HS Kingdon; and, most regrettably, Edgar Hyman, who for almost two decades had reigned over the Empire and been an entertainment pioneer.

The people who couldn't abide the humiliation of IW's ultimatum refused or resisted. In Cape Town, the well-known Fischer family and the respected Wilhelm Wolfram held out for as long as they could. Wolfram lasted for a year or two, the Fischers, quite astoundingly, for four.

Schlesinger came in like a blunderbuss. As one American magazine wrote, he 'fairly makes things hum'. His brash business style rubbed many people up the wrong way, especially those used to the more formal British manner of doing things.

But much about IW didn't sync with what the Rand was used to – where he came from, how he made his money, where he lived, who he fraternised with. He seemed to revel in his position as an outsider from the very start.

He had arrived from New York in 1894 at the age of twenty-three with nothing in his pocket, 'to try his luck.' Within a year he had made a fortune in insurance, and then in real estate, starting suburbs with names neither entirely American nor British, like Parkhurst and Orange Grove. Then he moved into agriculture, fruit canning, banks and retail stores. Each year, the list kept growing.

The Carlton Hotel opened in 1906, the same year as IW's favourite hotel in London, the Ritz. He moved in two years later. In his suite on the top floor, facing Eloff Street, he often held meetings as early as 6 am. He bought the Carlton in 1925.

Even his Jewishness was slightly off-kilter. He was not of German extraction from England (like Solly Joel, Barney Barnato, Alfred Beit, Lionel Phillips and George Albu) but Hungarian from America. His family's address for many years had been on Houston Street on the Lower East Side of Manhattan.

Instead of living in a mansion on the ridges of Doornfontein or Parktown, which he could easily afford, he chose the top floor of the Carlton Hotel. In his penthouse the lights burned from five every morning, and he went on till eleven at night. For him there weren't enough minutes in a day to do what he needed.

'If ever I saw a man with his soul aflame, it was IWS,' wrote one acquaintance, 'for no trouble was too great, no detail too small, no task too long, for him to undertake if it meant the success of the particular scheme on which his attention was focused for the time being.'

And in the middle of 1913, that 'scheme' was entertainment. With the Empire and a growing number of theatres in Johannesburg and Pretoria in hand, he travelled to Port Elizabeth, East London, Durban, Lourenço Marques, Bulawayo, to buy more ailing properties. So often did he travel on the Union Express that he joked with Sir William Hoy, the head of the South African Railways, that he was one of its best customers.

By the middle of 1913, signs were already going up above the entrances of Schlesinger's properties announcing that they were now part of a brand-new company called 'African Theatres'.

But what next? How could he stop an entertainment empire in free fall? What legerdemain was he going to perform to save them? The answer to that question lay far away, on two very different continents, in an industry that, typically, Schlesinger knew nothing about and which itself was in a state of flux like never before – the movies.

A CONFLUX OF APPARENT MIRACLES

It's hard to imagine today, more than a century later, how chaotic and messy the advent of motion pictures was – even the very word 'movie' was tussled over, considered by some Americans to be vulgar – with countless people trying to get in on the action. By 1913, it had built up into a global frenzy.

If, in the clandestine world of invention, there can be such a thing as a beginning, for movies it had come 20 years earlier, in the early 1890s. A number of men in England, America and Europe had been working on devices to show moving pictures – something more elaborate than just shifting slides in a magic lantern. Then, at about the same time, there were several remarkable breakthroughs.

In New York, a Scotsman named William Kennedy Dickson came out with the Kinetograph. What it filmed, though, could be viewed by only one person at a time, looking through a peephole in another machine called the Kinetoscope. The slightly more advanced Pleograph was brought out by the Polish inventor Kazimierz Prószyński.

Finally, in Paris in 1895, the brothers Auguste and Louis Lumière introduced the world to the Cinématographe, both camera and projector, which finally gave moving pictures wings to fly onto walls and screens. On 28 December, the first projection of a film before a paying audience took place at the Grand Café, near the Place Vendôme. It was hardly an auspicious start: the brothers could get barely 35 people to pay admission. 'No major daily newspaper covered the event. (But) within days, lines trailed down the Boulevard des Capucines for four hundred yards.'

In London the following year, 1896, the American magician Carl Hertz, famous for his vanishing birdcage act, was finishing off a run at the Alhambra of his popular show – 'Entertainment of Wonders and Conflux of Apparent Miracles' – and was about to set off on a year-long world tour, starting, as most tours of the Pacific region did, in South Africa.

The Alhambra happened to have two models of a brand-new British projector called the Theatrograph, one of which, kept for emergencies, Hertz kept bothering the theatre to let him take on his travels.

The ship to Cape Town, the Union-Castle line's two-year-old *Norman*, was the perfect place to test the new machine. The 'first truly "modern" Cape mail steamer', it boasted a beautifully panelled dining saloon, with light pouring through a dome, and a lounge with recessed settees, where Hertz set up his Theatrograph.

One can imagine the first-class passengers sitting enthralled as they watched the short films – five segments of 30 seconds each – barely noticing the strange west coast of Africa pass by outside. Hertz, after honing his new 'entertainment of wonder' at sea, was now ready for Johannesburg … and the Empire.

The ten-year-old City of Gold was more on edge than usual when he arrived, for it was only a few days after Dr Leander Starr Jameson, a close associate of Cecil John Rhodes, had led a force of 500 armed men from Bechuanaland to seize Johannesburg and precipitate a rising against the Boer government, which the Uitlanders accused of denying them political rights and of charging exorbitant taxes but delivering little in return. The raid failed, the men were quickly rounded up, and the ringleaders were sentenced to death.

'Those were stirring days in Johannesburg,' Hertz wrote. 'Martial law was in force … One night some shots were fired just outside, and everyone in the theatre jumped up and rushed out, leaving me standing there alone.'

Suddenly, cheering could be heard outside – the ringleaders' sentences had been commuted! The jubilant crowd came back inside, but it wasn't to watch Hertz but to drink and celebrate at the bar. 'When things had quietened down, we did big business and played to crowded houses.'

Of all the acts in his 'Entertainment of Wonders and Conflux of Apparent Miracles', it was the short showings of the Theatrograph, tagged on at the end, that had the audience on their feet.

'It is hard today to comprehend the full impact on audiences of 1896 of their first exposure to motion pictures,' was written of a very similar scene playing out in New York that year. 'Their amazement ... shows what a great jump it was from the mechanically produced moving images in the magic lantern.'

So popular was the Theatrograph that Hertz stayed on in South Africa for six months, long enough to befriend the mining magnate Barney Barnato and go to the races at Turffontein with him.

Posters outside the Empire declared it 'The Photo-Electric Sensation of the Day! The latest invention in photography, the most startling scientific marvel of the age.'

Cottoning on to its potential, the Empire's Edgar Hyman quickly got his own camera shipped out from London. Rather than waiting for film segments to arrive from abroad to show at his theatre, he would make his own.

His most famous excursion was in 1898, when he set out for Pretoria with his orchestra leader, David Foote, doubling up as his assistant. Their goal was to film President Kruger, who was known to be publicity-shy, as he entered the republic's parliament, the Raadsaal.

The film, even though it was only seconds long, was taken to Kruger's residence a while later, along with a small screen and a piano to play music to accompany the presentation.

'We have come to show the picture of His Honour going

to *raad*,' Hyman told Kruger's wife, Gezina.

The president, a fervently religious man who read the Bible regularly and knew many passages off by heart, immediately demanded that the piano be removed. 'What is this godless thing doing in my house?' he asked. He could be convinced, however, to allow an organ to be brought in, and then the show began.

By the following year, when the Anglo-Boer War broke out, Kruger would soon flee from the advancing British forces and Hyman started filming for the Warwick Trading Company in London. The war became a 'happy hunting ground' for foreign cameramen, and there were at least a dozen traipsing around the country, including even William Kennedy Dickson, the inventor of the Kinetograph. News, it soon became obvious, was a readymade source of entertainment for audiences always clamouring for something fresh.

When the war was over and people returned in even greater numbers than before, theatres like the Empire had to carve out space on their already bloated – and expensive – list of offerings. To vaudeville, plays, magic acts, opera, orchestras, comedians, dancers and acrobats, they now had to add moving pictures.

'"Bioscope fever" or "movie madness" had afflicted the country.'

Small venues opened that offered pictures only, often shown in basements or sparse back rooms. In the Royal Arcade on Pritchard Street, people flocked to the Popular Bioscope Café, a 'High-Class Tea-Room'. Even in the poorest neighbourhoods, such as Vrededorp and Chinatown, where you had to manoeuvre across a plank over a gutter and through a curtain, there was a projector flickering away. For the price of a cup of tea you could sit and watch a constantly repeating series of shorts, much the same as in London and New York.

'Bioscope teas were particularly popular at the New Egyptian Hall in Piccadilly, where in 1908 the lady from the suburbs could pause in her afternoon's shopping, and for a shilling enjoy a "dainty cup of tea and an animated display".'

Shortly after it opened in late 1911, the Orpheum showed a short,
locally made movie about a diamond heist. It was the first
and last one made in the country until 1916.

The American versions, 'nickelodeons' – where access cost a
nickel (five cents) – were usually located in storefronts, and despite
being uncomfortable and unventilated, were always packed.

By 1910, Great Britain had 5 000 of these small venues, the
US 10 000 (a number that would more than double in the following two years). Bigger premises came next, hybrids that could
accommodate mixed bills, both stage shows and pictures –
'bio-vaudeville'.

In Johannesburg, there was 'a band of fanatics … who used to
hire halls anywhere we could and, sewing two double-bed sheets
together, hung up the first cinema screens this country ever knew'.

Then came the Bijou, the Clifton, the Union Picture Palace, the
Gem, the Electric Theatre, the Apollo, the Adelphi – all names
taken from abroad. In 1910, so eager were audiences to get inside
the new 600-seat Tivoli Picture Palace, on President Street, that
it opened even before there were any doors or windows and 'the
operator had to be hoisted up into his box since there was no
stairway'. The projector was an old '"dog beater" machine…
turned laboriously by hand'.

Even more excitement was generated by the 'Mammoth Theatre
and Picture Palace' the Orpheum, on the corner of Joubert and

Jeppe streets, which advertised itself as 'The Most Magnificent Bioscope Theatre in the World, 1 500 Beautiful Upholstered Arm Chairs, Spring Seats, Foot Rests, etc. Eleven Pure Marble Statues imported from Rome at a cost of £800.'

Rufe Naylor, the young Australian who was well known at the racetrack, owned both the Tivoli and the Orpheum, even though his partner, a man named Marks Prechner, was less convinced about the viability of movies: 'They are a passing phase like roller-skating, but we must try to make something out of them.'

From cities and towns, the movie fad spread to every corner, even to small farm towns like Zuurbraak and De Rust. Peddlers who travelled the back roads sometimes got hold of a used 'dog-beater' they could set up on their wagons, 'tagging a show onto their haberdashery.'

'Townsfolk were forewarned with a dodger or handbill handed out beforehand.' Sometimes shows were held in the magistrate's court, the church hall or the hotel dining room. Even though the picture shook and wobbled and the film was often of the worst quality, people didn't mind. And they couldn't get enough.

Some of the better travelling 'bioscope men' had with them an 'apparatus generating oxygen, which had to be saturated with ether and burned on a piece of hardened lime, which then became incandescent and provided the rays for the bioscope machine'. It was a dangerous affair, and in Mafeking one night, one man's 'limelight plant' exploded, causing him to lose his arm.

For the public's insatiable demand there was an ever-growing supply of segments, 'short narratives, scenics (views of the world from moving trains), "actualities" (precursors of later documentary films), illustrated song slides, local or touring song and dance acts, comedies, melodramas, problem plays, stop action sequences, and sporting events.'

Mostly the films came from France, Germany, Italy, Denmark, Sweden, Britain and the US. The biggest studio in the world, Babelsberg, opened outside Berlin in 1912. In Italy, 200 production companies were turning out three short movies a day. Danish pictures, which saw their golden age from 1910, 'rivaled those of Hollywood for popularity on the screens of Paris, London, Berlin and New York'.

Other countries were also trying to get in on the act, including Japan, Russia, Mexico and Argentina. Even Australia, despite its distance from London and New York, produced no fewer than 50 narrative pictures in 1911. Most significantly, in 1906, it had made *The Story of the Kelly Gang*, about the famous outlaw and murderer. While most moving pictures internationally lasted no longer than 15 minutes, or one reel, it ran for a full 70 – the world's first narrative 'feature'.

But the US reigned supreme, if only because of its staggering output. By 1913, the country was exporting 32 million feet of film – at least 32 000 hours – a figure that would quadruple within the next decade. About half of that went to Europe.

In this vast and exploding landscape, South Africa was a blip on the screen. In 1913, it imported only 10 000 feet from the US (or less than a fraction of one per cent). Johannesburg might have punched far above its weight, importing the best stage acts since 1886, and South Africa was by far the biggest importer of film and had the biggest audience in Africa. But in world terms, it was a pinprick.

It was into this huge, crazy, boisterous, unpredictable, frenetic new world that IW was about to dive headlong and, it seemed, totally oblivious of what he was getting into.

With the paint barely dry on the signs for his new African Theatres, Schlesinger launched a second company called African Film Productions, or 'African Films'. His plan was to build a studio in the City of Gold, where he himself would make movies.

It was anyone's guess what they would be about, or how he would do it, but IW knew exactly. As with all his other businesses, he turned his attention to the northern hemisphere for ideas. Quite coincidentally, something fantastic was happening there.

A SPECTACLE ON BROADWAY

On 21 April 1913, one month before Currie's auction took place at the Empire, a different kind of crowd was gathering at another theatre, the Astor, in the heart of New York City. Lining up at the corner of Broadway and 45th Street, they were waiting to see a movie unlike anything that had been shown before.

So great was the event that the next day *The New York Times* carried its first-ever movie review – something it wouldn't do again for another six months. It called the showing at the Astor nothing less than 'the most ambitious photo drama that has yet been seen here'.

'There were thrills in almost every scene; some calling for enthusiastic applause and yet others which commanded profound reverence. Altogether it was a delighted people who rose reluctantly to leave the theater when the curtain fell on the last scene.'

⊏⊡⊏⊡⊐

To comprehend the exhilaration of the 'large, fashionable and enthusiastic audiences' who went to the Astor that spring day in 1913, it helps to know a bit about what was going on in movies in the US at the time. Despite all the cinematic offerings – an estimated 96 million feet of film a night were being shown at 20 000 theatres – the segments were small, similar and mostly unmemorable.

The reason, oddly enough, was the very man who had been behind the invention and advancement of motion picture cameras and projectors in the US, Thomas Edison. Like most production houses, his Edison Company was based in New York. By 1908, competition had become so fierce that Edison, in a bid to shut out smaller producers, decided to take action. As the owner of most of the patents for motion pictures in his country, he could.

He created a 'patent trust' – what became known as the 'Edison Trust' – a cartel that quickly crushed the opposition. Many of his competitors – Biograph, Essanay, Selig, Lubin and Kalem – joined the trust; if they didn't, they couldn't use Edison's equipment without fear of prosecution. At the same time, it became harder for foreign movies, especially the popular French ones, to access the US market.

A particularly bizarre regulation of the Edison Trust was this: movies could be only one reel long, which meant 1 000 feet, lasting no more than 15 minutes – earning them the name 'one-reeler'. The argument was that viewers couldn't endure more than that.

'(M)ovie audiences were believed incapable of enjoying more protracted entertainment. The (Edison) company also forbade the identification of actors because popular entertainers might demand higher salaries.'

By 1912 – just as the Empire Palace was starting to collapse – film companies in the US were starting to stand up to Edison. Some of them moved west, to California, not only to escape the legal reach of the trust but also to find a better filming climate. Others who stayed in New York began breaking his 'one-reel rule' and showing longer movies.

In July of that year, *Queen Elizabeth* was released by a New York distributor named Adolph Zukor, starring the famous stage actress Sarah Bernhardt. Called *Les Amours d'Élisabeth, reine d'Angleterre* in France, where it had been made, it was a full 40 minutes long. Even though it was a good deal shorter than *The Kelly Gang*, *Queen Elizabeth* was the movie that got noticed in the US – and proved that audiences could tolerate sitting for more than fifteen minutes to watch a movie.

Then, in April 1913, came the movie at the Astor. It wasn't one reel or two, but eight – a full two hours long – and it was being shown not at some small nickelodeon in the suburbs but in the very heart of Manhattan!

Suddenly, people used to watching single-reel comedies or Westerns in cramped storefronts found themselves in the heartland of the biggest theatres on earth – the New Amsterdam, the Belasco, the Lyceum and the 1 600-seat Astor – places once reserved for vaudeville, big plays and jaw-dropping magical acts, because it was believed that no movie could ever fill such huge auditoriums.

But this was no ordinary movie; it was the biggest ever made, an Italian spectacle called *Quo Vadis*. Based on an 1896 novel by the Polish Nobel Prize winner Henryk Sienkiewicz, it told the story of a clandestine love affair between a Christian woman and a Roman warrior in 64 AD, during the final days of the emperor Nero.

The movie sets were colossal, while the extras numbered in the thousands, with real lions wandering around a Roman arena and men racing chariots. The scenes of the burning of Rome were so exciting that 'the audience was unable to longer restrain itself and burst into loud and prolonged applause'.

Eight months later, while the record-breaking *Quo Vadis* was still showing at the Astor, another movie opened on Broadway, at Joe Weber's Theatre. The two venues and movies couldn't have been more different. Weber's was half the size of the Astor, and the movie was not a historical spectacle set in Italy but a modern-day tale shot on the streets of New York. But from the opening day, people were lining up all the way down Broadway, and then across the country, to see it.

The movie, *Traffic in Souls,* was a controversial and lurid story about white slavery – a scourge plaguing New York, where especially young women immigrants were being entrapped – making it 'equal parts melodrama, social indictment, and documentary'. A woman and her policeman boyfriend try to find her sister, who has been kidnapped and forced into prostitution.

The movie, which ran for an astonishing 90 minutes, became the biggest box-office hit of the year. Costing less than $6 000 to make, it grossed almost half a million dollars (the equivalent of more than $15 million today).

Within the next eighteen months, IW Schlesinger would approach the director of *Traffic in Souls*, George Loane Tucker, and the most famous actor in Italian spectacles, Bartolomeo Pagano, to come and work for him. Those were the first hints that he wanted to make movies like *Quo Vadis* and *Traffic in Souls* – big and commercial.

But in the middle of 1913, he still had no director, no actors, no writers, no studio, barely any facilities and no knowledge of how to pull them all together into a film company. What he did have was a handful of good men who knew how to use a hand-cranked motion picture camera.

Barely a few weeks after the auction at the Empire, the cameramen were already established in offices on the second floor of the theatre building. They had also started filming one of the bloodiest events in South Africa's history, which, quite unintentionally, prepared them for the sensational movies to come.

OPERATOR SHOT DEAD

At the 'handsomest theatre on the subcontinent', people were settling in again after the few weeks of closure for the auction in May. Old faces were joined by new ones, and in between the theatre people a new breed of entertainer – movie men – quickly started settling in.

On first glance, everything looked the same. Posters on Commissioner and Kruis streets urged passersby to come and see the American magician Arnold De Biere perform his Egg Bag, Clock Dial and Ten-Ichi Thumb Tie tricks. In a few weeks' time, people would be able to see 'Caesar's Five Forest Bred Lions – the most sensational and unique Animal act ever imported'.

Along the Empire's hallways scurried men carrying pieces of set furniture, crates of equipment for the multitude of coming acts, while women veered off into side rooms, their arms overflowing with costumes and fancy headdresses. The clicking of typewriters from the offices on the upper floors played off against the sound of the orchestra practising in the main auditorium.

But something else was happening too. In several of the rooms on the second floor, a handful of men, by the name of Crellin, Ayliff, Nissen, Humphrey and a few others, were setting up their roster of activities.

Arranged around the room were several film cameras, rectangular with hand cranks and heavy wooden tripods, weighing about 30 pounds each and probably made by Pathé or Bell & Howell, both prominent manufacturers at the time. The men made up a small camera unit.

Tommy Crellin had shot *From the Cape to the Zambesi*, the first-ever filmed tour of southern Africa, as well as the country's only narrative picture, *The Star of the South*. The one-reeler, about the theft of a diamond, had been shown in December 1911 at the newly opened Orpheum, although most people who saw it remembered the Orpheum instead of the movie. To boost ticket sales, it was retitled *The Great Kimberley Diamond Robbery*, but still ran for only four days.

The short movie, like the Orpheum where it was shown and the Tivoli, all belonged to Rufe Naylor, who, before selling to IW, had also started producing a newsreel that was a straight copy of one that had been launched in London three years earlier, the pioneering Pathé Animated Gazette.

In a world hungry for things to watch at the bioscope, daily events provided an endless source of material. Soon these were as popular as the movies that followed them, often more exciting too – railway crashes, floods, coronations.

In early May 1913, in the midst of IW's takeover of the entertainment business, Naylor's camera team brought out a series of shorts that included 'a motor fatality showing the wrecked car', a rugby match, the funeral of the mayor of Germiston, 'a Boy Scouts Church Parade', the opening of Braamfontein railway station and the 'Pony and Galloway' race meeting at Turffontein.

The following week, they were working for IW, under the banner of a newsreel that slotted in perfectly with his other new entertainment companies, African Theatres and African Films – it was called 'African Mirror'. Their first major assignment for him was also a lot more ambitious – and deadlier.

A labour dispute had started at Kleinfontein, a mine near the eastern end of the 60-mile Rand, at the beginning of May and grew quickly. Five strike leaders were arrested, causing more mines to join them in solidarity, followed by railway workers, who showed their support by closing railway stations. The unrest was not unusual for strike-prone Johannesburg, but then it took on proportions the government had never seen before.

The first segment of the news by African Mirror – referred to simply as 'the Kleinfontein strike film' – was shown at the Orpheum on 27 May. It 'excited a lot of interest … and tributes were held on all sides to the enterprise of (African Films) in sending a cinematographer so promptly to the scene of operations'.

As tensions across the Rand got worse, the prime minister, General Louis Botha, and his minister of defence, General Jan Smuts, tried to broker a deal – but in vain. By early July, with the government running out of peaceful options, a force of 8 000 men – policemen, soldiers, special constables – had been dispersed throughout the city.

Outside the all-important mining headquarters of Corner House and the nearby Rand Club, favoured by mine owners and captains of industry, the number of police and soldiers was especially high. Shops were boarded up to prevent looting. On the pavement in front of the Central News Agency, hundreds of people gathered, waiting for the afternoon papers with the latest news. Would the men march or not?

A strike was called for 4 July. A force of 18 000 white gold miners was to gather on Market Square, which happened to be right outside IW Schlesinger's headquarters, the Colonial & Banking Trust building. From there they would march through the streets.

'In the morning the city had been calm; many smart women were shopping; traffic, crowds, commerce, restaurant life, all were proceeding normally. In the afternoon the storm broke.'

At 1.30 pm, just before the protest was set to begin, it was banned by the government. When the thousands of protesters refused to leave, they were charged by men on horseback, and some fired back with their own guns. Then the crowd scattered through the streets, looting and burning shops as they went, even setting Park Station on fire. 'The blaze illuminated the sky for miles … The office of *The Star* newspaper was burned down. The wreckers danced around dead cavalry horses in the roadway as the flames roared upward. Night fell on a horrified town.'

The cameramen at African Mirror had been preparing for the event from 3 July. A dozen of them split into several teams, and over the next few days shot 2 000 feet of film: soldiers kneeling in the street preparing to fire on protesters; buildings being firebombed; a violent incident outside the Rand Club, where a mob refused to disperse and shots were fired at the military.

One of the ringleaders, a tall red-headed miner named JL Labuschagne, twice walked into the street, threw out his arms and cried, 'Shoot me!' The second time, when the crowd behind him began to surge forward, someone did fire at him and he died instantly. Labuschagne quickly gained hero status, and a pamphlet said he had in fact been shot in cold blood while trying to protect others.

Standing on a rooftop nearby was one of the African Mirror team, WE Clarke, who had taken up a position with a view over Market Square. During the action, so many people gathered alongside him that the roof under them started to give way and then collapsed. Clarke saved himself and his camera 'by tobogganing down on his back from a height of 25 feet'.

'For four days and nights twelve operators worked without ceasing … until it was too dark. All night long they developed and prepared the films secured during the day, and … went out with their cameras again, turning, turning, turning their film-reels, until their arms were ready to drop off.'

On 7 July, Botha and Smuts drove through from Pretoria to meet some of the mine owners at the Orange Grove Hotel, and then with union leaders at the Carlton. It was agreed that the dismissed workers would be reinstated, and a government commission was established to investigate the miners' grievances. 'A rumbling calm slowly returned to the town.'

Twenty-five people had died during the fighting, many of them bystanders, including a pianist, a dentist's apprentice, two commercial travellers, a 13-year-old named Monty Dugmore who had been selling copies of the workers' paper, the *Strike Herald*, and one of the African Mirror team. Even though the dead cameraman was never identified by name, it was a fact that would soon come in very handy.

By 18 July, a series of short films were ready to be shown – scenes of the bloody rioting, the charges by the dragoons, the destruction of property, the dead lying in the streets – and were publicised outside the Empire alongside posters of the magician De Biere. Titled *The Great Strike*, several short news segments had unintentionally turned into IW's first movie.

Every chance possible was taken to publicise the film before its first showing on 21 July: It was called 'The Civil War on the Rand' and 'The History of the World's Greatest Strike'; and all the posters bore the tragic words: 'One of our operators shot dead while taking the pictures.'

But on the day it was meant to open, signs went up declaring, 'The Strike Film(s) Will Not Be Shown'. A blanket ban by the military, the municipality and the police forbade *The Great Strike* from being shown in Johannesburg or any town along the Rand, 'lest they incite to violence'.

But in Pretoria, where no miners lived, and there was little chance the footage would cause trouble, the show did go on, at the Grand. It was the first time the public had seen what the African Mirror team had shot, and it was everything the publicity had promised.

'These included representations of the pontoon device at Vereeniging, whereby the strikers were enabled to cross the Vaal River to "pull out" the men at the Victoria Falls Power Station; the defence of the Power Station at Johannesburg and the Rand Club battle. The last-named film indicated clearly the movements of the firing line at the junction of Commissioner and Loveday Streets, and the shooting of Labuschagne.'

Ten more days passed, but across the Rand *The Great Strike* remained banned. Then, on 1 August at 11.15 am, an unusual gathering outside the Empire signalled that something might be happening. A group of policemen and judicial officers had walked down Kruis Street from the new green-domed Supreme Court in order to the watch 'the strike film'.

Sir Justice Wessels and Justice Ward, who were leading a commission of enquiry into the strike, wanted to see the footage 'in order to get a clearer impression of the events than (those that) could be obtained from the hearing of witnesses ... The film was taken at a very slow pace at times in order to enable the Commissioners to follow details and incidents closely.'

By the following week, it was decided that tempers had cooled enough and that people across the Rand could see the 'long-expected' movie. Audiences were advised that it would be shown 'for one week only, twice a day' at the Orpheum and the Grand – both theatres only a few blocks from the very site where the strike began – and it was 'certain to pack this capacious theatre at every performance'.

As predicted, people turned up in their numbers. The Orpheum was 'literally besieged long before the time for the opening of the doors ... At both sessions the house was crowded to its utmost capacity by an audience which followed each incident depicted with almost breathless interest.' At the Grand, 'the house was packed from floor to ceiling ... The film is remarkable, and is indeed a triumph of the bioscope art.'

There were fears that *The Great Strike* would itself incite violence, but that never happened. If anything, commented one reporter, 'A pleasing feature of the representation has been the entire absence of any hostile feeling or any demonstration whatsoever.'

For IW the movie was a triumph. It was still showing in places around the country one month later, and it firmly launched the name of African Mirror. Little did the cameramen who filmed

The Great Strike realise that it would be the best preparation they could get for the incredible challenges that lay ahead.

But IW still needed to find dozens of other technicians and artists, not only actors and directors and writers but also managers, carpenters, lighting specialists, anyone who had worked on a movie set before.

The obvious place to start looking was in London, almost 6 000 miles away. And by December 1913 African Films had found its first significant employee, a man who would become the most important person in the rise of IW's movie empire.

PART TWO
1914

The Film Crew

The adventurous newsmen of African Mirror followed violent bloody strikes in Johannesburg and the war in German East Africa. Shown here is LJ Humphrey and an assistant, probably near the Rufiji Delta.

THE KING'S CAMERAMAN

For the tall, handsome young Englishman, the last six months had been a whirlwind.

His name was Joseph Albrecht and he was employed by a film company on Wardour Street, a corridor of Soho between Leicester Square and Oxford Street. Along the route were at least 20 film production companies, gaining it a reputation as Britain's 'Film Row'.

At 89–91 Wardour Street, the American-born Charles Urban had opened his first premises in 1908, then a second at 80–82. The Ideal Film Company was next-door, at 76–78, and at number 173 was the Wardour Film Company. But the king of Film Row was the French-owned Pathé company, which had just moved from number 84 to larger premises at 103–109.

The biggest producer of camera equipment in Europe, Pathé had started a French newsreel in 1908, the world's first, and then an English version two years later, which it called Pathé Animated Gazette.

Into 84 Wardour Street, in the Gazette's first year, walked 16-year-old Joseph Albrecht, who had been around cameras since he was 12. In 1911, he was already filming his first big story, the coronation of George V – the biggest news event ever in the British Empire. After that, he filmed thousands of segments, including 'aerial experiments for the War Office from aeroplanes, balloons and dirigibles; (and) naval experiments in the Solent for the Admiralty when they tried to raise the submarine E11.'

When Albrecht heard that King George was in Yorkshire hunting with the Marquess of Ripon, he set out to get some rare footage of the private rendezvous. Following the royal entourage for miles by taxi, he then went on foot across the countryside, lugging his heavy camera all the way. Just as he arrived near the royal shooting box, with barely fifty yards to go, he was noticed by a detective. Trying to escape, he fell in a ditch.

'The clatter of my camera falling attracted the attention of the party, and I was just crawling out, covered with mud, when they spotted me, and I was their source of amusement for quite five minutes.'

In 1912, when Albrecht had just turned 18, he was sent by Pathé to cover the First Balkan War. Armed with his camera and a Mauser pistol, he crossed Germany, Austria and Hungary to reach 'dirty, sticky, muddy' Belgrade, the Serbian capital. He was forbidden by the army to take any photographs but sneaked off anyway and hired a cart and driver 'to get to the fighting somehow'. They didn't get far before the driver gave him away, and Albrecht was sent to Niš and then Üsküb (what is today Skopje), where more than two dozen journalists were holed up in the same hotel and rarely allowed to get close to the fighting. But Albrecht did so 'as soon as we dared'. After several months – and a few minor escapades – he was called home and managed to get out of Serbia without having his film confiscated.

On his return to London, he came down with typhoid, which left him bedridden for months. Back at work, he left Pathé to become chief cameraman for the new Éclair Journal, but his doctor warned him that he wasn't well enough to stay in London or Britain for much longer. He needed to move away from the cold, wet climate – and soon.

The young cameraman's options were severely limited. In Europe the climate was no better, but in America it was. And he had heard that exciting things were happening there.

'For a while I was very strongly tempted to go west,' he recalled later. 'Carl Laemmle, the first of the great American producers, was just opening a studio at a place called Hollywood and I thought something might be doing there. Then I heard about Mr Schlesinger.'

On the very same morning that his doctor told him he must leave England, he met a friend named Matt Reid, who worked for a new entertainment group in Leicester Square – the International Variety & Theatrical Agency.

Albrecht told him his news.

'That's funny,' Reid said, and pulled a cable out of his pocket. It was from Schlesinger, who was looking for cameramen to work in Johannesburg. Almost immediately, the young Englishman made up his mind and bought a one-way ticket on a steamship from Southampton sailing not west, but south.

Given IW's crammed schedule and an obsessive desire not to be interrupted, the first meeting between him and Albrecht would have followed a predictable pattern.

In about February 1914, after the Union Express from Cape Town pulled in to Park Station, Albrecht would have been picked up by Max Zasman, a young chauffeur who had just started working for Schlesinger. In a brand-new Napier sedan – IW, a lover of motorcars, had just switched from Talbots to the popular British model – they would have driven the short distance down Rissik Street and turned into Market Street before pulling up in front of the Colonial & Banking Trust building.

Inside, Albrecht soon got his first inkling of the man he would be working for. To avoid being bothered unnecessarily, IW had made it almost impossible for people to find him by creating for himself 'a secret chamber', his 'sanctum sanctorum'.

'You had to negotiate what was virtually a narrow rabbit-run type of passages, snake along past all of the directors' offices, up short stairs and down short stairs until finally a steep little staircase dropped about fifteen steps and would land you outside the doors of three or four offices. Then you would have to guess which one might be IW's.'

Once inside the 'sanctum sanctorum', Albrecht faced a man who couldn't have been more different from himself. He was barely twenty and English, IW about to turn forty-three and American. The one was travel-weary and perhaps a bit rumpled from the train journey, while IW, his bowler hat and cane always near at hand, dressed 'as though he was emerging from his Savile Row tailor in London ... His hands and finger nails were always impeccably groomed. There was never a hair out of place ... and he (always wore) the smartest pair of shoes and socks.'

Most noticeable, though, was IW's diminutive stature. Barely five feet and two inches tall, he only reached Albrecht's shoulder, a feature that had earned him the nickname 'the little man'.

One of the first things IW wanted to do was to show Albrecht Killarney. With both men in the back seat of the Napier, Max Zasman would have driven north, past Hospital Hill and the Old Fort, and then over the Parktown ridge, where the view suddenly opened up for miles, the Magaliesberg visible in the far distance. They turned onto Oxford Road.

Johannesburg, unbeknown to Albrecht, had much in common with the city that he had chosen not to go to – Los Angeles – even though it was more than a century newer. Built between and across a lattice of ridges, the one metropolis framed the Los Angeles Basin, the other the Witwatersrand Basin, from which came its popular name, the Rand. Their purpose, too, was equally self-evident: the one had oil wells and derricks, the other the telltale equipment of the gold mines, tall stacks above engine rooms, constantly rotating headgear and giant battery stamps. Instead of the Pacific Ocean on the horizon was an arc of shimmering flaxen-coloured pyramids.

Oxford Road was its Sunset Boulevard, the artery that ran out

In 1905 the mining magnate JB Robinson sold his bank
on Market Square to IW, who turned it into the
Colonial & Banking Trust. Deep inside its corridors
was his 'sanctum sanctorum'.

of Los Angeles through farmland like the new Hollywood, and
then along hills that were part of the Transverse Ranges. The
Napier, meanwhile, crossed hills of quartzite that led to faraway
areas like Melrose and Waverley.

On either side of the sedan rose mansions with names like
Dolobran, Northwards and Hohenheim, where some of the richest
men in the world had lived (or still did) – magnates, Randlords
and politicians such as Hennen Jennings, Lord Milner, Henry 'The
Oats King' Wilson and Sir Thomas Cullinan, whose name was
given to the biggest diamond ever found.

Albrecht's filmic eye would have quickly identified locations that could double for anywhere in the world. In front of them stretched a forest of eucalyptus trees called the Sachsenwald, a manmade lake with couples boating on it, and a wide avenue running down an axis between two ridges with what, in the distance, looked like an elephant carrying children on its back.

Near the eastern side of the Sachsenwald, Zasman slowed down and then turned the Napier through an unassuming farm gate. Ahead of them lay 26 acres of 'rocky koppies, broad slopes and wooded streams'. The previous owner, a man named Cook, had 'spent many thousands of pounds on the property (and) endowed it with a wealth of verdure and colour, while there is an artificial lake spanned in its narrowest part by a rustic bridge'. It had initially been called Cook's Estate.

When the property came up for sale in 1906, people were surprised that IW would pay what they thought was an exorbitant amount of money, £60 000, to buy something so far from the city. By this time, the name had been changed to Killarney.

Once Zasman brought the Napier to a stop, the two men got out. 'There were no roads and we started to stride through the thick grass of the veld.' When they stopped, it was at a place below the back of the Parktown ridge. IW had been there earlier with a contractor friend named James Thompson, who had helped him mark off an area with tape. He now told Albrecht what it was for.

'This is where we are going to have a film studio.'

HIS DOUBLE

At that moment, almost exactly the same scenario was playing out ten thousand miles away.

A man who had been in the entertainment business for not very long had just spent a lot of money, $165 000 to be exact, or just over £30 000, to buy a piece of farmland a good distance from the city centre, which people said he was crazy to do, and where he planned to build a film studio. The city was Los Angeles, and that man's name was Carl Laemmle.

Laemmle, besides being the person whom Albrecht had first wanted to work for, bore many similarities to IW. Almost the same age, and Jewish, they had both emigrated to America in the mid-1880s, IW with his family from the town of Eperjes in Hungary, Laemmle from Laupheim in Germany. And then, in their early forties, both had stumbled into a new profession – entertainment.

Indeed they were not unlike many of the American producers who were just starting out and would soon become the giants of Hollywood – the Warner brothers, Adolph Zukor (who came from a town in Hungary a few hundred miles from IW's family), William Fox and a man called Goldfish, who would soon change his name to Goldwyn.

'They came from the ghettos of Kiev and Minsk and Warsaw, and from little towns like Laupheim in Germany and Ricse in Hungary and Krasmashhilz in Poland. In turn-of-the-century America they took new names as they began to make their way in

'If ever I saw a man with his soul aflame, it was IWS,'
commented one acquaintance.

a new land ... They worked at petty trade, in menial occupations, among them a cloth sponger, a junk dealer, a glove salesman, a furrier, a pool hustler – and a jeweler who went bankrupt.'

Words used to describe them could easily have been applied to IW: 'visionary and enterprising'; 'driving perfectionist'; 'titanic temperament'; a gambler'; 'internationally oriented but with a deep love for his former ... homeland'; 'a cunning workaholic'; 'in love with million-dollar projects but someone who balked at high wages for stars'; a 'generous philanthropist'.

One of IW's acquaintances wrote a rare description of him that could have fit any hard-nosed Hollywood producer: 'Small in stature, he had an enormously strong personality and dominated everyone … he stood no nonsense, and I never heard him give anyone any praise. I doubt if he knew the meaning of the word "gratitude". He certainly never said "Thank you!"'

IW also shared with Laemmle and Zukor his diminutive height, although it was Zukor, measuring an inch or two shorter than Schlesinger, who was also referred to as 'the little man'. Of them all, though, the one whom IW was watching most keenly, the one he would come to copy the most, was Carl Laemmle.

In 1906, at the time that IW was buying Cook's Estate, Carl Laemmle was still working as a bookkeeper and office manager in Chicago.

He invested in a nickelodeon called the White Front on busy Milwaukee Avenue, and it was so successful that he bought others. Soon he went into film distribution and then production. He formed the Universal Film Manufacturing Company, and in 1912 moved his headquarters from Chicago to New York.

Suddenly under the sway of the monopolistic Edison Trust, Laemmle refused to play ball, and the following year he released the controversial six-reel white-slavery movie *Traffic in Souls*. With the staggering profits from the film, he moved Universal's headquarters to the West Coast.

In Los Angeles, it was still early days. Movies were being made on small properties – in barns, roadhouses, wooden shacks – so when Laemmle bought the 230-acre Taylor Ranch in the San Fernando Valley, behind some ridges that would soon become known as the Hollywood Hills, and announced that he would be building the biggest studio in the world, people decided he was crazy. So much so that they called his venture 'Laemmle's Folly'.

Construction began on a $30 000 headquarters for Universal – big and solid, unlike the flimsy structures that until now had been the norm. There would also be an outdoor stage the size of a football field that could handle eight productions at a time, a barracks to house a 'troop of expert cavalrymen', a bunkhouse for cowboys, tepees for 75 Native Americans, restaurants, shops, a post office and even space for the studio's own police force.

In another innovation, members of the public would be allowed to visit Universal's grounds, and while sitting in specially constructed bleachers they could watch a real movie being made. One of the first of these, when the studio opened in 1915, was the 'fake flooding' of a town with more than 150 000 gallons of water.

The very first movie made on the Universal property, *Damon and Pythias*, would – just like *Quo Vadis* – feature 'a great chariot race of the kind that later became famous on the screen in *Ben-Hur*'.

The chariot race, like a lot of other things Laemmle was doing, IW would soon replicate in the City of Gold – the studio head-quarters with manicured gardens, the fake flood, the village for indigenous people, the bleachers for spectators to watch movies being made. It was as if he had someone secretly feeding him regular updates from deep inside Laemmle's organisation.

In the middle of 1914, that was quite possible. While 'Laemmle's Folly' was still a construction site, some of IW's agents happened to be close by on another mission that had nothing to do with movies. They were in San Francisco to inspect the progress on the upcoming World's Fair.

For the Panama-Pacific International Exposition of 1915, more than 20 grand pavilions from different countries were being built on a 650-acre site between the Presidio and Fort Mason. There would also be numerous exhibition halls, or 'palaces', to display food production, mining, transportation and liberal arts, all centring on the 435-foot-high Tower of Jewels.

IW was leading a charge in South Africa to have the next World's Fair in Johannesburg; it was already being referred to as the 'Golden City Exposition of 1916'. On 24 May 1914, shortly before he left for his annual trip to England and New York, he told a newspaper, 'My agents in San Francisco report very favourably on the prospects of being able to induce many of the exhibitors at the Panama Exposition to come here after that is over.'

It wouldn't have been difficult for his agents, once they had finished in San Francisco, to go to Los Angeles and check out Carl Laemmle's new studio. Copying other businesses was something Schlesinger did well, and repeatedly, although sometimes he did it on the sly.

In 1919, the author and politician Sir Percy Fitzpatrick accused IW's agents of infiltrating his orange-growing scheme in the Sundays River area of the eastern Cape. Schlesinger was already busy developing 'the biggest orange estate in the world', at Zebediela in the northern Transvaal, but seemed to also be eyeing an area that Fitzpatrick saw as his own.

One agent in particular, the former theatre owner HS Kingdon, happened to be in London doing work for IW. He wrote to Fitzpatrick claiming – falsely, it later turned out – that he'd had a falling-out with IW's property company, African Realty, and wanted to work for an honest company, namely Fitzpatrick's.

'I declined,' the author wrote in a letter to the Colonial Office, 'because a scoundrel does not become any better in my judgment by also being a traitor.'

If it wasn't Schlesinger's agents who made it to 'Laemmle's Folly', someone else close to him did. Within a year, the copying of what was happening at the Taylor Ranch had begun at the Killarney farm. The one studio would be christened Universal City, the other the City of Film.

AT SEA

As IW settled into his cabin on the *Kinfauns Castle* in Cape Town harbour on 20 July 1914, there was a commotion outside. Throngs of passengers moved onto the decks to watch a jubilant cavalcade make its way onto the quay below them.

A large procession of coaches led by a four-horsed drag and a band, and surrounded by crowds, came down Adderley Street and stopped alongside the steamer to let several people alight, each of them wearing brightly coloured garlands around their necks. On all sides was a 'tumultuously applauding' crowd.

Two of the new arrivals, a small man and a woman, were Indian, and next to them stood a taller white man, his most distinguishing features a thick crop of dark hair and full moustache. Attached to the coach was a banner reading, 'Bon voyage to the great Indian patriot, MK Gandhi, and family, also Mr. Kallenbach. God be with you until we meet again.'

Speeches were made, letters of appreciation from community leaders were read, and the two men were praised for all they had done to help Indians and coloured people in the country. It was an emotional event, and people cried openly. The Indian man thanked South Africans for all they had done for him, but he said many challenges still lay ahead. After twenty years in the country, he was going home to India. Then the garlanded trio walked up the gangway to the Union-Castle steamer, where hundreds more telegrams of gratitude awaited them in their cabins.

The *Kinfauns Castle* was not without its luxuries, but IW, who sailed to Britain and America at least once a year, had a special passion for the *Mauretania*, the fastest ship in the world.

Numerous articles appeared in newspapers at home and abroad about the historic departure of Mohandas Gandhi aboard the *Kinfauns Castle*. At the bottom of page two of the *Rand Daily Mail* was also a brief report that – in the custom of the time – listed passengers from the Rand who were on board. Besides the Grey-Colliers and their daughter, as well as George Garson, Gordon Cheape and a dozen or so others, there was 'IW Schlesinger'.

There is no record of whether the two most famous men on board the *Kinfauns Castle* met up after it set sail, although given the length of time at sea – eighteen days – and the limited number of people on board, it is more than likely that they did. Schlesinger and Gandhi had several things in common: their arrival as immigrants in South Africa (in 1893 and 1894); their acquaintance with General Jan Smuts; and, perhaps most importantly, their connection to the Empire Palace.

In his long fight for the recognition of Indian rights in South Africa, Gandhi had been allowed to use the Empire to make his rousing speeches. It was there on 11 September 1906, with the place 'packed from floor to ceiling' with 3 000 people, that he launched his campaign of passive resistance, *satyagraha*. Even though IW did not yet own the theatre, he knew the man who did – Edgar Hyman – and he would have kept up with the news of Gandhi's zealous activities in Johannesburg.

Any meeting on board between the two men isn't likely to have lasted for long, for IW had plenty of work to do before he reached London and had no doubt already set up his maritime 'sanctum sanctorum' where he could avoid being disturbed.

In a speech IW once made to his insurance agents – who, as he put it, should have 'the proper beezum in their egos' – he urged them to use every minute of every day industriously. Some would succeed and some wouldn't, and 'the whole story in a nutshell is that those who fail cannot employ the 1 440 (minutes of the day) to the best advantage'.

On board the *Kinfauns Castle,* the other passengers listened to the band playing on deck during the day, before it moved into the lounge after dark, or they drifted between the drawing room done in satinwood and 'furnished with a Broadwood grand piano and with sofas and lounges of dark mahogany sumptuously upholstered in silk' and the smoking room 'designed after the manner of an old Dutch interior' or the 'luxuriantly fitted up' first-class saloon and a second oak-panelled saloon on the upper deck. IW, meanwhile, went over his schedule for London – assisted by a young man identified only as 'LJ Baxter'.

In addition to his usual round of business, dealing with the bureaus for his companies African Realty, the African Life Assurance Society and several others – most of which had their London offices on Regent and New Broad streets – Schlesinger now also had to conduct meetings with 'likely exhibitors' for the proposed Golden City Exposition, where he would '(put) the scheme forward in its fullest sense to commercial London and America'.

Most importantly, though, he would officially open his new

entertainment headquarters on Leicester Square, the International Variety & Theatre Agency, which combined his interests in both theatres and movies. One of IW's first acts when he got to London would be to buy 'a circuit of film theatres'. As for his African Film division, he needed to find actors, directors and technicians he could send to South Africa, as well as stories that could be turned into movies.

The only event to shake IW out of the hectic routine of 'working like a machine' – as it did everyone else on board – happened barely a week after they sailed from Cape Town. On 28 July, one month after the assassination of the Archduke Franz Ferdinand and his wife in Sarajevo, came the news that Austria-Hungary had declared war on Serbia. By 4 August, Germany, France, Russia and Britain had joined in.

When the *Kinfauns Castle* sailed into Southampton harbour several days later, the passengers had barely disembarked before the ship was requisitioned by the Admiralty, and within days she had been converted into an Armed Merchant Cruiser.

Gandhi's plans to travel to India were delayed, and he would only get there in January 1915. Kallenbach, who had been supposed to join him, was, as a German citizen, taken to an internment camp.

As Schlesinger and LJ Baxter made their way through London to the Ritz Hotel, it was already clear that his dream of a Golden City Exposition in 1916 was dead; no one in the northern hemisphere would be interested in building pavilions and fairgrounds in South Africa when most of the potential exhibitors were at war. Even Baxter had given up on IW and had already made up his mind to enlist in Kitchener's New Army.

In all the uncertainty, it seemed quite possible that IW might pull back on his decision to make movies. But at his new headquarters near Leicester Square, IVTA House, the home of the International Variety & Theatrical Agency, it was clear that the machinery of his new entertainment conglomerate was in full swing. There was no turning back.

THE GREAT SEARCH

Just off Leicester Square in central London, the building at 3 Leicester Street was like a babel of entertainment.

On each of the four floors of IVTA House, people were rushing about, with phones tinkling, typewriters clattering and voices raised to be heard above it all. Scattershot conversations ran the gamut of entertainment – plays, vaudeville, theatres, films, comedies, newsreels, cameras, production.

Could they get Harry Lauder? How much would he cost? And the new Italian spectacle Cabiria? *Had anyone seen that? What about* Traffic with Souls? (No, they would have to speak to the office in New York about that one.) *How was the deal going to create a worldwide agency? Had anyone been to the musical that was just finishing at the Aldwych? Or the play at the Prince of Wales? Would they work at the Empire? Did anyone have the details of the film manager they interviewed yesterday? And the two actors from Brighton, would either one be good as a leading man?*

Through all the bustle, the news came in that IVTA was about to clinch a deal with the all-important Rickard and Bandmann theatre circuits that covered Australia, India and the Far East. A press release was immediately composed for the newspapers and new entertainment magazines; as was the custom in the entertainment media, they were already predicting stupendous success.

'It will be one of the largest booking agencies in the world, particularly if it links up with the Orpheum and Keith circuits of the United States' – an even bigger agency – 'as now seems very probable.'

The compact building – which, quite fittingly, found itself halfway between the theatres of the West End and Film Row – was quite unlike anything in the entertainment world.

In just one year IW had created a strange, multi-tentacled beast: not only a theatrical agency (IVTA) but a company that owned theatres and bioscopes (African Theatres) and another (African Films) that not only distributed movies but would soon be making them. Schlesinger had become both impresario and movie producer.

It was on the movie side, however, where his real vision lay. He had assembled an unprecedented, all-inclusive corporate structure – production, distribution and exhibition – under one roof. This was the model that Hollywood would adopt only five years later, giving rise to the much-maligned 'studio system' that reigned for the next three decades.

But in most other respects, IW was way behind the rest of the world. Not only did he still have to build his studio at Killarney, and find technicians and actors to work there, but he needed product – stories they could turn into movies.

His main source, as it was for every other moviemaker in the world, was novels. By 1914, a number of authors had already found favour in movies: Sir Arthur Conan Doyle, Daniel Defoe, Robert Louis Stevenson, Thomas Hardy, Jonathan Swift, although the most popular by far was Charles Dickens. IW's agents weren't allowed to go for those authors, however, for he had stipulated that he wanted very particular stories – ones that were set in South Africa.

Lucky for them, the last few decades had produced a glut of suitable titles: tales of women in search of love on the veld; outcasts and fugitives seeking redemption in Africa; farmers finding diamonds on their land that villains then tried to steal.

Sir Henry Rider Haggard came to Johannesburg in 1914 and stayed at the Carlton Hotel. IW desperately wanted to make a movie of the author's bestseller *King Solomon's Mines*.

At the top of IW's list was a very famous novel of the time, Olive Schreiner's *The Story of an African Farm*, about three children in the Karoo and the arrival of the confidence trickster Bonaparte Blenkins. There was also Charlotte Mansfield's *Gloria, a Girl of the Veld*, about love and illicit diamonds; John Buchan's *Prester John*, whose hero learns of diamond smuggling, the mythical kingdom of Prester John and a snake-shaped ruby necklace; William Westrup's *The Man Who Was Afraid*; and Bertram Mitford's *The Gun-Runner*. Three titles came from a prolific Irishman who wrote as Tyler de Saix or under his real name, Henry de Vere Stacpoole: one of them was about two children stranded on an island after a shipwreck – *The Blue Lagoon*.

The adventure stories of gun-toting heroes in search of long-lost treasure, of which there were plenty of examples, all seemed to be trying to copy one book in particular: *King Solomon's Mines*, the bestseller by Sir Henry Rider Haggard. 'Were the title page torn out the reader would unhesitatingly put down the book as coming from the pen of Mr. Haggard', read the review for one of the novels. For another: 'a cross between Haggard and Robert Louis Stevenson'. For a third: 'not unlike (the style) of the clever master, Haggard'.

Like Haggard's hero Allan Quatermain, who was in search of a lost kingdom, the protagonists were also always on a great quest: for sunken treasure (*The Reef of Stars*); a plant that supposedly helps its possessor become indescribably rich (*With Edged Tools*); the ten lost tribes of Israel inhabiting an underground city (*Isban Israel* or *The Buried City*); a cipher with a secret code to find a cache of hidden diamonds (*The Vulture's Prey*); and, in Andrew Balfour's *The Golden Kingdom*, a mysterious tribe of white people.

None of these books had reached the heights and fame of *King Solomon's Mines*, but no one had ever attempted to make a movie of it either. IW wanted the rights to the bestseller, probably more than any other, and negotiations were undertaken to secure them. But his agents quickly found out that it was going to be almost impossible.

SHOWING ON TIMES SQUARE

In late October, IW was at sea again, heading west on the *St Paul*, a steamer of the American Line. He had sailed this route more than a dozen times each way since his clandestine departure from New York two decades earlier.

For that very first trip, at the age of twenty-three, in 1894, he had bought a ticket in steerage, probably on a steamer of the Ellerman & Bucknall Steamship Co, which had just started sailing between New York and Calcutta. Telling no one of his plans – not even one of his seven siblings – IW left a note for his parents, Abraham and Lena, saying that he was heading to Africa and would come back either a pauper or a millionaire.

After he returned the first time, a very rich man, his voyages became an annual pilgrimage. Unlike the Cape Town–Southampton route, where the choice was usually the Union-Castle Line, the Southampton–New York crossing had many more options. The *Majestic*, the *Normandie*, the *Berengaria*, the *Olympic*, the *Leviathan* – the very names of the vessels suggested grand luxury.

His favourite of them all – because it was the fastest in the world – was the Cunard liner *Mauretania*, and if there was a ticket available for that ship, he would take it. He also travelled on its sister vessel, the *Aquitania*. But for some reason – perhaps it was his belief 'in the less inexplicable side of things', the supernatural – he flatly refused to travel on Cunard's third great transatlantic liner, the *Lusitania*.

As the *St Paul* sailed through the Narrows into New York harbour, and past Ellis Island and the Statue of Liberty, passengers could see an almost-completed skyscraper rising in the financial district – the biggest office block in the world. For IW it had special significance because it was his old employer, Equitable Insurance, for whom he had worked intermittently as an agent in New York and South Africa. Part of this visit, in fact, was to discuss buying Equitable's interests in Africa.

The steamer docked at the 23rd Street pier, and waiting for IW on the quayside was a man who could have been his doppelgänger. Very short, impeccably dressed, his neatly combed hair slightly darker, he was IW's youngest brother, Max. MA, as he chose to be known, was also the main representative of IW's interests in America.

Over the past decade, three of the Schlesingers – besides MA, there was an older brother, Samuel – had established a way of doing business that worked well for them. Ideas, mostly American, were taken back to South Africa, applied, and then spread into other territories – the rest of Africa, Great Britain, the Far East.

IW named the African Realty Trust after two companies he had seen listed in a Manhattan newspaper. All the equipment for the African Life Assurance Society – right down to the desks, his telex address and the format and content of his weekly newsletter, African Life Jottings – he had got from the US. So too the canning machinery for his pineapple estate in the eastern Cape; in preparation, MA had visited the pineapple-growing region of Hawaii, although the brothers later boasted that their fruit was far better. There seemed to be no business they wouldn't attempt, no territory they wouldn't enter.

'I am an out and out expansionist,' IW once told a British reporter, in what was perhaps the most public declaration he would ever make about his philosophy. 'My experience is that if we don't expand, we go down. Moreover, if I were a politician I would do everything in my power to expunge (from South Africa) the word South. My aim would be a United States of Africa.'

After Samuel's sudden death in 1910, MA was in control of the New York office, and he would also lead the entertainment business. A brief story on 23 June 1914 in the influential trade publication *Moving Picture World* noted that a 'colossal venture' in Johannesburg was being undertaken by IW Schlesinger, 'the strongly silent director of African Films'. There were no details given, but there were really none to give.

In New York, the heart of the entertainment world – and about to become even more so, now that war was distracting Britain and Europe – IVTA House had no equivalent. And it wouldn't have one for some time to come.

Unlike London, where IW had offices in Regent Street, New Broad Street and Leicester Square, in Manhattan all his interests were located at a single address, 10 Wall Street. The building was mostly occupied by financiers and small banks, although it had probably been chosen for its location – right next-door to the New York Stock Exchange and round the corner from Equitable Insurance.

To get from 10 Wall Street, in the south of Manhattan, to 207 West 110th Street, in the north, where MA lived, the Schlesinger brothers would have driven along Broadway – once known as Bree Street, like Johannesburg's – which would have taken them straight through the theatre district and Times Square.

By October 1914, things there had changed dramatically since the historic showing of *Quo Vadis* a year earlier. Motion pictures were now becoming part of the entertainment mix. At 47th Street, just a few blocks from the Astor, where the Italian spectacle had played, people were lining up outside the very first movie-only theatre, the 3 000-seat Strand. At the Knickerbocker a play called *The Girl from Utah* had recently replaced a movie that had done so well – predictions were that it would run through the winter – it had been transferred to the Globe.

'To say that never before had such a presentation of a motion picture been given in this country seems well within the bounds of conservative statement,' wrote one reviewer.

The movie, *Cabiria*, was another Italian historical spectacle and had taken two years to make, with a cast of five thousand and shooting in five countries, including Egypt and Switzerland. Set during the Second Punic War (218–201 BC), the main story was about a young princess on the run who is then saved by a slave. The mammoth sets included the Temple of Molloch, where an insatiable god is fed live children. The director had even recreated the sacking of Carthage and Hannibal's crossing of the Alps on elephant-back.

At the New York premiere, instead of a Wurlitzer organ playing repertory music, there was an orchestra of 50 and a choir performing a specially composed score, which had been done only once before, in 1908. The movie itself was an unprecedented 12 reels, or 126 minutes!

IW quickly paid 'the biggest price ever' to get the rights to show *Cabiria* in his theatres in southern Africa, and he told his agents at IVTA House to approach the main actor, Bartolomeo Pagano – who had played Maciste, the slave-warrior in the movie, and who would soon become world-famous – to come and work for him in Johannesburg.

Now that he had started construction on his studio at Killarney and had a team of cameramen led by Joseph Albrecht working away at the Empire and was buying up novels to film, he needed to find a director able to helm a picture as grand and sprawling as *Cabiria*.

THE MAN WHO MADE TRAJAN

The middle-aged man on the movie set in Santa Barbara, California, had lively, penetrating eyes set off between his high forehead and aquiline nose. Lorimer Johnston was self-confident, well-travelled, multi-talented, smart, experienced and a proven creator of spectacles. He was exactly what IW needed.

In his chequered career, Johnston had crossed the Atlantic many times. For six years, until the mid-1890s, he had carried the odd title of 'Bearer of Dispatches for the President', a post that was done away with during Grover Cleveland's second term in office. Afterwards he began acting in plays, and then writing them, and since 1911 he had directed movies. For a year 'he had studied in the studios of Rome, Paris and Copenhagen'.

In New York, Johnston had made dozens of one-reelers before following the growing tide of moviemakers to California, where he had started making bigger productions, such as *The Esterbrook Case* and the five-reel espionage thriller *The Envoy Extraordinary*.

But it was another movie that probably first drew IW's attention. In late 1913 – while *Quo Vadis* was still playing at the Astor – Johnston directed *In the Days of Trajan*. Set in the second century AD, during the reign of the titular emperor, the movie was released at the same time as another Italian epic with a similar name, *The Last Days of Pompeii*.

Trajan was only two reels long, and *Pompeii* six, but the two movies were publicised side by side in *Billboard*, with Johnston's being made to sound just as huge: 'with an immense cast ... A spectacular feature ... with stupendous settings and most gorgeous costuming.'

A year later, he wrote a scenario for Carl Laemmle at Universal about the biblical character Samson, a man not unlike the slave-warrior Maciste in *Cabiria*. *Samson* went on to become one of the biggest movies of the year.

'Never has a picture been more heralded than this,' the publicity declared. By April 1914, 'Universal's Greatest Masterpiece' was showing to 'crowded Theatres on Broadway and in other big show places from San Francisco to New York'.

For IW, Johnston ticked all the right boxes. An American from Hollywood who could write and direct a movie like the Italians. In early 1915, Johnston was approached to come and work in Johannesburg for two years and 'a very large salary'. African Films, he was told, was 'backed by unlimited capital', and he would have 'absolute power'.

It was an offer he could hardly refuse. He had already directed more than 60 movies and written a dozen, and he was getting on in years, a lot older than many other directors. It was time to finally make a name for himself.

A departure date was set for September 1915, although Johnston wasn't yet clear what he would be working on. IW was buying up the rights to so many novels and had his eye on a growing number of possible spectacles, but which ones would he finally choose to make?

WAR!

By February 1915, IW was back in South Africa, where his entertainment empire was quickly taking shape.

That month he bought four more theatres, all in Cape Town, giving him a total of 40 in the country, their turnover a staggering £750 000. He was also planning to build several theatres that would match the largest ones in London and New York. Lorimer Johnston, 'a prominent film producer of America', was to arrive soon, and 'cinema stars will be introduced from overseas'. Movie production, it was declared, was 'on the eve of fruition'.

The team of cameramen under Joseph Albrecht had, during IW's absence, come into their own as a crack group of newsmen. Albrecht saw the newsreel as a kind of newspaper, and his operators as journalists heading into a world of danger and adventure. Albrecht himself went to Swaziland and Basutoland and was planning trips to 'the impenetrable forests of Knysna and the Addo Bush'. 'It is unnecessary to point out,' African Films said in a statement, 'that such enterprise is full of danger, but the intrepid cameraman … scorns such a notion.'

Every week the news segments were gaining popularity, especially their coverage of the war.

'The African Mirror series presented on the screen last night was easily the most interesting bioscope production one has seen for a long time,' one reviewer wrote at the close of 1914, harking back to the exciting footage of *The Great Strike*. 'There is every reason why local pictures should be better than those which come from over the water.'

By November theatres were advertising 'African Mirror and the Latest War Topicals'. There were 'stirring scenes' of 'Machine Gun Drill in Booysens' and 'the trouble in this country', especially the event that took up much of the camera team's time in the closing months of the year, 'The Unique Local Topical – The Rebellion.'

Several former Boer generals who were opposed to the Union of South Africa's decision to fight alongside Britain, their former enemy, had hatched a plot against Prime Minister Louis Botha. On 15 September 1914, two of them, Christiaan Beyers and Koos de la Rey, were driving from Pretoria to hold secret talks in Potchefstroom.

In Johannesburg, unbeknown to them, the police had set up roadblocks to intercept the murderous Foster Gang plaguing the city. After avoiding the first pair of policemen who tried to stop them, near Orange Grove, Beyers instructed their driver to take a 'dark road' past IW's farm, Killarney – an area he knew well – and then Villa Arcadia, the mansion of Sir Lionel Phillips. Using tracks and side streets, they finally came out in Vrededorp and then Fordsburg. Near Langlaagte station, when they didn't stop for two more policemen, they were fired upon. The popular De la Rey was fatally wounded and died in Beyers's arms; two weeks later, the first shots of the Afrikaner Rebellion went off.

The African Mirror team was soon taking scenes from different parts of the country. Even though the news sometimes took weeks to get to theatres, audiences couldn't get enough of it.

'The war film – an excellent one, depicted scenes of the Rebellion – Piet de la Rey's commando on the veld, Van Heerden's contingent at Rustenburg, prisoners brought in by the loyalists, and other incidents … the photography of which seems lately to be better than any of the imported "Gazettes" – perhaps owing to the pellucid atmosphere of the Rand.'

Skirmishes continued through the rest of 1914, with Botha's

army chasing an ever more scattered group of rebels. On 8 December, the charismatic General Beyers and a group of about 30 men were trapped at the Vaal River, which divided the Transvaal from the Orange Free State. Under fire, he tried to cross the river on his horse, but the animal, spooked by gunshots, started going in circles. Beyers finally let go and tried to swim back to shore but drowned. It was a tragedy that would come back to haunt IW on his biggest movie.

Once Botha had quelled the uprising, in February, IW's cameramen joined him and General Smuts to film the war in Africa. After several months in German South West Africa, they crossed the continent to follow the British East African Expeditionary Force. Their protracted exploits provided African Mirror with 'a remarkable series of films which were continuously shown under the title "With Our Boys in German East"'.

In Johannesburg, anti-German sentiment was especially high after the Afrikaner Rebellion, and it only got worse in the second week of May 1915, when the Cunard liner *Lusitania* was sunk by a U-boat south of Ireland while sailing from New York to Liverpool. Out of 1 962 passengers and crew on board, 1 198 died, mostly from hypothermia and drowning.

Reaction was swift in the City of Gold, as it was in Britain and America, with many believing that the incident would push the US into the war. On 12 May, any business that was German-owned or whose proprietor had a German-sounding name 'received the attention of the mob'. Rioters burned the German imperial flag outside the Town Hall, attacked stores like Schiller's Lighting, Stern's Hairdressing, the opticians Bull & Oehman, the jeweller Wehrley and Hildebrand's chocolate shop. Numerous small bioscopes – 'which are, or are believed to be, in the hands of enemy aliens' – were wrecked.

The Hotel Norman, the Hotel Bristol, the German Club and Buttner's Beer Hall were broken into, and furniture, musical instruments, pianos and pictures thrown from balconies into the street and set on fire. Angry crowds plundered a food warehouse in Newtown, as well as liquor stores owned by the Nebels, Rolfes, Libermans and Belstedts, pouring gallons of whisky into the street and setting it alight. At least 100 businesses were attacked, more than 60 infernos battled by the fire brigade, and an estimated £250 000 worth of property destroyed.

On 13 May, 'hundreds of men and woman all in an ugly mood who had been smashing shop windows and setting fire' to dozens of businesses marched through the streets to Market Square, where they came to a halt outside a building on the southern side. Despite a name that sounded very English, Colonial & Banking Trust, most people knew that IW owned the company, and to them the name 'Schlesinger' sounded very German.

By the time the rioters arrived, IW was ready for them. He stood at the top of the front steps, as well dressed as always, brusque, unfazed, his New York accent discernible when he began speaking.

'I am an American citizen,' he called out. 'If you want to burn down my place, you can bloody well do so.' For the benefit of those who didn't know, he added, 'It is insured by a South African company.' That company – the African Life Assurance Society – was, of course, his own.

The rioters left.

AN AFRICAN IN LONDON

Sailing out of New York on the same route as the *Lusitania* on 4 September 1915 was an American ship, the SS *St Louis*.

A few days earlier, the German ambassador had assured US Secretary of State Robert Lansing that his country's submarines would not fire on foreign liners without a warning or first making provision for the transfer of non-combatants. But that was cold comfort to anyone out in the middle of the icy Atlantic, where vessels were being torpedoed with growing frequency.

For the director Lorimer Johnston, the risk probably seemed worth it, the payoff potentially huge. Shooting movies for IW Schlesinger meant big budgets, huge productions, no limits, 'absolute power'. He was on his way to the new Hollywood.

Luckily for the American and the other passengers on the *St Louis*, their voyage passed without incident, and five days later they sailed into the mouth of the Mersey River. Liverpool Riverside station was conveniently located quayside, although traffic at the normally busy terminus had died down since the *Lusitania* tragedy.

Within a few hours of boarding a southbound London & North Western Railway train, Johnston and the dark-haired woman accompanying him, Caroline Frances Cooke, were at Euston Station. From there it was only a short taxi ride through Bloomsbury to Leicester Square and IVTA House.

IW arrived in London more than a week later, having sailed north on the *Dunvegan Castle*. His and Johnston's visits to the city would overlap only for several weeks, after which IW would sail on to New York, and Johnston south. During that time, decisions needed to be made about the movies that the American director would start shooting in Johannesburg.

The focus was narrowing, but numerous titles were still being tossed about. There was John Buchan's *Prester John*, Olive Schreiner's *The Story of an African Farm*, De Vere Stacpoole's *Blue Lagoon* and Haggard's *King Solomon's Mines* and its sequel, *Allan Quatermain*. As for historical spectacles, IW finally opened up about subjects he was considering for a possible production: Cecil John Rhodes, the Zulu King Dingaan, the 1820 British settlers.

On the day that IW arrived in London, 25 September, something happened that would profoundly affect his decision. *The Birth of a Nation* opened at the ornate Scala theatre on Charlotte Street, in Fitzrovia, about a mile away from IVTA House.

America's very first historical spectacle, *Birth of a Nation* was Hollywood's answer to *Cabiria* and *Quo Vadis*. Billed as the '8th Wonder of the World' when it opened in New York, the movie's publicity claimed '18 000 People. 3 000 Horses. 3 Years to Produce. $500 000. The Supreme Picture of All Time'. Like *Cabiria*, it was twelve reels long, and its director, DW Griffith, was being hailed as a genius, his movie the first ever to be screened at the White House.

'No description can give an adequate idea of the excitement and movement of these scenes played over a wide extent of country,' wrote the *Daily Mail* the following day, 'but there is little doubt that this series of pictures of great American historical events will prove a big attraction.'

The story in the movie focused on two families caught up in the Civil War of the 1860s – the Stonemans from the abolitionist North and the Camerons from the Confederate South – and the ensuing Reconstruction. It opened, famously, with a recreation of the assassination of Abraham Lincoln.

Besides being the biggest movie America had ever made, it quickly became a flashpoint. The reason was that one of the main characters, Colonel Benjamin Cameron, was based on a real person who had helped found the racist Ku Klux Klan in 1865.

Black characters in the movie were almost all 'represented as uncouth, intellectually inferior and predators of white women'.

'Negroes and Their Friends Call Production "Cruel and Untrue",' ran a headline in New York's *The Sun*. The film was 'a public menace ... not art, but vicious propaganda', wrote the author WEB Du Bois, adding that 'a new art was used, deliberately, to slander and vilify a race'. Protests 'solidified the foundations' of the six-year-old National Association for the Advancement of Colored People, of which Du Bois was one of the founders.

'The ground of my protest,' added Frederick Howe, the white chairman of the US board of movie censorship, 'is that the play affects 10 000 000 citizens who are degraded by it. One half deals with war and the other half portrays the negro as a lustful and degraded creature.' The mayor of Chicago, William Thompson, banned the movie from being shown, and was soon followed by the mayors of Denver, Pittsburgh, St Louis and Minneapolis.

In Britain, most of the protest came from a group called the Anti-Slavery and Aborigines Protection Society, which 'sought to monitor abuse and injustice in relation to colored people'. But otherwise the reaction was noticeably muted: 'There were ... no well publicised debates or objections to this film's racist representations, no attempts to censor or ban the film at local exhibitions and no public disturbance such as those which accompanied the film in the United States.'

A lone voice of dissent came from a man living at 25 Carnarvon Road, Waltham Forest, northeast of the city. Solomon Tshekisho Plaatje was a black South African intellectual, politician, journalist and linguist who would later translate a number of Shakespeare's plays into his native language, Setswana.

Plaatje was the general secretary of a recently established political movement, the South African Native National Congress. He had come to London the previous year to protest the Natives Land Act of 1913, which put into law 'a strict curtailment' of land rights, whereby 'the South African native found himself, not actually a slave, but a pariah in the land of his birth'. After the rest of the delegation went home, Plaatje stayed on.

Like Mohandas Gandhi, Plaatje would have been on IW's radar. Unlike the Indian, Plaatje loved movies; after returning to South Africa, he would start a small touring outfit, 'Mr Plaatje's bioscope', riding his bicycle to non-white communities to show all-black movies.

But in 1915, movies were not the link between Plaatje and IW. Through the Colonial & Banking Trust, Schlesinger had come into contact with two other founders of the Congress, Pixley ka Isaka Seme and John Dube. Before the 1913 Land Act came into force, the Congress started a company to enable Africans to buy land. When it ran into financial difficulties, a partnership was formed with Schlesinger, whose company often advertised its services on the front page of the Congress's paper, *Abantu-Batho*.

When *Birth of a Nation* was shown at the Scala, Plaatje watched the public's enthusiastic reaction in disgust. Already 'friendly with members of the (Anti-Slavery and Aborigines Protection) Society,' he wrote to the British Home Secretary, Viscount Simon, asking why the film was 'permitted to libel the black face in England and the British Empire'. How could the film be shown 'at a time when black races by the thousands were dying in defence of England and the British empire'. He drew 'attention to the offensive nature of the film ... demanding that it be withdrawn'. Wiping its hands of the affair, the Home Office replied that since 'the Film Censors had already licensed the play, the government could do nothing'.

The matter did not end there, however.

William P Schreiner, the South African High Commissioner at the time and brother of Olive Schreiner, 'widely regarded as one of the South African public figures most sympathetic to African interests', was keenly aware of *Birth of a Nation* and its racist story-line. He went to see the movie and was in contact with two leaders from the Anti-Slavery Society, whom he assured that he had taken unofficial steps to prevent it from being shown in South Africa.

In the coming weeks and months, Griffith's movie opened across the British Empire, in Australia and Canada, as well as in parts of Europe and Latin America, where it drew crowds. The one place it didn't open was at IW Schlesinger's African Theatres – although that had nothing to with him.

In early 1916, the British government took the unusual step of banning *The Birth of a Nation* in South Africa – a restriction that would stay in place for 15 years, until 1931.

But a seed had been planted. If only for its sheer scale and spectacle, *Birth of a Nation* was the American movie that IW wanted to copy.

'THE REAL WORK OF MY LIFE'

By late October 1915, a month after the premiere at the Scala and a few days after IW sailed for New York, Lorimer Johnston was back at sea, for the last and longest stretch of his journey to South Africa.

When the director boarded the *Llandovery Castle* at Southampton, he once again had as his companion the actress Caroline Frances Cooke. Dark-haired and big-eyed, she was a good head shorter than him and eighteen years younger.

Cooke, who was married to the director, had been the lead actor in many of his movies, including his biggest, *The Envoy Extraordinary*, in which she had played the Countess of Northstone, wife of the prime minister of a 'great power' facing the threat of a war. Johnston's movie had been made before war was declared, and American publicity made much of his uncanny prediction. Now, it was a real war the movie couple was entering.

As they sailed through the English Channel towards Spain, into the North Atlantic, and then southwest to skirt the bulge of Africa, it seemed mad to be setting off on the adventure of a lifetime as the conflict in Europe was growing more brutal by the day.

At Gallipoli, the fighting was entering its eighth month, with tens of thousands of lives already lost. During a three-week battle around the village of Loos, in France, the British lost at least 60 000 men killed, wounded or missing.

The *Llandovery Castle*, barely a year old, was still freshly painted in the Union-Castle's distinctive livery, a lavender hull and red-striped funnel. It stood out against the other passenger steamers, many of which had already been requisitioned by the Royal Navy and painted in camouflage colours, and were carrying troops and nurses to the front. Its sister ship, the *Kinfauns Castle*, had already been involved in the dramatic hunt for the German light cruiser *Königsberg*, which had been causing havoc in the Indian Ocean. The marauding ship was eventually trapped in the Rufiji Delta, south of Dar es Salaam, in the middle of May and sunk.

Johnston, who was known to be a fast worker, had plenty to keep him busy on the 18-day voyage. 'Dogged, determined, and knowing his own mind is how I would set him down,' one journalist wrote of him at the time. 'There is no damn nonsense about Mr Johnston. He … knows exactly what he wants, and wastes no time or space with ornamental verbiage.'

In preparation, he had already gone through at least 80 history books and novels. Some of them that had been acquired by African Films he could quickly turn into scenarios: Bertrand Mitford's *The Gun-Runner* and Charlotte Mansfield's *Gloria*. There was also an original story that IW – a fervent supporter of the Boy Scout movement – had come up with, *The Silver Wolf*, about a boy who persuades his thieving father to hand himself over to the police.

Cooke, who had written the scenario for a 1914 movie called *The Story of the Olive*, about a young settler in early California, chose a similar title for her first effort for African Films, *The Story of the Rand*. It dealt with a young mother who, after killing her abusive husband, escapes with her daughter from England to Johannesburg.

On 2 November, while the ship was sailing somewhere off West Africa, Johnston celebrated his fifty-seventh birthday. It was the start of a year full of promise and possibilities. 'I am fully convinced,' he wrote to a friend in New York, 'that (in Johannesburg) I will do the real work of my life in the production of pictures.'

When they sailed into Table Bay about ten days later, he was received like a celebrity. The *Rand Daily Mail* called him 'the producer in chief' of a new industry of 'cinematograph films on a large and ambitious scale (to be produced and exported) to the important cities of the world.' 'Mr Johnston is a very famous man in the film world,' crowed IW's own brand-new movie magazine, *Stage & Cinema*, 'having been producer with the Santa Barbara Motion Picture Company, the Flying A Company, Universal, and later with the Vitagraph, undoubtably the premier film producing company in the world today.'

Johnston himself declared: 'I am going to put on a number of pictures that will exploit the ancient and present – and I will prognosticate the future – history of South Africa.'

Once again, the titles of several possible pictures were mentioned, most notably *The Story of an African Farm* and *King Solomon's Mines*. 'I have already been in contact with Rider Haggard,' said Johnston, 'and I hope to get his assistance on the spot.'

As for the spectacles – would IW mimic *Cabiria* or the newer *Birth of a Nation*? – they seemed to be closing in on three particular subjects, one Afrikaner, one English, one African. The subjects IW was keen on had changed slightly since they were last mentioned.

'I will produce pictures of "The Great Trek" and the leading incidents in the life of Cecil Rhodes,' Johnston said. 'When I get going, I want to produce a Chaka (sic) picture that will astonish the world.'

EMERGING FROM THE CHRYSALIS

The Palm Court was quiet. As the early-morning light poured into the glass-roofed atrium, a towering tree in its centre just like at the Ritz in London, waiters were setting set up for coffee and breakfast at the polished tables dotting the grand room.

Walking through the Palm Court to the lobby, Lorimer Johnston passed a doorman and exited onto Eloff Street in front of the Carlton Hotel, the clatter of a tram reminding him of the noise that he had heard through the night coming into his balconied windows. In some ways, it could have been New York or London.

Shops were still closed. Cuthberts, then Blinmans and Chud-leighs – too many new names for him to remember, too many windows to look into. Thrupps was full of sweets and biscuits from England. Atop the Wolff and Elias Building on Market Street, next to the Library Hotel, stood a sculpture of Mercury. As sleepy-eyed shoeblacks began setting up on street corners, the aromas of bread baking and kitchens firing up filled the air, while tables were being laid at the Corner Lounge, the Carlton Grill and Madeleine's.

And the theatres! Even the Carlton had one. Two streets away, on Jeppe, there was the Bijou, boasting: 'We Have Delved Among all the Superlatives of the English Language to Find the Word to Aptly Describe "The Master Key".' At the Orpheum, the Trempers were on stage, as were the Granville Trio and Selma and James, while on screen was *Portrait in the Attic*. At the Palladium, John Galsworthy's *Strife* was publicised, quite appropriately in a city obsessed with labour turmoil, as a 'Great Strike Drama'. Every theatre, the American would have noticed, belonged to IW.

Johnston kept going east and crossed Kruis Street. To his left, the road ran straight into the impressive domed Supreme Court, while in front of him lay his destination – the Empire. The week's main offering was the show *Step This Way*, 'An All Star London Cast – Jay Whidden and Billy Kuming – The Boys Who took London by Storm'…accompanied by '20 of London's Prettiest, Smartest and Best Chorus Girls'.

Once the director entered the building, he took the steps to the offices and workshops on the upper floors. The first movies he was to make at African Films were to start shooting in early 1916, less than two months away, and there was plenty of work to do before then.

He could immediately see that the engine of IW's movie company, at least for the moment, was the cameramen. So popular had African Mirror become that every motion picture at IW's theatres was now expected to open with not only the latest episode of cliffhanger serials like *The Purple Mask* or *The Adventures of Ruth* but news from home and East Africa and abroad.

Every Monday, copies of the weekly segments – what they called 'engagements', up to 12 of them – were ready to be distributed around the country in circuits, each one of four engagements. The men who weren't in East Africa travelled further afield, to 'remote and faraway places, seeking adventure, so that it may be photographed in either camera or motion picture machine'. Stills they took were used in IW's magazine, *Stage & Cinema*.

If it wasn't news they were filming, it was scenics or travelogues or educationals. That year already, African Mirror had produced 'A Holiday at Port Elizabeth', 'Farming by Dynamite', 'The Victoria Falls', 'A Ride to Camps Bay' and 'The Cape Times Printing Works'. Tommy Crellin had gone to Howick Falls in Natal, and Albrecht to Pretoria, Rustenburg and Kloof. He had filmed a tram travel the five miles from Eloff Street, near the Carlton, to

Joseph Albrecht, on the right, had just turned 23
and was already indispensable to IW. On the left is Ralph Kimpton,
who met IW's scorn soon after this photograph appeared.

Orange Grove, one of the suburbs IW had created, providing 'one of the most astonishing testimonies of the rapid growth of the town'.

What the cameramen were facing when they began working with Johnston, however, was something they had never done before – a narrative movie, filming actors on sets or out in the open, artifice instead of reality. None of them could have guessed that in only a few months, the two would collide right in front of them with disastrous consequences.

Unlike the well-oiled team of cameramen, the actors and technicians Johnston met were a motley bunch. They came to the Empire from all over the world and had varying degrees of experience in acting or film – some of them none at all.

Mabel May, Dick Cruickshanks and his wife, Florence Creagh, who had all been part of touring theatrical groups from England, decided to stay and try their hand at acting in front of a camera. Denis Santry, smart and insightful, his hair always neatly combed, was a political cartoonist. John Maxfield, from Yorkshire, was a botanist. Holger Petersen, Danish, only 20 years old, had tried his hand as a miner for a short time and failed, but was luckily blessed with the good looks that would make him perfect as a screen hero or villain. Ralph Kimpton had been a stage manager in London. The famous circus master himself, Frank Fillis, now almost sixty, would train men and women to do stunts, ride horses and eventually even steer chariots. Fillis's daughter, Adele, 23, pretty, a horse rider, also signed up, as did Fillis's son, Frank Junior. Benjamin Franklin Clinton arrived from San Francisco to be a studio manager, even though his experience was in writing. Sam Stern, a New Yorker, was already in town doing vaudeville and comedy acts. And MA Wetherell, whose initials stood for Marmaduke Arundel, was a 36-year-old Englishman, six foot tall and not unhandsome, with a taste for new experiences. He had been a policeman, a ranch hand and a hunter; why not try movies next?

Besides them, Lorimer Johnston had hundreds of others to meet who wanted to act in his movies. For months already, inserts had been put in IW's theatre programmes looking for people who could ride, swim, cycle and shoot, and in the hope that they could act, giving 'facial expression to the emotions aroused by certain imaginary occurrences'.

For Johnston, however, that still wasn't enough. 'I am in touch with some artistes here,' he told one newspaper, 'but I am bringing other artistes from England and America. I have selected from the Vitagraph Company some very celebrated people, and one code word cabled to America would bring them here.'

That code word, presumably, was 'Spectacle!'

Most importantly, Johnston had to visit the place where he would bring all these people together, the studio at Killarney, the City of Film. By now it had been under construction for almost a year.

If anyone was capable of judging the quality of the studio, it was Johnston. He had worked for production houses in Rome, New York and Los Angeles, including for Carl Laemmle. He had even been in Los Angeles on 15 March 1915 for the magnificent opening of Laemmle's Universal City, the model for IW's Killarney studio.

Even before the studio building was complete, filming began on an open-air stage at Killarney in early 1916, in full view of houses in Houghton.

What Johnston saw below the Parktown ridge impressed him greatly. 'I found already on my arrival,' he wrote to the New York impresario Robert Grau, 'studios started, and by the end of February (1916) we will have a plant that will compare more than favourably with 90 per cent of our American studios.'

The formidable main building was, he said, 'decorative to the landscape instead of a detriment, as so many of our studio "shacks" are at home'. Made of cut stone and concrete, it would eventually measure 20 000 square feet on each of its two floors. There were to be offices for IW, his directors, managers, scenario editors and writers; a place for posters to be created; a section for African Mirror; a library and reading room; kitchen and dining room and mess hall; and ateliers for carpenters and costume makers. Across the property Johnston saw them building an open-air stage and water features, garages for vehicles to be used in movies, a place for animals to be trained, the list went on. In almost every respect, it felt like Carl Laemmle's Universal City.

'And not only will pictures be produced, but the films themselves will be manufactured here from raw materials,' one journalist wrote. 'Thus when the city finally emerges from the chrysalis stage of construction it will be a scene of great activity, and the home of a busy, thriving population.'

As construction at the City of Film hurried along, and before Johnston started shooting his first movie there, which was meant to happen in early 1916, one last thing remained to be done. He had to experience IW's 'wand of witchery'.

THE WAND OF WITCHERY

As 1915 drew to a close, Lorimer Johnston packed enough clothes to last him for two months. With him as he boarded the train at Park Station was Henry Howse, a colourfully boastful English cameraman who had been in the country for only a week.

Ahead of them lay an exhausting journey of 2 500 miles – the equivalent of crossing North America or going from London to St Petersburg and back. First, they were heading north to Rhodesia, then south to the hinterland and the eastern Cape coast at Algoa Bay, and finally to Zululand, in the northeast, before returning to the City of Gold.

'I shall go wherever it is necessary to get the proper environment,' the director declared, like an explorer, before setting off. In America, he added, speed and footage were the most important things when shooting a movie, but his policy in Africa would be very different. 'I want to get pictures that will be scenically, historically and atmospherically South African.'

They took with them at least one camera, to film scenes along the way. These would serve two purposes: first, they could be used as scenics by African Mirror later on; and second, they would be a filmic record for possible future movie locations. It was IW's very own reconnaissance mission.

Shooting on location, as Johnston knew only too well, was a rarity, even more so when it was in the exact setting where the story was meant to take place. If movies were not filmed indoors, in front of fake scenery or a painted canvas, or on a flimsy set in a confined lot, they were filmed in countryside that could double for the real place. In the US only a few months earlier, claims were made that a popular six-reel Western, *The Squaw Man*, had been filmed in Utah, Arizona and Wyoming, but in reality 'the company never left southern California'.

IW wanted to be more like Giovanni Pastrone, the Italian director of *Cabiria*, who had travelled incredible distances, to Tunis and Egypt, and had actually taken elephants to Switzerland to recreate Hannibal's famed crossing of the Alps. Verisimilitude was what he was after, no matter how much it cost to get it.

IW's insistence on using real locations seemed to be tied inextricably to his passion for the country, which he wanted everyone to see. One of the few things that he ever wrote for publication was about the South African landscape, which he found 'seductive and wheedling'. As a young insurance salesman, covering many thousands of miles by foot, bicycle, donkey and Cape cart, he had often slept under the stars.

'It seems to beckon and lead you as with a wand of witchery,' he wrote of the countryside. 'It insinuates itself into your consciousness and slowly envelops you as with a mantle of peace until you resign yourself to its gentle influence and are content. The wide horizons, the great open spaces swept by the sun-washed air of a vast and virgin Continent, have always held a strong appeal for me.'

Joseph Albrecht had been the first person IW sent off to see what he had seen, and now Johnston and Howse were next. The 'wand of witchery' tour was becoming almost mandatory before you could shoot one of IW's movies.

As the train rattled along, though open veld and past clefted koppies and breathtaking mountains and subtropical shoreline, Johnston and Howse must have bonded quickly. One can imagine them swapping tales of Hollywood and derring-do.

Howse was much closer in age to Johnston than was the young Albrecht – there was only seven years' difference between them – and his experience was considerable. To hear him talk about it, he made his life sound more like a fantastic fiction: 'Were it possible to make up a composite life of Robinson Crusoe, Midshipman Easy, and Captain Cook ... I really think some idea of my career might be obtained from the result.'

He had travelled to 35 countries, including China and Tibet, some of them several times, and often to record the activities of William Booth, the founder of the Salvation Army. Three times he had stood trial for his life in front of 'Bedouin brigands', and in 1909 had filmed a 500-mile trip up the Yangtze River. He also claimed to have sailed as a cameraman with Sir Ernest Shackleton on the *Nimrod*, where he 'looked death in the face every day ... and even madness'. It was only by the 'narrowest margin of good luck' that he missed going with Robert Falcon Scott on his doomed expedition to the South Pole.

Between the two of them, Johnston and Howse had clocked up decades of experience, yet neither had been to Africa before, let alone made a film there. Now they were about to become the first men to make feature movies on the continent – not only multi-reel pictures but huge spectacles.

By the time they got back to Johannesburg in January 1916, Johnston was full of enthusiasm and ready to start filming: 'I have just returned from a tour of 2 500 miles, visiting Rhodesia, Swaziland, Zululand, Natal, Orange Free State, Basutoland, Cape Colony and Transvaal. I have made this trip to familiarise myself with the actual locations for the pictures I am to produce.'

The slate of movies he was going to direct came up again, and details were provided that hadn't been made public before, which seemed to make them all that much more of a certainty: 'We have contracted with Sir Rider Haggard to picturize "King Solomon's Mines", combined with "Allan Quatermain," and shall make this a massive production in five reels. We are constructing a power system to use in the Cango Caves, the actual place Haggard describes in the novels …

'I shall also produce "The Story of an African Farm" by Olive Schreiner, "Gloria" by Charlotte Mansfield and "The Great Trek", and a five-reeler to be called "Dingaan".' The last-named film, he promised, 'will use thousands of Zulus in their own country (so) you can see how great a production I shall make.'

The 'wand of witchery' tour had done its trick. Johnston was smitten and wrote to his friend Robert Grau in New York about the great and thrilling challenges that faced him: 'The more I have seen of Africa, the more I am convinced of the great possibilities for cinema art.'

It sounded almost too good to be true – and it was.

PART THREE
1916

Into the Valley of Death

The very first big scene from *Winning a Continent*, in Dingaan's kraal.

SENSATION

Like the cork popping off a New Year's champagne bottle, 1916 began with excitement and a frenzy of energy.

Suddenly, film crews and actors were all over Johannesburg. In the city centre, actors performed on the steps of the Town Hall, and cameras were set up along the main shopping thoroughfares of Eloff and Pritchard streets, and inside busy arcades.

Crowds gathered on Market Square one day to watch a man dressed as the devil act out his role for *The Major's Dilemma*. On being filmed for *£20,000* on Von Brandis Square, the American actor Frank Harrison later recalled: 'After being drenched with soapsuds, smothered first in flour, then in soot, I had the pleasure of seeing myself on the screen.' The shooting of *A Kract Affair* 'held up the traffic in Eloff Street', watched by a crowd of 1 500 people, 'some amused, some mystified'.

'The opening of the New Automobile Club ... and the beautiful house of Denis Santry, and other pretty homes in Parktown Heights have been utilised for locales.'

For *The Story of the Rand*, written by his wife Caroline Cooke, Lorimer Johnston took his crew to film at Crown Mines, Langlaagte, Geduld Mines, Springs and into the protected sanctum of the Rand Club.

A scene took place with Cooke and others 'in Indian servant disguise' mingling among guests at an organised function held on the Killarney farm. 'Quite a mild sensation was caused by the

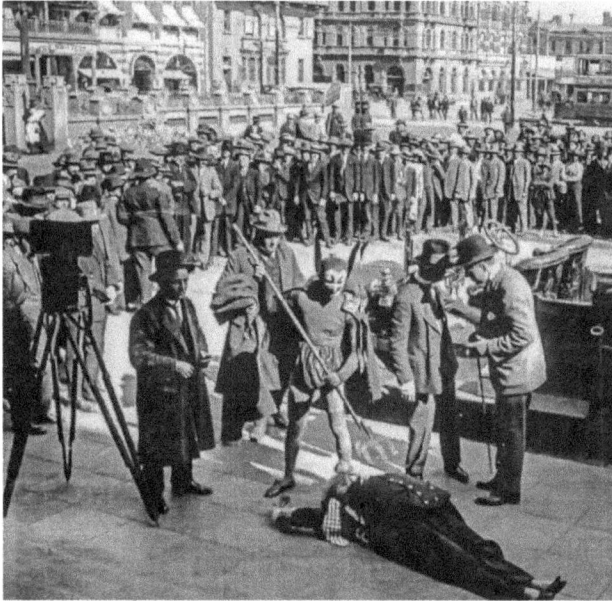

Lights! Camera! Audience! A scene from the 1916 movie *The Major's Dilemma* drew crowds of curious onlookers to Market Square.

appearance of the artists with their painted faces (and) by the quick and nervous remarks of the producer, who was interrupted by a fat-headed policeman who apparently imagined that some anarchic episode was about to be performed.'

Soon the film crews would be going further afield, to Parys on the Vaal River to shoot *A Splendid Waster*, and to Swaziland, where the Queen's royal guard of 500 warriors played extras in *A Border Scourge*.

For IW, after two years of travelling between Johannesburg, London and New York to amass his movie teams, it was all suddenly paying off. The chrysalis had emerged.

At the third AGM of African Films, held early that year at the Empire – the theatre had almost become his good-luck charm – it was announced that the company had already imported two million feet of film – up from the 10 000 feet it bought from America in 1913 – and was opening offices in India and Egypt. IW now owned all of the most important theatres in the country, except for the final holdout, Fischer's Elite Bioscope in Cape Town.

'Mr Schlesinger is never content to stand still,' wrote the *Rand Daily Mail*. 'He is always trying to perfect any business he takes in hand.

'From all parts of South Africa inquiries are received, and there is no doubt that at some near future date this country will be assisting the British trade in no small degree by offering some of the world's best photoplays, produced and entirely completed in one of the Mother Britain's youngest colonies.'

The prediction that African Films would soon be a global player was astonishing, especially given the fact that, apart from his newsreels, IW hadn't yet released a single movie.

A QUIET ENTRANCE

On Monday 29 May 1916, a brief one-reeler played at the Orpheum. It was so short and took place so late in the evening that it was almost overlooked.

The programme began with the 'comedy cyclists' Newhouse and War, the male impersonator Rhoda Paul and the comedienne Gracie Grahame. Then, at the tail end of the night's fare, came 'The first South African Drama released by African Film Productions Ltd' – *A Zulu's Devotion.*

For anyone who had lived through the weeks of hype leading up to *The Great Strike* – the posters, the daily news reports, the banning, the inquest, the unbanning, the new posters, the publicity of the camera operator dying, and finally its successful showing – the release of the very first movie from African Films passed with little fanfare.

The one-reel drama, directed by Lorimer Johnston, was about 'a faithful Zulu farm-hand who frustrates the schemes of a couple of half-caste stock thieves and rescues his little mistress from their clutches'. One journalist wrote that it 'got a big round of applause, and it was quite evident that the picture was much to the liking of an audience big enough to pack the place from floor to ceiling'. Another called it 'a distinct success', adding that 'The old Zulu, too, acts his part splendidly'.

There was some consternation, however, that 'a Zulu herd boy' was allowed to arrest a white man, one of the stock thieves, although patrons were later told that the two men were in fact 'half-castes', 'a fact which might have been explained (beforehand) to the audience'.

The name of the actor playing the title character, quite unusually, was listed in the newspapers alongside Holger Petersen, Caroline Frances Cooke and Marmaduke Wetherell. His acting name was Goba, but his real name was Archibald Zonzo Goba, and he would become the most important African actor at IW's studio. How that had happened is unclear, but one story held that he had been the head gardener at Killarney.

With *A Zulu's Devotion* he had 'taken to 'movie work' like a duck to water, and ... before long will be a familiar figure on the world bioscope screens'. Soon he was joined at Killarney by several other Africans who would play lead roles: Tom Zulu, Umpikayiboni and Msoga Mwana.

The Zulu nation clearly intrigued IW. The prominence of stories about its three most famous kings – Shaka, Dingaan, the half-brother who killed him, and Cetshwayo, who was at the centre of the Anglo-Zulu War of 1879 – put them at the centre of several possible movie spectacles.

At the end of 1913 already, his cameramen went to film the funeral of Cetshwayo's son, Dinizulu. Joseph Albrecht had travelled to Zululand several times, and had shot extensive footage for documentaries, one of which, *The Natives of Zululand*, included a traditional wedding and a council meeting.

During their 'wand of witchery' tour, Johnston and Howse found a Zulu who would become one of the lead actors. At the local police station in the town of Stanger, north of Durban, there was 'a head boy of the police ... who rejoiced in the name of Bicycle ... a fine looking Zulu of the royal breed (who) was picked to be King Dingaan'. It was agreed that he would come to the City of Film with his family for the production. By the time he arrived, a suitable screen name had been chosen for him: Tom Zulu.

It was Johnston, according to the film historian Neil Parsons, who did the most to promote the advancement of African actors at the studio. Goba later wrote him a letter 'thanking me for the fame I've given him outside Zululand by showing his likeness in all parts of the world'.

A Zulu's Devotion, besides fitting in nicely with IW's fascination with the tribe, was a direct copy of an American movie made seven years earlier, *The Zulu's Heart*. The director, most significantly, was DW Griffith, who had gone on to make *The Birth of a Nation*.

The difference between the two Zulu movies was that Griffith had used the hills of New Jersey as a substitute for Africa, and the African characters had been played by white men in blackface, a practice that would continue in the US for many years to come.

The newly named Tom Zulu arrived at the City of Film shortly before Easter 1916. The 'family' the studio had agreed could accompany him included his 'wives, children and followers', numbering several hundred people.

To accommodate them – and serving much the same purpose as the tepees erected at Universal City – a copy of a Zulu village had been constructed on the farm. There were about 70 beehive-shaped huts, and most of the material to make them had come from the Sachsenwald plantation. Running between the huts were grass palisades.

Tom Zulu took the central hut, which was about ten times larger than the rest, a beacon standing out in the Johannesburg veld. The kraal of almost six dozen structures, which was finished even before the studio headquarters, was quite clearly meant to be the centrepiece in an upcoming spectacle. But no one seemed to know yet which one. *King Solomon's Mines*? The story of Shaka? The Dingaan picture that Lorimer Johnston promised would 'astonish the world'?

Until filming began, the newly arrived men were given jobs as gardeners, water carriers, 'teaboys', carpenter's assistants and painters, or they tended to the 100 cattle and 400 sheep that IW had bought to graze in the nearby veld. The women looked after the small gardens around their huts and did beadwork.

The new set became known simply as 'the village'.

MEN OF SPEED

On weeknights, IW had taken to going home via the Empire, 'so that he could see what was going on'. Afterwards, Max Zasman drove him out of the city, past the glimmering mansions of Parktown into the quiet grounds of Killarney.

Since taking over the Empire, he was spending more of his nights not at the Carlton but in a modest building, 'a very simple shack' whose most distinctive feature was being lined with hundreds of books. An African housekeeper made dinner for him before he retired at eleven, and by five the next morning he was up again.

The 'shack' was everything the Carlton wasn't, not only in size and luxury but also in location. In his penthouse, he was in the heart of the city, and virtually at the top of it, and was seen every day by the hotel staff. His Napier motorcar drew so much attention when it was parked on Eloff Street that he eventually told Zasman to wait in the back instead. From there, though, he was back in the public view again as they drove along Commissioner, Simmonds and Market streets to Market Square. He couldn't have chosen a more public setting, which was strange for someone who detested being in the spotlight.

'He disliked … being photographed … (and) he avoided newspaper interviews and only gave them strictly on business matters when it was in the interest of the (Schlesinger) Organisation.' Social gatherings and cocktail parties were anathema, 'and (he) abhorred dinner parties at private houses.'

But at Killarney, far from the city centre, off Oxford Road, hidden away between the trees, IW could avoid all of that. Initially, after he bought the farm in 1906 and started spending more time there, two other people also lived on the property, the paint manufacturer Herbert Evans and the contractor James Thompson, who had helped IW mark off the studio boundaries.

Away from prying eyes, IW could also receive visitors without being noticed. In a city infamous for its divisions, that was perhaps wise, for callers at the shack were from every quarter – Afrikaner, Jew, Englishman, mining magnate, politician, civil servant, businessman, military man, theatre impresario, criminal lawyer.

There was Solly Joel, the mining-magnate owner of the Carlton Hotel; the prime minister, General Louis Botha; the Randlord Sir Lionel Phillips; Sir William Hoy, the brilliant Scotsman who created the South African Railways out of four separate networks after Union; the defence minister, General Jan Smuts; the industrialist Sammy Marks; Johannesburg's first public prosecutor, Frederic Krause, who in 1899 had persuaded the retreating Boers not to blow up the mines, and who had prosecuted the great charlatan and murderer Baron Ferdinand Karl Ludwig von Veltheim – and lost; the diamond tycoon Sir Abe Bailey; and Sir JB Robinson, from whom Schlesinger had bought the bank on Market Square in 1905 where he now had his headquarters. Robinson's name was also part of a major landmark in the city, the Robinson Deep mine, which would soon play an incredible role in IW's movies. The idea to use it had perhaps even been sparked in the modest shack.

Of all the visitors, the most unusual was a handsome military officer immediately identifiable by his handlebar moustache. General Christiaan Beyers was a lawyer and a sportsman whose religious convictions seemed at odds with his vanity.

Side by side, they must have made an unlikely pair, the sturdy Afrikaner with deep Calvinist beliefs and proud of his good looks, and the small American Jewish business tycoon who had a love for telling 'Yiddisher' stories. But Beyers was 'one of his great friends'.

The men shared a passion for cars. Even though IW may not have known how to drive, and always needed a chauffeur, he loved speed, and his efforts to promote motor vehicles earned him accolades like 'the well-known patron of sport and automobilism on the Rand'. He had launched car and motorcycle races to Rustenburg and Durban and got his cameramen to film them for audiences to see at his theatres. When one of the racing films played at the Orpheum in 1914, the winning Rudge-Whitworth motorcycle was put on display in the foyer.

In 1903, IW had also started the Transvaal Automobile Club. While it was seen by some as an alternative to the elite Rand Club, which was thought to exclude Jews, the TAC was no easier to get into – you had to own a car to join, which very few people could afford. By 1910, there were only about a thousand cars on the Rand and in Pretoria, half of the total in the entire country.

In the middle of September 1913, when the club turned ten, General Beyers was the guest of honour, and presented a new four-foot silver cup, donated by IW, to the winner of the latest automobile race, which was a Ford. The TAC was now located in a building on Killarney, and it was such an important event that IW turned up and had African Mirror film it for a 'Grand Automobile Night' at the Empire ten days later.

Beyers had just returned from a visit to Europe, where he met with the German monarch, Kaiser Wilhelm II, a man he greatly admired. With the threat of war already in the air, he used his speech at the club to talk about the use of motor vehicles in battle. Much success, he said, had been achieved with them in the Balkans conflict, and 'the time (is) not far distant when a lot of cars (will) be required by the Government for use, if necessary, in warfare'. After IW responded, 'three cheers were given for General Beyers and Mr. Schlesinger'.

The evening was tragically prescient. The Union Defence Force's motorised brigade would be launched in that very same building one year later, on 7 November 1914. The event was officiated by

General Smuts, seeing that Beyers had by this stage joined the Afrikaner Rebellion, was on the run and would soon be dead.

Even though IW was out of the country when the Rebellion began and when Beyers drowned, he was 'shocked and surprised' by the news of his friend's actions and death. On his return from London, he went to Pretoria to visit Beyers's widow, Mathilde König, who, like anyone supporting the Rebellion, was facing public anger. IW wanted 'to ensure that she was not without funds and despite any odium which might attach to this, he helped her through this crisis'.

Besides cars, however, IW and the general also had something else in common: a passion for the Afrikaner.

Before the Anglo-Boer War, Schlesinger, like 'the great majority of Americans, was anti-British and pro-Boer'. At the opening of the Three Castles tobacco factory in Johannesburg, owned by the three Holt brothers, he had even met President Kruger, to whom he tried in vain to sell a life insurance policy with Equitable.

While Schlesinger travelled the length and breadth of the country for Equitable, 'insuring the lives of the Boer farmers (he) laid the foundations of (his own) great insurance company and learned to know the Afrikaner Boer, for whom he always had a sneaking regard'.

In time, IW progressed to travelling with a Cape cart pulled by four *skimmel*, or dappled, horses, his companions a doctor – to carry out medical examinations on prospective clients – and a Malay driver, and they would be away for months. 'We lived with the Boer farmers. They gave us what they had – tough goat meat and brown *semels* bread (made from bran) and bad coffee – but they were always hospitable and kind.'

At the outbreak of the war, in 1899, there was a rumour that Schlesinger had accepted a post as an assistant to the Boer general Lukas Meyer and would join his commando. It was Meyer who, five years earlier, had helped the Zulu prince Dinizulu defeat his brother at the battle of Tshaneni.

When IW realised that by aiding the Boers, he would lose his American citizenship, and could even be executed, he soon left the country to take up a post with Equitable Insurance in Ireland, where he stayed until the war ended in 1902.

Those early years – crisscrossing southern Africa – clearly had a profound effect on Schlesinger, not only the 'wand of witchery' that the countryside exerted over him but the Afrikaners he met: 'Being fond of children he was able to establish immediate bases for friendship with their big families.'

Over farm dinner tables and campfires, they told him the history of their ancestors, the Voortrekkers, and their trek into the hinterland to escape their British overlords at the Cape. 'Without claiming to understand Afrikaans, he could follow the stories of many of the Boers, thanks to his knowledge of German.' Sometimes the speakers were old men and women who themselves had been children at the time of the historic events they told him about.

Maybe it was his friendship with Beyers, Smuts and Botha. Maybe it was those early days travelling about the countryside, listening to campfire tales 'from some of the last of these pioneers'. Maybe he just wanted a big story to tell. But by the middle of 1915, IW had at last decided what his first movie spectacle would be – a retelling of the best-known and most sacred event in Afrikaner history.

THE HISTORIAN

No one in the country knew more about Afrikaner history than a man living in Pretoria named Gustav Preller. He had even thought up the name by which the Afrikaner's most famous historical event was known – *die Groot Trek*, or the Great Trek.

A portly man with an engaging smile who had just turned 40, Preller wore many hats – newspaper and magazine editor, author, literary critic and a main proponent of the new language, Afrikaans. In 1905, he published *Piet Retief*, a book that covered the events of the trek north from the Cape and the battle of Blood River. So popular had it become that it was already in its ninth printing.

Preller lived in Pretoria, a place where IW had canvassed early in his career, and which he fondly called 'a small city with a big heart'. There were 'no stately avenues, as in Stellenbosch or Kenilworth; no acres of consistently beautiful grounds, as in Parktown (but) some of the noblest structures in South Africa,' most notably the seat of government, the Union Buildings, which opened in 1912 and 'dominates the better part of the town'.

Preller lived just below the Union Buildings, in the suburb of Arcadia, and in 1915 he received a visit from IW. The Afrikaner was a great supporter of General Louis Botha, and it was quite possible that the prime minister himself had organised the meeting. Schlesinger and Preller immediately 'began discussions', and their attention was soon focused in equal parts on the two major incidents in *Piet Retief* – the Great Trek and Blood River.

In 1838, thousands of Boers who were unhappy living under British rule in the Cape Colony set out to find their own territories. One of the trek leaders, Piet Retief, led his group north, crossing the Orange River, going east over the Drakensberg and then moving down towards the Indian Ocean. Eventually, Retief's party reached the Kingdom of the Zulu, ruled by the powerful Dingaan, who had come to power by murdering his half-brother, the great Shaka.

In a bid to negotiate a deal for land, Retief went to Dingaan's kraal, accompanied by about 100 'elite' men and his young son, and a number of Khoisan auxiliaries. It was their third attempt to see the Zulu king. They were asked to leave their weapons outside the kraal as a show of good faith, but Dingaan, suspicious of their motives once they were inside, had them all killed.

At the close of that year, another Boer leader, Andries Pretorius, and a group of 500 men were camped by a river in the same area when they were set upon by Dingaan's men – a force said to total some 20 000. Vastly outnumbered and facing certain death, they swore an oath before God that if they survived, they would always commemorate that day – 16 December. In the ensuing battle, 3 000 Zulu died and only three Boers were wounded. So many bodies floated in the water that it became known as 'Blood River'.

As the discussions between IW and the author went on, 'Preller became enthusiastic about the idea of making a film record of "the greatest incident in Boer history".' But there was one obvious problem: he had never written a film scenario before. He knew the history, facts, details, anecdotes, but he would need someone to help him assemble a plot and a storyline.

That was where Lorimer Johnston came in.

The American director had been working non-stop since his arrival. He had made *A Zulu's Devotion*, *The Artist's Dream*, IW's Boy Scout drama *The Silver Wolf* and Caroline Cooke's *Story of the Rand*, and was moving on to *The Splendid Waster*, *The Illicit Liquor Seller* and *The Gun Runner*, but in truth, he had been biding his time, waiting for this moment, to make the first spectacle and 'the real movies of my life'.

But IW suddenly had other ideas. He had changed his mind about Johnston, and now wanted someone else to direct his first epic movie – someone bigger, someone more famous. And by Easter 1916, that man was on his way.

'COME MAKE BIG MOVIES IN AFRICA'

Ten miles southwest of Leicester Square, just across the river from Kew Gardens, was a dark-brick building that had once been an ice-skating rink. St Margarets now served a very different purpose, the headquarters of the London Film Company.

As a bitterly cold wind blew down St Margarets Road towards the Thames in early 1916, a pretty young woman sat at a table with two men in a drawing room that had been created for the drama being filmed, an adaptation of Sir Arthur Conan Doyle's novel *The Firm of Girdlestone*.

Standing near them was the director, with big intense eyes, hair parted on the left side and a round-tipped nose on the edge of which rested his metal-rimmed spectacles. Harold Shaw was about to turn 40 and had been working continuously since his arrival in Britain almost three years earlier.

In 1913, after acting and then directing for several studios in America – including Carl Laemmle's Universal – Shaw was approached by the London Film Company to come and make movies in Britain. It was a big gamble for the American.

Compared to Italy, France, Germany, Denmark and his own country, British movies fared poorly. The country 'frequently struggled with establishing itself as a major distributor of notable, critically acclaimed films (with) the public favouring the grandeur and excitement of American pictures and distinguished stars.'

The London Film Company's idea was to import Shaw to

produce movies in the American style – slicker, more thrilling, more like the white-slavery hit, *Traffic in Souls*. Shaw was friendly with that movie's director, George Loane Tucker, and asked him to come to London too. Tucker accepted.

The duo quickly brought out a series of hits. First there was *The Prisoner of Zenda* and its sequel, *Rupert of Hentzau*. Then came *The Manxman*, based on an 1894 bestseller by Hall Caine; *Trilby*, with the famous stage actor Sir Herbert Beerbohm Tree as Svengali; and the Sherlock Holmes mystery *The House of Temperley*.

Conan Doyle himself was charmed with the result: 'My little brat has been so trimmed up by (Shaw) on film that I hardly knew him, but I am very glad indeed to acknowledge my offspring.'

By early 1916, Shaw had made a staggering 34 movies and was ready to return to America. On 1 March, a farewell dinner was held at the nearby St Margarets Hotel, where, to lots of 'hurrahs' and 'cheers', Will Jury, of the English distributor Jury Pictures, said that Shaw and Tucker had 'taught the British trade how to produce films' and had shown 'that a British firm could produce films equal to any'. The duo had changed the face of British film.

Ten days later, on 11 March, Shaw told a newspaper that he had received offers 'on this side and the other' of the Atlantic, but that he hadn't made up his mind yet and would only do so after taking a much-needed rest and visiting his father, whom he hadn't seen for seven years, in California. Shaw and his girlfriend, a young American actress, were scheduled to sail to New York on 30 March.

In the next two weeks, something happened to make him abruptly change his mind. After a journalist friend told him that the United States was not intending to join the war, the director was left disheartened. So much so that he vowed not to 'set foot on his native land until President (Woodrow) Wilson's attitude towards the (German) submarine atrocities has become more clearly defined'.

'Since my country persistently declines to protect her citizens against the Teutonic sea-murderers,' he wrote to his family, 'I must forego the pleasure of visiting you, my dear father.'

But that left Shaw in a fix. He had given up on the London Film Company and was unwilling to move back to his former movie home, Los Angeles. Where could he go?

Both Shaw and Tucker were obvious targets for IW. By now, IVTA had become a player in London and IW was gaining show business clout. His network included the theatre owner Sir Oswald Stoll, who was about to take over the London Opera House; the film director Sidney Morgan; Bertie Samuelson, who had a studio at Worton Hall; the financier Isidore Ostrer; and the impresario Walter de Frece, whose wife was the male impersonator Vesta Tilly, both of them friends of Solly Joel.

In Shaw and Tucker, IW saw two fellow Americans who, besides now being more attuned to the way things worked in the Empire, were making the kind of movies IW wanted, American style. So, in the same way that they had initially been poached by the London Film Company to make American movies in England, IW approached them to make their movies at his City of Film.

It was a crazy request. Not a single movie made by African Films had appeared on a screen anywhere in the world (*A Zulu's Devotion* had yet to be shown). The studio was still being built, and there was no script yet for a spectacle, just Gustav Preller tinkering away at his attempt in Pretoria. But that didn't stop IW from inviting both Shaw and Tucker to join his enterprise.

'Come and make big movies for me in Africa,' he said.

One of the two men said yes. It was Harold Shaw.

The scene had a sense of déjà vu about it – and then several times over.

At the end of April, an American couple, a director and an actress, boarded a ship in Southampton and sailed into dangerous seas, where beneath the surface plied the 'sea-murdering' U-boats.

The director Harold Shaw with the towering Tom Zulu,
playing Dingaan. The actor was found by Lorimer Johnston working at a
police station in Stanger and brought to the City of Film.

The tide of war had turned slightly against the Germans, at least
at sea, where the Royal Navy had just started using depth charges
and had sunk their first German submarine in March.

The ship sailing south – once again, part of the diminishing
Union-Castle fleet – was the two-funnelled *Norman*. It was exactly
twenty years since the same vessel had taken Carl Hertz to South
Africa, during which voyage he had entertained passengers with
his Theatrograph machine. And it was barely six months since
Lorimer Johnston had made the same voyage on the *Llandovery
Castle*, with dreams of movies on an 'ambitious scale (for) the
important cities of the world'.

Like Johnston's wife, Harold Shaw's travelling companion had regularly acted in his movies. Dark-haired, doe-eyed and not yet 23, the American Edna Flugrath was the eldest of three sisters who had all gone into the picture business 'at the insistence' of their mother, who had already shepherded the youngest sibling through 30 movies by the age of 15. Mrs Flugrath had been asked by Edna to join them on the trip to Africa but had declined.

When the American couple got to Cape Town, they followed the same route as Johnston and Cooke. They stayed at the Mount Nelson Hotel and gave copious interviews, with Shaw telling the press that he wanted to make the logo of African Films 'as famous as the (London Film Company's) beefeater'.

Shaw's arrival was presented as a segment for African Mirror, and one newspaper said he had been given nothing less than 'carte blanche instructions to use the entire Dark Continent as background'. Flugrath was 'earmarked as the leading lady' in an upcoming epic, which still hadn't been identified.

In Johannesburg, the repetition continued, as if it was part of the IW Playbook. Like Albrecht and Johnston before him, Shaw was packed off to tour the subcontinent, to experience the 'wand of witchery'. In May, when he reached Rhodesia, he told the Bulawayo Chronicle that he was busy studying African life and scenery and hoped to make a movie about Cecil John Rhodes.

The actual movie spectacle that IW was planning, about the Great Trek and Blood River, was for some reason still being kept a secret. Maybe it was because Schlesinger knew that as soon as the news broke, there could very well be trouble.

THE BLOODY RIVER

There was much beating of drums around Easter 1916, with the media full of promises and ballyhoo.

While Shaw and Flugrath were still at sea, *Stage & Cinema* told its readers that 'the public of both hemispheres may expect soon to find a new and telling factor in their picture houses – the hitherto neglected South African Factor'.

African Films had created its own logo, with 'the trademark of "The Springbok"'. And why not? Carl Laemmle's Universal was using the world globe and Adolph Zukor's Paramount the Matterhorn. It was still two years before the most famous logo burst on the scene, the lion of Goldwyn Pictures. The springbok, African Films stated, would shake up the movie world.

'The public are tiring of the stereotyped subjects!' it declared in bold capital letters in Britain's *Kinematograph Weekly*. 'FRESH FACES, FRESH SUBJECTS, FRESH IDEAS, and FRESH ENVIRONMENTS are URGENTLY NEEDED. THE AFRICAN FILM PRODUCTIONS, LIMITED will endeavour to supply this demand for the OPEN MARKET with something entirely new and different for your programmes.'

As the hype built up, numerous topics for a movie spectacle were still being thrown around: 'Rhodes, the Empire Builder', 'Dingaan, the South African Hannibal', David Livingstone, Henry Stanley, Shaka, Dick King, Lobengula; stories set around Blood River, Victoria Falls, Shangani River, Majuba, Rorke's Drift, the Matopos, the Zimbabwe Ruins and 'the gold and diamond fields, and such incidents as the Matabele and Zulu Wars'.

But right after Harold Shaw arrived, and in a very simple statement, it was announced that the first epic would be about the Great Trek and Blood River.

If it had been a mad idea to try to create Hollywood in Africa, it was an even crazier one to turn the most famous piece of Boer history into a movie. A quagmire and a boobytrap all rolled into one – that's what IW was stepping straight into.

Resentment among the Afrikaners against the British ran deep, the combined result of the Anglo-Boer War defeat in 1902; the deadly concentration camps, where some 26 000 Boer women and children died (as did at least 20 000 Africans); the uneasy peace between the two sides; the declaration of Union in 1910; and finally, in 1914, the Rebellion.

One of the former Boer generals, a studious-looking lawyer and judge named Barry Hertzog, had started a pro-Boer opposition party that by June 1915 had set up in three of the four provinces. Like General Beyers, Hertzog and his National Party were opposed to South Africa joining the British war effort.

Hertzog regarded Botha and Smuts as too lenient with Africans, too conciliatory to the British. Even though Botha was seen by many as a fair man who had achieved wonders, Afrikaners began siding with one of two camps, Botha's or Hertzog's.

Johannesburg, meanwhile, was the tinderbox at the centre of the discontent. There were so many strikes – organised, wildcat, white miner, black miner, railway navvies, tram workers, rubbish collectors, engineers, the building trade, musicians, police and schoolteachers – that the African Mirror team would soon make a short film called *City of Unrest*.

Into this scene of resentment, historical friction, political uncertainty and racial acrimony stepped IW, a rich American Jew, who announced his intention to make a movie about two events that were sacrosanct to the Boer.

It spelled trouble from the start, which was why one of the very first people whom IW approached was the prime minister. Botha was so enamoured with the idea of a Great Trek movie that he even offered government assistance, in the form of military equipment that was now obsolete: a cannon and Martini-Henry rifles.

Botha also took the magnanimous decision to be the guest of honour at the premiere, whenever that happened. With the buy-in of the prime minister himself, IW could have easily concluded, what could possibly go wrong?

'LITTLE TIME FOR SLEEP'

Two fictional families, a romance between their offspring, a real assassination, an almighty battle, all set against an important historical event. The scenario for IW's spectacle that Harold Shaw and Gustav Preller finally came up with was strangely familiar. It had all the same elements that drove *The Birth of a Nation*.

In the South African version, the two families were named Landman and Faber. The handsome young Jan Faber loves Johanna Landman, whose parents are about to join the doomed Boer leader Piet Retief on his trek into the interior.

Shaw squeezed as much drama out of the physical journey as he could, the Boers setting out 'with hopeful hearts and with complete confidence in providence...On they plunge, the oxen hauling, slipping and struggling, now swallowed up in undergrowth of thorns and jungle, now toiling through sandy wastes while great clouds of dust mark their adventurous tracks.' And then they came to the raging Orange River.

Two villainous Portuguese traders, Perreira and Diaz, one of whom is also in love with Johanna, are unhappy about the Boers journeying into territory where they themselves are trading with – and cheating – the Zulu. They race ahead of the pioneers and turn Dingaan against them.

A warrior named Sobuza, expelled by Dingaan after refusing to help murder the ruler's mother and child, is taken in by a local missionary, who sends him south. Almost dead from exhaustion, he meets the northbound Retief, who restores him to health. The Boer leader becomes Sobuza's 'king, chief, savior', and the Zulu acts as a guardian to him and his young son.

After Retief and the boy are killed, Sobuza plays dead and then steals off to warn the others waiting at a place called Weenen, but he arrives too late: 'Women and children are butchered; wagons are burnt and a vista of indescribable confusion follows – a scene without precedent in the annals of cinematography.'

The battle of Blood River follows soon after. When it is over and Dingaan learns how many of his men have been lost, the two Portuguese villains are executed. Dingaan's followers desert him and he is left with only 14 people. In another fictional twist, Sobuza kills Dingaan with the very assegai used to kill the Boer leader.

Even though *The Birth of a Nation* hadn't been seen in South Africa, Harold Shaw and IW had both been in London at the time of its celebrated opening. Besides the story of two fictional families caught up in real events, the assassination and the bloody battle, both films were based on bestsellers. Thomas Dixon's novel *The Clansman* and Preller's *Piet Retief* had also, quite coincidentally, both been published in 1905.

The very titles of the two movies sounded the same too, although, in an apparent game of one-upmanship, IW went for something much bigger than 'a nation' – a continent. His film would be titled *Winning a Continent*.

At the Empire and the City of Film, things built up to a crescendo throughout the first half of 1916.

Lorimer Johnston, despite being sidelined, proved that he indeed 'wastes no time', and filmed a series of one-, two-, four- and five-reelers one after the other, while Joseph Albrecht was so busy that he 'got little time for sleep'.

An American named Benjamin Franklin Clinton had arrived from San Francisco to join the team. Even though his most notable contribution in the US, indeed the only one, had been to write a short film directed by DW Griffith in 1913, he was given three comedies to direct: *The Water Cure*, *A Kract Affair* and *£20,000*.

Joseph Langley Levy, an Englishman who was the editor of the *Sunday Times*, started writing scenarios alongside Johnston and Shaw. Albrecht and the actors Dick Cruickshanks and Marmaduke Wetherell also tried their hand at writing. The idea of a movie about Rhodes was still so prevalent that a scenario was being worked on by Levy, Shaw and the journalist and satirist Stephen Black, who had returned from working at the *Daily Mail* in London. But by mid-1916 the focus was almost entirely on the Blood River epic.

Researchers, carpenters, mechanics, builders, artists, costume makers all worked into the night. Under Preller's watch, every detail was followed up, from something as small as a Boer ceramic pipe to old Bibles to the replication of old Cape Colony bank notes. They even tracked down the treaty between Dingaan and Retief, which was said to have been discovered on the Boer leader. Dozens of old ox-wagons were found or recreated, and, for the extras who would be playing Boers, they collected saddles, bridles, powder horns and rifles. 'The whole Transvaal and Orange Free State were scoured for old-time muzzle-loaders, particularly elephant bores; with great difficulty 300 authentic pieces were gathered.'

In the costume department, a massive job was under way, stitching together outfits for at least 6 000 people. For the male trekkers, there needed to be jackets, trousers, neckcloths, waistcoats and hats made of straw or beaver's plush; for the women, dresses with full skirts and multilayered petticoats, and the distinctive poke bonnets done in layers of silk and linen quilt.

For the much bigger force of Zulu, meanwhile, they needed grass skirts or *moochis*, decorative headdresses, ornamental tufts made from cow tails, and 22 000 flashes for their elbows and knees, all fashioned out of goatskin. In addition, they had to make 12 000 assegais ('both for throwing and stabbing') and

Costumes and weapons for soldiers and warriors
were made by the thousands.

5 500 knobkieries – a short club-like stick with a knob on top.

Like *The Birth of a Nation*, IW wanted a musical score, 'the first film in the Commonwealth to have its own orchestral arrangement'. Silent movies, typically, had a pianist or organist playing classical or repertory music, or just improvising. *Cabiria* had a score by the Milan composer Ildebrando Pizzetti, and *The Birth of a Nation* featured music by the composer-conductor Joseph Carl Breil. In Pretoria IW found a Dutch composer, Henri ten Brink.

The intertitles – the cards inserted between scenes to explain what was going on and provide the dialogue – were to be in two languages, English and Afrikaans, on either side of the screen. It was probably the first time it had ever been done.

The movie itself also got an Afrikaans title to stand alongside *Winning a Continent*. It would be *De Voortrekkers*.

MAGIC

From dawn one Sunday morning in early June, the Zulu village at the City of Film was a hive of activity.

The cameras were set up first. Joseph Albrecht and Henry Howse had been joined by the newly arrived William Bowden, who had shot several movies in London. They positioned the cameras in the central yard, and at another point high enough to capture long shots across the grass roofs and palisades when it came time for the warriors to race frantically between them.

Standing with Shaw was his assistant, Ralph Kimpton, an Englishman who had mostly done stage work until now. The English actor Dick Cruickshanks, playing the ill-fated Boer leader Piet Retief, had his short, light brown hair covered in a dark wig and leather hat, his face then given a heavy beard. Opposite him, in all his royal regalia to play Dingaan, was the tall, 'regal-looking' Tom Zulu, standing well over six feet and weighing about 250 pounds.

According to Shaw's scenario, there were to be four big scenes in *Winning a Continent*, and this was the first – the killing of Retief, his son and more than 100 of his men at Dingaan's kraal.

To play the warriors, the men in the village were joined by several hundred more Africans. Migrant labourers who worked for the city, they lived at a municipal compound, probably the Salisbury and Jubilee Compound in the city centre. For African men, the compounds were virtually the only accommodation option, other than the location at Klipspruit or freehold in

Alexandria and Sophiatown. One of the slums, Vrededorp, had even been visited and photographed by the African Mirror team to focus on the terrible conditions there.

Sunday was the workers' day off, the only day they could be used as extras at the City of Film. From that day in June onward, Sunday also became the day for shooting big scenes, even when African extras weren't needed.

The extras were all given goatskin flashes, *moochis*, headdresses and ornamental tufts, as well as their weapons, assegais and knob-kieries. Split up into groups, with many of them not speaking English, they were given instructions by translators spread among them. At various points throughout the day, they were instructed to sit in rows, stand, chant, dance, gather around the white men, clash, slay them.

During a break for lunch, Albrecht watched the daily rushes, or 'first flashes', of what they had shot that morning. The men standing closest to him watched over his shoulder, some of them stunned. 'I can still remember them clapping their hands in front of their mouths in amazement,' he recalled later. They called it *mtagati*, magic, and Albrecht became *mhlamena*, the man who eats in the middle of the day.

That afternoon, everyone moved to another part of the property, a site higher up on the back of the Parktown ridge, where they filmed pioneers being chased around the countryside by the Zulu warriors.

'A rocky outcrop had been chosen to double for an infamous site known as the "Hill of Vultures", from which the bodies of the dead pioneers would be tossed … The scene showing the Retief party being dragged from Dingaan's kraal to the "Hill of Vultures" was shot on the koppie to the right side of Houghton kloof, now forming part of that beautiful flora reserve called "The Wilds".'

Less than a mile away, across the valley, there were houses being built in an affluent new suburb called Houghton. Anyone out for a stroll that Sunday afternoon, as was the custom, would have seen a truly disturbing sight – African men in battle dress chasing white men, felling them and then disposing of what looked like lifeless bodies over a small cliff.

The day passed without incident, but it wouldn't be long before everyone, and not just people living nearby, knew about the strange goings-on at the City of Film.

SCORPIONS

In late June, IW's theatres were full of his new movies. *The Silver Wolf* was playing at the Orpheum, *A Kract Affair* was on a double bill with *The Vortex* at the Bijou and *The Illicit Liquor Seller* had pride of place opposite Charlie Chaplin at the Carlton.

Driving north along Eloff Street to Park Station, a group of people led by Harold Shaw would have passed some of IW's other bioscopes too, the Vaudette and the Tivoli and the Grand. At that moment, it felt very much like IW's town.

After being dropped at Park Station, they boarded the Union Express. Accompanying Shaw were his assistant Ralph Kimpton, Joseph Albrecht and some of the cameramen, technicians and make-up artists, in addition to the main actors for the upcoming scene: Dick Cruickshanks as Piet Retief and Caroline Cooke as his wife; Holger Petersen and Edna Flugrath as the young lovers; Marmaduke Wetherell as her father; and a new arrival, Percy Marmont, who had been touring with the Liverpool Repertory Company.

Ahead of them lay the second major shoot for the spectacle, the trek of the pioneer ox-wagons across the Orange River. The closest railway stop to their final destination was the town of Colesberg, 400 miles southwest of Johannesburg. From there they had to reach Alleman's Drift, the actual site of the crossing almost eight decades earlier.

'Nothing incongruous must be allowed to enter into a picture,' Shaw said, echoing Schlesinger's wish to make his movies as close to reality as possible.

The overnight journey was, for most of them, a respite, a time to relax. They had been running between productions. Cruickshanks, Cooke, Wetherell and Flugrath had worked together in *Sonny's Little Bit*, Johnston's movie about a young boy's attempts to catch a German spy. Henry Howse worked on *The Silver Wolf* and *The Water Cure*. The biggest production so far, *The Splendid Waster*, had taken most of them on another train journey, to Parys, where Wetherell, playing the drunk protagonist, had to swim across the Vaal River to escape the police.

But the movie that most of the crew were probably talking about was the one at the Carlton, *The Illicit Liquor Seller*, which had 'a special significance given the tragic happenings at Florida'. The same weekend in June that it had opened, a family called the Smellies had been violently killed west of the city. The wife was raped and her husband and daughter butchered, apparently by men who had got drunk on illegal liquor. Within days, the police had arrested four suspects, who belonged to a gang called the Ninevites.

'By June 22, the fast work of police and an African from the phenomenal police Native Suspect Staff found that the Ninevites gave orders that ten men under a lieutenant, Isaac, should patrol the West Rand to rob and steal but not to kill ... They had been drunk in the hills outside Florida when Smellie and his wife and daughter came walking through the area. One of the signs was that Mrs Smellie had many wounds in her, and it was a known Ninevite promotion to plunge many knife wounds into the belly of a white woman.'

IW's movie imitated the successful *Traffic in Souls*, not only in the way it focused on a real-life tragedy but also in its storyline of a lawman and a woman teaming up to fight injustice. Wetherell, who now sat among the others on the train to Colesberg, had played the policeman boyfriend of a young woman (Mabel May) whose father is selling liquor illegally to Africans.

The combination of the tragic Florida news and the uncertainty of what lay ahead of them at the Orange River must have left a sombre pall over the movie passengers, and over Shaw in particular. Even though he had already filmed the crowd scenes and the clashes at the village in the City of Film, he was now facing one of the biggest shoots that had ever been done on a movie, a train of dozens of wagons full of people making their way across a river.

In his colourful preparatory notes, Shaw had predicted that 'the stream is in flood and the crossing is fraught with dangerous menace'. Little did he know that those words were about to come true.

The fleet of 30 ox-wagons trundled across the 35 miles of rough track to Alleman's Drift, where the crew set up camp alongside the Orange River.

Even though it was desperately cold, they needed to be ready for an early-morning shoot the next day. Big campfires were built, and after dinner the actors sat around them in the darkness trying to stay warm.

Suddenly, Edna Flugrath jumped up screaming. A large tarantula, and then several more, as well as scorpions, were all around them, drawn to the warmth of the fire. And then, just as the actors were settling in for the night, it started raining heavily.

'The following morning,' Albrecht recalled later, 'the oxen were inspected and the wagons loaded up with all the household gear of the voortrekkers, including period furniture, *rustbanks*, etc, all to be used with the trek scenes. We passed through thick thorn bushes across the sand valley and began crossing.'

The actors took their places on wagons, Cape carts and horse-back in preparation. As they headed down to the riverbank, Shaw asked Albrecht to get some shots from the middle of the river. The young Englishman went into the water until it was up to his armpits, holding the camera above his head. After the night's rain, the water level had risen considerably, and so had the strength of the current.

Albrecht began filming oxen 'swimming past' with their wagons in tow, some of which drifted his way and almost collided with him. The women on board, he could see, were 'genuinely frightened'.

At one point, a Cape cart carrying Edna Flugrath and 'an elderly Boer woman' and their driver was suddenly carried away by the stream and drifted straight at Albrecht. He yelled at them, but they couldn't do anything until, with the cart almost reaching Albrecht, the driver managed to get the horses under control.

But then the horses got spooked again. Holger Petersen, who had been riding ahead of the others, came back to help, 'providing an unrehearsed incident which appears in the film'. Flugrath, at this point, was practically fainting, 'but the old Dutch lady (next to her) never batted an eyelid'.

There were many close calls that day, but when it was over, Albrecht had some great shots. At one point, he had been in the water for almost three hours straight and there hadn't been a single disastrous incident. The next time they filmed around water, they wouldn't be as lucky.

FINDING AN ARMY

By August, filming on the spectacle had ground to a halt because they still had no location for the big battle scene.

The plan from the start had been to film at Blood River, the very place where the conflict had happened. That was what IW wanted, verisimilitude. It would have meant moving dozens of ox-wagons, several cannons and thousands of extras and their costumes a distance of 240 miles from Johannesburg.

But 'transport and other difficulties' on the Orange River shoot – a hint that they had been plagued by more than just scorpions and an overnight flood – suddenly made IW change his mind. He wanted a more convenient location closer to Johannesburg, a city that had no rivers to speak of.

As time was running out, a possible solution was offered by a mining company. East Rand Proprietary Mines, which was known by its initials ERPM, owned a piece of land just a few miles east of the city centre 'in a fairly wild condition and crossed by a small stream'. The place, called Elsburg, was perfect in every respect, except the stream needed to be a river. So, IW ordered one to be made.

Construction began immediately on a dam that could feed the narrow waterway. Even though Johannesburg's supply of water was precarious – the Vaal River Barrage was not yet built – IW managed to get the Rand Water Board to sell him two million gallons, about 20 per cent of the city's daily consumption. It was enough to fill a trench 50 feet wide, ten feet deep, and almost as long as two rugby pitches.

At the same time, a massive operation had begun to find the extras – Africans and Europeans – to battle it out on the banks of the new river. And that was where the real trouble began.

Lying in a wide crescent several miles long just north of the Elsburg valley, but out of sight of it, were the ERPM mines Cason, Angelo, Comet and, the most important, Driefontein.

On the mines, as in municipalities, the labourers lived in same-sex compounds. The men came from across the subcontinent – Zululand, Basutoland, Pondoland in the eastern Cape, Portuguese East Africa. Conditions in the mine compounds were cramped and volatile, often unhealthy, although some mines were better than others.

At Driefontein, the manager in charge of the labourers was AP Norton. Along with two of his assistants, G Blair Hook and Mark Foxcroft, he approached his men. Would any of them, Norton asked, be willing to form part of a Zulu army for a movie?

In order to show what was required of them, a demonstration was scheduled for early October. One week before the Blood River shoot, several cameramen from African Films arrived at Driefontein, set up 'a sham fight' and then filmed it. Six hundred of the mineworkers, in the presence of 'all the other boys in the compound', acted out what was meant to happen on the day of filming. To replicate the action as much as possible, guns were even fired in the background. The day 'went off satisfactorily'.

After the footage had been developed, it was shown to the miners at the ERPM Hall 'to allay any suspicions that might exist. They were satisfied that it was purely play,' Hook later recalled, '(and I) was quite convinced that they understood.'

Out of the volunteers, 3 000 were chosen. They were divided into six *impis* (regiments) of 500 men each – one consisting only of Zulu, the rest a mix of other men. Overseeing them, besides Norton, Hook and Foxcroft, were 38 compound managers and assistants, in addition to numerous African supervisors, called *indunas*, and 'many interpreters (who were) necessary to transmit instructions'.

At a meeting a few days later that included Harold Shaw, Norton, Hook, mine managers and a representative of the Department of Native Affairs, it was agreed that the police should also be present on the day of filming. Inspector Henry Freame Trew, who was filling in as assistant commissioner of police for the district, was put in charge. He would lead a contingent of 82 white policemen, some of whom would be on horseback, and 12 African constables.

Trew's main concern was crowd control – they were expecting a lot of spectators. Word about the filming had spread quickly, and because it would be a Sunday most people would be free to come and watch. Apart from the residents of nearby towns, there would be many miners; those who hadn't been chosen as extras were given the chance to see the others performing.

Trew estimated that the crowd could grow to as many as 15 000.

⌷⌷⌷⌷⌷

People in the towns nearby Elsburg weren't the only ones who heard about the shoot.

Rumblings among the public had started in April already, even before the scenes acted out on the 'Hill of Vultures' near Houghton. Now it was being reported that thousands of men would be re-enacting Blood River. Articles and letters appeared in several newspapers, and 'there was considerable opposition to the film being taken, and telegrams of protest had been dispatched to the Government'.

The sudden flood of photographs in IW's magazine *Stage & Cinema* of scenes that had already been filmed, as well as large portraits of the two main African actors, Goba as the good warrior Sobuza and Tom Zulu as Dingaan, didn't help calm things down.

There were three major points of concern, especially among the more conservative Afrikaners, many of them supporters of Hertzog's National Party: filming on Sundays, the Sabbath, which was for them a day of rest; the possibility that the depiction of events cherished by them might be inaccurate; and the explosive idea of making black and white men fight, even if it wasn't for real.

'Set a few hundred natives on the "mimic" war path,' wrote *The Transvaal Critic*, the country's oldest established weekly, 'and Heaven knows what will be the end of it … It is quite time the Government put its foot down once and for all on the idea.'

The government, however, knew full well about IW's movie. Probably the first person he had told was Louis Botha, who had not only given it his blessing but had offered assistance. IW had also employed Gustav Preller, a well-known and respected Afrikaner author and historian, to write the scenario.

But the public outcry kept coming. In September, a month before the shoot of Blood River, Preller wrote a letter – on stationery headed 'African Film, The Empire Building' – to the minister of justice, Nicolaas de Wet, to quell any unease. De Wet was the very man who had dealt with the 1914 Rebellion against the government.

In this 'time of tumult, wars and rumours of wars, and such dreaded things (*meer sulke aardighede*)', wrote Preller, 'local authorities would probably immediately suspect a "third rebellion"'. He wanted to reassure the magistrates of the towns around Elsburg, who could possibly shut down the re-enactment if they suspected trouble, that there were no 'traitorous intentions'.

At the last minute, IW contributed his own strange solution, which was meant to alleviate friction but probably did the exact opposite. He instructed that the white people hired as extras, who would come from the nearby towns of Alberton and Germiston, be evenly split politically. Half were to be 'supporters of Botha and the other half of General Hertzog and the nationalists'.

The task of finding the white extras fell to a man named Leonard Streeter, who was also the local representative on the East Rand for the *Rand Daily Mail*. He was asked by African Film's general manager, Alfred Smith, to obtain the services of 300 men, 200 women and 100 children for the shoot.

Streeter, not being able to speak Dutch, went to Stoffel Herselman, a taxi driver, to ask for help, as he spoke Dutch and had better contacts in the two towns. Herselman also had to make sure that 125 of the men were able to ride a horse.

On set, the guns to be used by the white men were to be handed out by a Union Defence Force officer identified only as 'Major Pretorius'. He also had to show the men how to handle the old muzzle-loaders and Martini-Henrys. 'To fire these guns was no easy matter ... even to the otherwise experienced marksmen.'

Other than the firing practice, however, there was no rehearsal planned for the white extras. They were told to arrive early in the Elsburg valley on the Sunday morning of the shoot, and head to the main tent to pick up their costumes and weapons. No other instructions were given to them.

THE VALLEY OF DEVILS

At 6.15 on the morning of Sunday 15 October, the mineworkers, already outfitted as warriors, left Driefontein. To the compound manager, AP Norton, it must have been an incredible sight, although to anyone who didn't know what was happening, it was probably terrifying.

Almost 2 000 African men in full battle dress, armed with traditional weapons and oxhide shields, marched in a tight crowd, stomping their feet so that dust rose off the road. From the west, meanwhile, marched a second contingent of 1 000 men, similarly armed and lively. The six regiments headed for the ridge above Elsburg.

In the valley, preparations had begun long before dawn.

'From early morning a seemingly endless stream of horsemen and wagons laden with women and children marked the skyline, and numerous motor cars passed along the dusty and uneven roads running east and west,' wrote one newspaper.

Joseph Albrecht, having set up his camera on the side of the ridge with the other cameramen, beheld the magnificent sight below him of the half-moon shape of the wagons, 'most impressive in the early morning sunlight'.

As the white extras arrived, they collected their costumes at the dressing tent and proceeded to the laager, where they were meant to receive final instructions. Those who needed weapons got them from Major Pretorius.

IW made one of his rare appearances for the historic event, joining Harold Shaw, Ralph Kimpton, the *Sunday Times* editor Langley Levy, the general manager of African Films, Alfred Smith, and – quite fortuitously – Detective CE Young from the Boksburg CID. Gustav Preller went to join the people inside the laager.

Six cameras had been set up at various points along the ridge, for the first shots were to be taken from a distance. Behind the cameras, the number of curious onlookers quickly multiplied. 'As the news had spread, an enormous crowd of spectators assembled to witness the proceedings.' Near them, and at various points along the ridge, the policemen under Inspector Trew took up their positions.

Trew walked down to meet with Shaw, and, accompanied by Detective Young, they went to speak to the people in the laager. Not far behind the wagons was the newly created dam that would soon flood the Elsburg stream.

Through a translator, Shaw explained to the white extras, the younger men in particular, that he was filming historical episodes and they should 'play the game' to help him make a successful picture. He begged them not to 'irritate' the Africans in any way.

'Away over the hilltops (one) could hear the chant of 5 500 natives.'

When they appeared, the Africans were 'all dressed up in their warrior finery, marching to the appointed place under the control of the compound managers … The set route they were to take in the charge of the laager had been marked off.'

They were met by Shaw, who took three or four preliminary shots to show 'the advance and warlike manoeuvring' of the *impis*. Once again, as he had done at the laager, he went over what needed to happen.

The plan was to shoot the battle in three movements: the first, a half-moon charge downhill from the ridge on the eastern side of Blood River; the second, and most important, the crossing of Blood River and the approach to the laager; and the third, the warriors back on the ridge again.

The stampede of the men down the hillside went off without incident, and the men stopped at the bottom as they'd been instructed. For the second big movement, Shaw indicated a point where they should move to next, across the river and in the direction of the laager; his assistant, Kimpton, who was dressed in a white suit, was standing in the distance as a marker. It was imperative that the charge was to stop before they reached the laager.

The white extras, it was already clear from their movements, were less organised. Some of the men were on horseback, the rest in and around the laager. 'Ammunition was given out only for the latter.' From early on that morning, the newspaper editor Langley Levy noticed, there was 'desultory firing all the time', but he didn't think there was anything strange about it.

At 10 am, the main battle charge started. After Harold Shaw gave the signal, the warriors came towards the newly created Blood River, went over it and continued on to the laager.

'All the while they were approaching the camp the natives kept up a weird rhythmic whistle, like the whistle of a gale through the rigging of a ship, only many times magnified. The effect was so strange and almost unearthly that it carried a threat into the very marrow of one's bones.'

Before they reached the point where they were meant to stop, several white men outside the ox-wagons started firing their rifles, first into the air and then directly at the warriors. Men on horseback who had been near the dressing tent stormed past the laager and into the middle ground, also shooting. None of their actions were part of the script.

The closer the warriors got, the more shots were fired, and some of the men fell. The blank ammunition had been replaced with something else. Some Africans were getting scorched on their bodies and faces, while others were bleeding, and they quickly

A rare photograph showing some of the spectators in the background who came to watch the filming at Elsburg.

decided to fight back. Instead of stopping, they kept on going, rushing at the wagons and pulling horsemen from their saddles.

'Not only the natives were angry, but the Europeans also had their blood up,' one spectator recalled later.

It all happened so quickly and looked so much like part of the film action that it took a few moments for the people in charge to realise something had gone terribly wrong. Inspector Trew, looking through his field glasses from some 300 yards away, initially thought that the conflict was planned. When he saw a rider being violently pulled to the ground, he galloped down.

Shaw jumped on a cannon and frantically waved his hands in the air, shouting, 'For the Lord's sake, stop that firing!' But no one could hear, or they just chose not to.

Inside the laager, some of the extras around Preller were still getting dressed when the shooting started. He knew something was wrong when the warriors who were meant to stop kept rushing towards the enclosure. He tried in vain to intercede, but 'it was difficult to stop the shooting because of the noise and din.'

The ERPM men led by Norton, Hook and Foxcroft, joined by the *indunas*, raced down the ridge at the same time as Trew, even though they had been told to stay out of view of the cameras. Norton confronted some of the whites, 'but they took no notice'. At that point he heard one of the men exhort the others, and even though it was in Dutch he understood the words.

'Shoot the devils!'

As the police and compound leaders got some of the warriors to move to the east bank of the river, another group of them resumed attacking the laager. Hook and Foxcroft galloped off and stopped them in time, although more Africans had 'mustered with the object of coming to (their) assistance'.

The spectators had no idea the danger they were in, which Inspector Trew was grateful for. If they had shown signs of fear, he believed they too would have been attacked in earnest.

In the chaos, some of the warriors who had penetrated the laager went out the back and found themselves blocked by the dam. They tried to cross, not realising that it was ten feet deep in places and they couldn't swim. After they had been helped across by men from the mine, the dam surface was littered with abandoned shields and assegais.

As the angry men were escorted up the hillside, they began chanting war songs, and one of the *impis* broke away and started running back down the slope towards the ox-wagons. A group of policemen managed to head them off.

Norton was furious and told Inspector Trew that his men were justifiably angry, and they wanted revenge. If the filming was allowed to go ahead, he said, he couldn't guarantee there wouldn't be more bloodshed. The miners' intention was 'to kill every man in the laager'. It was only because of his and Hook's interference that 'a great catastrophe was averted'.

When Trew advised IW and Shaw that further filming would have to stop, they assured him that the white extras would be kept inside the wagon enclosure for any further filming, and there would be no contact between the two sides. It was imperative that filming continue, as this was their one and only chance to film the battle. If the cameramen had obtained any footage so far, it would have been spoiled by the chaos and the sight of Trew, Norton and the others running and galloping between the actors.

To recreate Blood River and set up the scene again would cost a fortune, and it would set them back many weeks that they did not have. There was also a very good chance that the local magistrates Preller had tried to appease would forbid further shooting.

But the police and mine managers were adamant – filming had to stop. After several hours of rounding up the warriors, the carnage in the veld around them was evident. As many as 135 people were injured, 120 of them African, some seriously. Thirty-five men had to be admitted to hospital, four with gunshot wounds, and at least one miner was unaccounted for.

It was hard to imagine that things could get worse, but they did.

The next day, the news was confirmed. A man was dead.

Detective Young dragged the dam at Elsburg that morning, in search of the miner who was unaccounted for. His body was found in ten feet of water, 'standing upright with his toy assegai still in his hands'.

'It seems that at this point a deep hole existed and he stepped into it. From the appearance of the body, death must have been due to heart disease,' said the district surgeon, who concluded that he had drowned. ERPM said the missing miner's name was Faduk.

That same day, 16 October, Inspector Trew was approached by someone who told him there had been a plot to wreck the day's shoot. The white extras' provocation of the warriors 'was not due to them getting out of hand, but was deliberately planned so as to cause trouble. There is evidence that unauthorized persons did obtain uniforms and rifles.'

Trew was convinced there had been sabotage, especially given the growing public opposition to the movie. But the informant refused to make an official statement, and a police investigation turned up nothing.

Detective Young began running tests on some of the fake weapons that had been used in the battle. He obtained several shields, at least one of the rifles and some of the blank ammunition. He would give his results at the inquest into the death of Faduk, which was scheduled for the middle of December.

PLAYING AT MURDER

A temporary flash of disappointment was followed by a flood of outrage.

One newspaper noted that thousands of people who had arrived on the afternoon of the shoot 'were deprived of a really grand spectacle'. But others focused on the chaos and what they saw as an exhibition of mockery and blasphemy; they blamed the prime minister, his government and the police for not taking earlier warnings seriously.

'Kaffirs Play at Murder While Officialdom Looks On!' ran a headline in *The Transvaal Critic*. Two days before the shoot, the paper had predicted there would be trouble. 'Who sanctioned kaffirs acting with whites?' it asked.

The *Rand Daily Mail* criticised the wisdom of putting 'a few thousand South African black bucks together and (telling) them to play at blotting out whites', while the Afrikaans daily *De Burger* 'launched an unequivocal attack on Sabbath-breaking', accusing the producers of mocking the Afrikaner.

The costumes for the Boers looked like they had been made of cretonne and blinds, and the day of filming would go down in history as a day of bloodshed. If IW had wanted to create a movie to 'make some of the American producing houses open their eyes', he shouldn't have done it 'by placing white women and children in danger among a lot of black savages'.

Three days later, before the publicity could get any worse,

African Films invited a 'favoured few' to the Empire to see exactly what had been filmed at Elsburg. In the audience was a journalist from the *Rand Daily Mail* who described in thrilling terms what was depicted in the raw footage taken on that fateful day, calling it 'Realism too Realistic'.

After watching 'the dusty cavalcade (and) an endless procession of dusky figures' approach the stream, where they pitch camp and 'the huge trek-wagons are lined up end-to-end to form a laager', the men inside make 'all manner of warlike preparations ...

'Then the spectator is spiriting over the hills and a couple of miles away to where a huge horde of natives is gathering. They have been gathering since daylight – groups of dusky warriors, in full war paint, bearing their shields and every form of native weapon. They come from all sides: the sky-line is always alive with marching Kaffirs until a fearsome impi has been assembled for the attack on the Boer camp.

'It is an amazing sight when they move off ... In the distance they seem nothing so much as an immense army of black ants ... moving swiftly and inexorably across kopje and valley towards their objective. There seems no end to their number, and from the savage visages in the foreground to the crawling specks on the distant horizon, the whole line is barbed with assegais which are ever moving in wild, fantastic rhythm.

'At one moment they are a compact mass of men, rolling up the steep slope of a kopje, and pouring down into the valley like a stream of black lava. A little later, and they have flung themselves out into the form of a wide crescent for the rush on the camp.'

The ensuing chaos on set, however, was barely a footnote in the article, except for the mention that there had been some 'premature firing', the Africans 'smashing on right up to the laager ... (and they) swarmed up to the right of the wagons like bees, and something in the nature of a hand-to-hand fight developed'.

The death of Faduk was also mentioned, but the journalist added that 'so far from being the utter failure which is commonly stated (what he saw) is as yet 2 800 feet of very exciting film'.

Only later did it come to light that there had been footage to show because of Joseph Albrecht. When the trouble had started in the valley, he made sure to focus the cameras on the running masses and to keep the mounted police and non-actors out of the field of the camera as much as possible: 'By this means I was fortunate enough to obtain sufficient shots of the mass attack and the retreat of the warriors to save the expenditure of this big day.'

Within a month, public anger had died down so much that the camera team went to Elsburg again. This time, however, everything was strictly controlled and there was no publicity. No outsiders were allowed on the set, and a much smaller number of men were used – only 400 Africans and 75 whites. All of them were 'clerical, manual and mining men' from ERPM, and the compound manager AP Norton was in complete control. Inspector Trew was there too but took a much smaller contingent with him – 20 mounted policemen.

Albrecht and the cameramen stationed themselves in the valley this time, between the men, filming 'suitable mid-shots and close-ups'. At sunset, he took the final frame, 'a fine picture of wagons trekking through mountain fastnesses'.

SABOTAGE

The suspicion that something devious was afoot lingered.

Even though Inspector Trew was unable to prove sabotage, there were those who remained convinced of it. In early December, just as everyone was preparing for the inquest into the death of the miner Faduk, something else happened to rouse suspicions again.

Winning a Continent was almost complete, and the pressure on everyone involved with the film was intense. The premiere, set for 16 December, was less than ten days away, and they still had one scene left to film. Even though it was a small scene, they were cutting things dangerously close.

One hundred thousand feet of film had been edited down to 10 000 feet, or almost two hours of running time. The single copy of the film – most producers kept two copies, in case something happened to one of them – was being stored at the Empire.

Just as everyone was heading to lunch that day, clouds of black smoke started pouring out into Commissioner Street.

'We heard alarms of "Fire!"' Albrecht recalled later. 'You can imagine how we felt with nearly a full year's work in peril ... We all made one dive for the "Voortrekker" negatives and carried them out higgledy-piggledy into the street. I shouted to my companions to leave everything else and so we rushed up and down until it was out of the building.'

The fire was said to have started in some large cases of old, highly flammable film, which were being sealed for dispatch when 'a drop of solder set the whole mass ablaze'. But there was also the possibility that someone had done it intentionally and tried to burn down the Empire to get rid of the movie.

When the inquest into the death of Faduk started a few days later, at the Boksburg Police Court, the issue of sabotage was raised again. A headline on the first day read: 'Was there a Plot to Wreck the Film?'

Almost the entire technical and production crew were called in to give their version of the events of 15 October – Schlesinger, AP Norton, G Blair Hook, Gustav Preller, Harold Shaw, town councillors, managers from the mines, Leonard Streeter and Stoffel Herselman, as well as mine *indunas*, white extras and miners who had been wounded.

Their testimony drew a picture of how the day had quickly descended into chaos.

A lawyer for ERPM described how the miners had been given a demonstration and shown a film of what was expected of them on the day, and so were fully prepared. As for the pioneers, other than a briefing by Shaw just before the action, it seemed they had been given little direction.

According to Hook, the miners had done everything to the letter, 'entering heartily into the spirit of the thing', while the whites appeared to do things on the fly. 'Two or three said to the natives, "We have shot you; now lie down." They, the Europeans, had evidently not been instructed.'

Confusion had reigned at the costume tent. According to one of the white extras, anyone could just walk in, join the line and get a costume, until all of them had been handed out. Another said that everybody was looking around for instructions, and he estimated there were at least 80 extras who weren't meant to be there.

The studio general manager, Alfred Smith, tried to blame Streeter and Herselman – the men he had delegated to find white extras – and their 'faulty organisation'. Herselman had been told to provide 'troop-leaders', which had not been done.

Detective Young produced the results of his armaments tests to show the court. The shields were made of papier-mâché about a quarter of an inch thick. Using one of the rifles from the set, he found that at point-blank range the discharge made a hole over an inch in diameter, and at a foot the hole measured as much as five inches. Tests were done by firing sand, and it was found that the force of the powder 'drove the sand through the shield with considerable force'. Young said the trouble had been caused by some of the mounted pioneers: 'These men were riding all over the country and blazing away indiscriminately.'

Inspector Trew told the court what he had been saying from the start – that the young riders were to blame. 'The white men continued firing at close range, and even when the natives were retiring, the white men, in spite of (myself) and others expostulating, still fired at them.'

The accusations went back and forth, and the evidence was often contradictory. One witness said there were women and children on set, while Smith said there were none. There was testimony of men shoving stones and sand into their rifles, while others said there was no sand in the area. One mine manager saw men hiding among the rocks to shoot. The *Sunday Times* editor, Joseph Langley Levy, dismissed the men's gunfire as nothing more than 'high spirits and exuberance'.

Several of the miners described how they had been attacked or tried to flee the fighting. One who had been hit across the head said there were men standing outside the laager firing, but he saw no sand or stones being put in guns. Responding to an accusation that some of the African extras had been carrying real knives and battle-axes, an *induna* identified as Barberton said this wasn't true. Several miners agreed with him.

Barberton added that the Africans had been told that they were 'going to play'. They all understood perfectly well that guns would be fired at them, but they didn't expect to be hurt.

One miner, who showed the burns he had sustained, had heard talk about sand being put in the guns, but he could not say whether this was true or not. He heard Shaw and others repeatedly shouting at the white men to stop firing.

A miner named Jacob testified that he had been shot in the chest. So did another, who said the shot had come from only eight yards away, but he didn't see who fired. A third said there were definitely stones in the guns.

An official from ERPM who was assisting on set that day, Cecil Surmon, said he saw about 15 Africans getting into difficulty in the water, and assisted some of them to get out. During that time, though, he saw nothing occur that might have caused the death of Faduk.

THE PREMIERE

On 11 December, while the inquest was still going on, the final scene for *Winning a Continent* was filmed at Killarney. Fortunately for the editors, it was also the very first scene of the movie – showing the pioneers leaving for the hinterland. Within hours it had been developed and added to the start of the main reel.

The next day, 12 December, the single copy of the film was entrusted to IW's driver, Max Zasman. He drove it to Pretoria, where it was shown to the prime minister and several senior government members.

'General Botha was very deeply affected and was not ashamed to confess that certain portions of the film had moved him to tears.' Congratulating Shaw later, Botha said the American had depicted 'the history of my people in a manner at the realism of which I can only marvel'. Ferried back to Johannesburg, the same copy was shown to several hundred businessmen, journalists and 'influential people' invited by IW. Throughout the screening there were outbursts of applause.

'These are scenes which stamp the name of Harold Shaw as one of the finest living producers,' wrote the *Sunday Times*. *Winning a Continent* would be 'a success in every part of the world ... (The) verdict was ... that a great work had just been completed.'

All that remained was the premiere, and for that IW had planned something unique, unprecedented and quite bizarre.

Early that week, with the movie barely completed, people from distant parts of the country began a pilgrimage. Farmers, railway workers, civilians – they all set out by rail, ox-wagon or Cape cart for Krugersdorp, 20 miles west of Johannesburg.

Forty-four 'special trains' were made available to bring in some 10 000 people, and 30 000 in all were expected to descend on the town. Lodgings were booked out, campsites were prepared, and provision was made for trains to be parked on sidings in nearby towns to provide additional accommodation.

By Wednesday 13 December, those who had come by ox-wagon had formed a laager around a monument on the main road dedicated to the battle of Paardekraal in 1880. But the big event was three days later, on Saturday 16 December, when General Botha was scheduled to lead a massive parade to mark the anniversary of Blood River. The day was now known as Dingaan's Day.

There were events all around town. Thousands of people dressed up as pioneers visited the refreshment tents – 'All the leading caterers of the district have established quarters on the main road running to the south of the laager lines' – or attended church services.

Soldiers who had fought in the campaigns in East Africa and South West Africa came to pay their respects, as did a troop of Boy Scouts. Money was gathered for the erection of a monument to Piet Retief and his followers.

'Venerable men and women, children of those who pioneered the way with the old Voortrekkers, were present in large numbers, and one of the most impressive spectacles of the whole of the ceremonies ... was the appearance on the balcony of the Monument on Saturday afternoon of aged orators who gave their graphic story of the Great Trek.'

Throughout the celebration, at three separate venues around town, people were also able to see the very first showings of *Winning a Continent*, which was advertised only by its Afrikaans title, *De Voortrekkers*. At the Wanderers Ground, which was big enough to admit thousands, it was being sold as 'The Great Mass Exhibition'.

Even though *Winning a Continent* was the biggest movie ever made in the British Empire, and one of the biggest in the world, IW had chosen the site of its premiere very carefully. Instead of Johannesburg's Town Hall, which could seat 3 000 people, or one of his picture palaces, the first showings would be in a small Afrikaner town named after the Boer leader Paul Kruger. The date, in particular, was crucial: the anniversary of Blood River, 16 December.

The reception that audiences gave the movie, especially after the antagonism among many Afrikaners during its filming, was incredible.

'When not attending the ceremonies, (the people's) most popular form of entertainment was witnessing the display of "The Voortrekkers," which was screened at repeated intervals in a large bioscope tent within the laager lines, at the Town Hall, and the Vaudette.' At the Town Hall, shows ran every two hours from morning to night.

Many who attended even paid one shilling apiece for a poster showing the face of their hero, Piet Retief, probably not even realising that he was portrayed by the Englishman Dick Cruikshanks.

'The birth of a Great African Industry,' wrote the *Rand Daily Mail*, 'admitted by all who have witnessed (it) as the Greatest Film Picture ever produced in the history of the Cinema.'

One person not attending the festivities was IW. Besides not liking to be seen in public, he had more than enough to keep him busy, including the next movie he was planning to make. Like *Winning a Continent*, it would be a spectacle, but an even bigger and more expensive one.

PART FOUR
1917

In the Shadow of King Solomon

An unidentifed actor portraying Cetshwayo
readies for battle.

THE RISE OF QUATERMAIN

In the first week of 1917, a British officer scouting an area near the mouth of the Rufiji River, south of Dar es Salaam, was hit in the head by a German sniper's bullet. He died instantly.

Within a day, his death was being reported in newspapers around the world, for that man was none other than Sir Frederick Courteney Selous, the 'great hunter, explorer and naturalist'.

'I mourn his death,' wrote his friend the former American president Theodore Roosevelt. Even the commander of the German forces in East Africa, the formidable General Paul von Lettow-Vorbeck, the 'Lion of Africa', was said to have written a letter of condolence.

Despite being 63 when war broke out in 1914, Selous didn't hesitate in signing up, and was finally assigned to the 25th Battalion of the Royal Fusiliers, formed by members of the famous paramilitary group the Legion of Frontiersmen.

Adventurer, man of exploits, extremely handsome – his 'wonderful eyes (were) as clear and as blue as the summer sea' – and a man who, it was said, 'even the elephants could not kill', Selous sounded like some fantastic hero of fiction.

Many of the news reports of his death had one thing in common – they brought up the name of Allan Quatermain, the hero of one of the best-selling books of all time, Sir Henry Rider Haggard's *King Solomon's Mines*. The widely held belief was that the author had based Quatermain on Selous.

The *New York Tribune* wrote that the fictitious hero's adventures 'were only a little more bizarre than those with which the original of the pen picture had to deal with in real life ... Captain Selous was Quatermain'. Frederick Selous was, added *The New York Times*, 'The Original Allan Quatermain'.

King Solomon's Mines was by now thirty years old, but it remained incredibly popular, and the news of Selous's death revived sales.

'Once in a while when we want to give our imagination a treat,' wrote the *Los Angeles Times*, 'we try to remember the flights that others have taken ... (and) we never seem to be able to improve upon Rider Haggard's "She" and "King Solomon's Mines." Haggard ... certainly knows how to make pictures in the mind.'

The story of Allan Quatermain had its genesis in South Africa. In 1875, barely 19 years old, the young Haggard found work as a secretary to the governor of Natal, Sir Henry Bulwer. He often stayed at the Royal Hotel in Durban.

During his ten years in South Africa, Haggard learned about adventurers like Selous and the American scout Frederick Russell Burnham. In 1885, when Haggard returned to England, his brother made a bet with him that he couldn't write a book as successful as the latest one by Robert Louis Stevenson, *Treasure Island*.

In just six weeks, Haggard turned out *King Solomon's Mines*, which went on to outsell *Treasure Island* and made Haggard a rich man – at least for a while. Between 1887 and 1894 he was earning an astonishing £10 000 a year (£500 000 in today's figures), double what Stevenson earned, and far more than other novelists. A later novel, called *She*, which first came out in magazine form in 1887, sold half a million copies.

Quatermain himself was the quintessential adventurer, searching for a lost world, diamonds and treasure, and meeting warriors and witch doctors, good and bad, with plenty of escapades along the way.

Accompanied by his friends Captain Good and Sir Henry Curtis, he sets out from Cape Town on the steamship *Dunkeld* and lands in Durban with a secret map. There, Quatermain's base, like Haggard's had been, is the Royal Hotel.

'Eventually we dropped anchor off the Point and in the windows of the houses of the Berea sparkled a hundred lights ... The next day we went ashore and I put up Sir Henry and Captain Good at the little shanty I have built on the Berea and which I shall call my home.'

For someone like IW, entranced as he was by 'the wand of witchery' exerted by the South African landscape, *King Solomon's Mines* was an obvious choice to turn into a movie. The story had been on his mind for a long time.

In 1894, the year that IW left New York, *The New York Times* declared southern Africa to be 'The Land of Solomon's Mines', with 'an inexhaustible supply of gold'. You just needed to dig to find it, and if the goldfields of Johannesburg or Barberton were too crowded, you only had to head north to Mashonaland, the land of King Solomon, Ophir and the Queen of Sheba.

Now that IW had proved he could make a movie spectacle, and *Winning a Continent* was turning into a wild success, he switched from history to pure adventure. *King Solomon's Mines* had also been mentioned so many times over the past two years, especially by Lorimer Johnston, who spoke of a 'massive production', that it was clearly at the top of IW's list.

But nothing had been said about Haggard's novel since early 1916. And the reason was that, despite insinuations to the contrary, IW had never managed to get the rights. Haggard had sold them to someone else in Britain who was planning to make his own movie.

On Film Row in London, Joseph Albrecht's old stomping ground, a small studio had opened in 1915. Situated at 93–95 Wardour Street, it was called Lucoque Productions.

One of the first things that its owner, a young lawyer named

Horace Lisle Lucoque, did was to negotiate with Haggard's literary agent, Alexander P Watt, to buy the film rights to six of the author's novels for seven years. Even though they included *King Solomon's Mines* and its sequel, *Allan Quatermain*, the one that interested Lucoque the most was *She*.

Before the end of that year, and without any experience in film-making, Lucoque started shooting the story of two adventurers who go in search of a lost kingdom in Africa and encounter a tribe led by a mysterious white queen named Ayesha, who reigns as the all-powerful 'She-who-must-be-obeyed'.

It was the kind of strange, titillating story about 'Darkest Africa' that had fascinated movie producers from the very beginning: a one-minute version of *She* came out of France in 1898, a one-reeler by Thomas Edison in 1908 and another by the US studio Thanhouser three years later. Lucoque would barely finish filming his own adaptation when an American studio started planning an even bigger one.

Lucoque's version, the fourth, was released in February 1916 and seen by two million people in its first five months. One of those people was Haggard himself, although he waited until October to see it, and then noted cryptically in his diary, 'It is fair, considering all things, though somewhat distressing to an author.'

In contrast to Haggard's *She*, nothing had been done with *King Solomon's Mines*. IW started making advances to Lucoque as early as 1915. In a sign that things were happening, the Englishman started distributing some of African Films' productions in Britain, and his cameraman William Bowden came to work at the City of Film. But in the end, it came down to money.

IW promised Lucoque that *King Solomon's Mines*, if made at the City of Film, would have 'massive casts and grandiose sets worthy of Italian and recent Hollywood epics'. Lucoque, who was perpetually in financial trouble, eventually gave in.

In October 1916, just as *Winning a Continent* was being

completed, Lucoque agreed to a deal. There was one important condition: the Englishman, despite his lack of experience, would get to direct not just one of the most expensive movies in the world, but two.

ON TOP OF THE WORLD

Lorimer Johnston had, by this stage, had enough. He was fed up.

He had been promised the world by IW – *King Solomon's Mines*, *The Story of an African Farm* and numerous spectacles – but he had ended up making none of them. Even his biggest movie for IW, *Gloria* – a full five reels long, released in late 1916 – had got lost in the buildup to *Winning a Continent*. Six months before his two-year contract was over, just after *Gloria* was released, he resigned.

Johnston wasn't the first person to leave the studio early either, and under less than happy circumstances – nor would he be the last. Benjamin Franklin Clinton, after directing three comedies for African Films, had gone back to the US disenchanted by his experience.

In late 1916, he gave a stark appraisal of the African Hollywood to the American media. In no way, he said, did the light compare to California, despite what people kept saying – 'It has a peculiar yellowish tinge, which makes it very hard to obtain clear distinct photographs' – and the African workmen who did most of the 'mechanical work' around the studio 'lacked imagination'.

On 3 February 1917, Johnston and Caroline Cooke stood on the platform of Park Station, surrounded by a group of well-wishers, mostly Americans. To avoid crossing the Atlantic, where German U-boat attacks on Allied shipping were increasing, they chose to sail east, via Australia.

Among the people who had come to see them off were Harold

Shaw and Edna Flugrath, who had got married several weeks earlier at the Johannesburg magistrate's office on Government Square. With Clinton and Johnston now gone, Shaw was the only full-time director at the City of Film.

His name also suddenly seemed to be everywhere. In a well-coordinated blitz that started before *Winning a Continent* premiered, his British movies were shown at the Carlton, the Bijou and the Orpheum. And then, a few weeks later, they were brought back again. If a movie starred Edna Flugrath, her name was advertised in bold letters too. Even a musical co-written by Shaw called *His Own Way* had opened at the Empire in August 1916.

And then came the cherry on top for the American, *Winning a Continent*, which was hailed as 'The most important cinematograph production in this or any other country' and is 'now universally known as Harold Shaw's masterpiece'.

At Easter, several months after its premiere, the spectacle was brought back to the Palladium. By the following month, it had been seen locally by a quarter of a million people.

On the first Friday in May, a private screening of *Winning a Continent* before 'a small and distinguished audience' took place in London, at the Alhambra, right across Leicester Square from IVTA House. It was attended by the South African High Commissioner, William P Schreiner, and General Smuts, who had been invited to London by Prime Minister David Lloyd George to join the British war cabinet.

During a speech at a dinner in his honour two weeks later at the Savoy Hotel, Smuts exhorted people to see the movie: 'The history of South Africa is in many respects one of the true and great romances in modern history. One of the most wonderful episodes in that romance you will probably have the opportunity soon to see in a cinematograph film which will be produced here in London called "Winning a Continent", in which scenes from the great Boer trek into the interior are represented. I hope you will all see it.'

The king himself, according to *The Bioscope*, had expressed a desire to see the film, and a command performance would be held at Buckingham Palace. In the West End, the movie had been chosen by Sir Oswald Stoll to open his new Stoll Theatre near Covent Garden, which had previously been the London Opera House.

And then came the reviews. *Winning a Continent* was declared to be greater than not only *The Birth of a Nation* but also DW Griffith's more recent – and far bigger – production, *Intolerance*. The 17 May issue of *Kinematograph and Lantern Weekly* called it 'one of the greatest achievements in the history of film-making'. 'It is said that more people were employed in the filming of this picture than any other thus far produced.' *The Bioscope* added: 'Nothing finer than the native battle scenes could possibly be seen or ever imagined.'

Harold Shaw was now one of the few directors in the world who could claim to have created such a colossal and expensive movie. *Winning a Continent* had cost $100 000, the same as Griffith's *Birth of a Nation*. Ahead of him lay an even costlier project, although what it would be about wasn't immediately clear. *King Solomon's Mines* had already been assigned to Horace Lisle Lucoque, who was only scheduled to arrive in early 1918, more than six months away. So what did IW have in mind for Shaw?

The most likely subject seemed to be Cecil John Rhodes. Shaw, during his 'wand of witchery' tour, had spoken to people in Rhodesia about the possibility of such an epic. He had also made contact with Colonel Johan Colenbrander, a well-known adventurer who had had personal dealings with Rhodes. The editor of the *Sunday Times*, Joseph Langley Levy, and the playwright and satirist Stephen Black had both been working on a scenario for quite some time.

Talk also still lingered of a Shaka spectacle, or one about Dingaan. But no, it would be one that hadn't even been mentioned before. What IW had in mind was a war movie, the biggest one ever.

THE WAR MOVIE

It was another very risky idea.

The world was 'war-worn and weary' of the devastation across Europe. Names like Gallipoli, Ypres and the Somme were grim reminders of how many people had died, and of the horror of men suffocating to death from poison gas. On 17 February 1917, the SS *Mendi*, carrying more than 800 men of the South African Native Labour Corps to serve in France, was rammed in fog by a British merchant vessel, with most people on board lost. Even IW's own magazine *Stage & Cinema* ran an article that month saying, 'Keep clear of all war topics!'

But IW was fresh off a historical spectacle that was becoming a box-office success. And there was much about the new movie that would be just like *Winning a Continent*: a famous local story, heroes, Zulu warriors and a miracle battle. It was the story of the Anglo-Zulu War of 1879.

Forty years after Blood River, the Zulu king Cetshwayo – whose father, Mpande, had vanquished Dingaan, his half-brother – believed he was being forced into an unfair land agreement with the British. The land that they would fight over was very desirable, so much so that a young colonial official at the time wrote about it in almost lyrical terms.

'The country impressed me enormously. Indeed, on the whole I think it the most beautiful of any that I have seen in the world, parts of Mexico alone excepted. The great plains rising by steps to the Quathlamba or Drakensberg Mountains, the sparkling torrential rivers, the sweeping thunderstorms, the grass-fires creeping over the veld at night like snakes of living flame, the glorious aspect of the heavens ... all these things impressed me, so much that were I to live a thousand years I never should forget them.'

That official was the young Henry Rider Haggard.

At the beginning of 1879, when Haggard had been in the country for four years, 15 000 British troops gathered under the leadership of Lord Chelmsford in the town of Pietermaritzburg and marched north into Zululand to confront Cetshwayo. Barely 50 miles from Blood River was a mountain that, because it was shaped like an abomasum, part of a cow's stomach, the Zulu called 'Isandlwana'.

There Chelmsford left an ill-equipped force of 1 300 men, as well as several hundred civilians, including a contingent of poorly armed Africans, before setting off after the Zulu king at his royal seat of Ulundi. No position could have been worse to secure, and Cetshwayo, with his much larger force of 30 000 warriors, seized the advantage.

On 22 January, he attacked the vastly under-defended Isandlwana. Most of the soldiers and civilians were killed, while the Zulu lost a thousand men. Two officers, lieutenants Nevill Coghill and Teignmouth Melvill, would famously be awarded the Victoria Cross posthumously for trying to save the Union Jack from being captured before they were killed crossing the nearby Buffalo River.

From Isandlwana, the Zulu marched on. Six miles away lay Rorke's Drift, a mission outpost and former trading store that had been turned into a supply station and emergency hospital. A small force of British troops was left in the charge of John Chard and Gonville Bromhead, also lieutenants.

When 4 000 Zulu attacked Rorke's Drift, there were only 150 men to fight them off. They put up a long and brave defence of the hospital, which repeatedly came under attack and was set on fire as the soldiers tried to move the patients to safety.

After ten hours of fighting, the Zulu fell back. Miraculously, the British had lost only 16 men, the Zulu 20 times that number, with another 500 seriously wounded. After six months of fighting, Cetshwayo was defeated by Lord Chelmsford at Ulundi, which was destroyed in a blaze so immense that it could be seen from miles away.

Harold Shaw got to work on the scenario with Horace Rose, the editor of *The Natal Witness*, a newspaper based in the town that had played a major role in the war, Pietermaritzburg.

The storyline they came up with was, like *Winning a Continent*, a sprawling one – even more sprawling – of lovers, families, soldiers and outlaws caught up in war, romance, kidnapping and treachery.

Gert Moxter, a Dutch farmer, and his daughter, Marie, live on a remote farm on the banks of the Buffalo River. Engaged to marry Preston Fanshall, a handsome English farmer, Marie is also coveted by Carl Schneider, a rapscallion farm overseer employed by her father.

When Carl makes unwanted advances, an old servant named Gubo, who is Marie's protector, steps in but gets hit with a sjambok. As a result, Carl is banished by Moxter, and the two men, white and black, vow vengeance against each other, 'one out loud, the other quietly'.

A second love story plays out among the Zulu, where Cetshwayo's chief messenger, Tambookie, loves the young Melissa, although the evil witch doctor Dabomba claims her for himself. When she rejects him, Cetshwayo orders her thrown off a cliff, but Tambookie saves her.

Warned by Preston of the oncoming Zulu war parties, Moxter, Marie and Gubo leave the farm and take refuge at the vulnerable station, Rorke's Drift. Preston, who goes to join the British at Isandlwana, is wounded but escapes to Rorke's Drift, where he is treated by Marie and Gubo. During the fighting at the station,

Moxter is killed, Preston struck down and Marie taken hostage.

The villainous Carl Schneider has, in the meantime, gone to Pietermaritzburg, where he plots revenge. His knowledge of the terrain gets him the job of guide to the Prince Imperial, son of Napoleon III, who has come to fight alongside the British.

At Rorke's Drift, they hear news of Marie's kidnapping, and the prince says he will find her. Behind his back, Carl conspires with Dabomba to trap the prince and kill him, and his reward will be Marie.

Overhearing the plot, Gubo follows them. The prince is killed and Carl is taken to the Zulu kraal, where Marie is being kept hostage, overseen by Tambookie and Melissa. They help save her, but Gubo is killed. His body is wrapped in the British flag. The two pairs of lovers are united, and Lord Chelmsford marches to victory at Ulundi.

Harold Shaw had two titles in mind for the movie – both referring to the Union Jack – *The Flag and its Glory* and *The Symbol of Sacrifice*.

THE BELLY OF THE BEAST

So much was happening at the City of Film that the significant departure of two men in April 1917 went largely unnoticed. They sailed east to America, across the Indian and Pacific oceans, not only to avoid the dangers of the Atlantic but to do business along the way.

Ernest Wyrley Birch was a Canadian who had played the part of a kindly minister in *Winning a Continent* but was now filling other roles for IW, while Alfred Smith was the general manager at African Films who had disastrously neglected the costume tent on the day of the fateful battle at Elsburg.

Smith had somehow managed to avoid blame, and, in a way, had even been promoted. He and Birch were being sent on a buying spree across half the globe. IW was looking for new markets, and they were paving the way for him to establish a theatre-and-film network stretching from the Arabian Sea to the Sea of Japan.

In Java, the Straits Settlements, Bombay, Hong Kong and Yokohama, they made contact with theatres that IVTA could provide with theatrical acts and movies. At the same time, three movie companies were launched: India Films Ltd in Bombay; the Federated Malay States Films Ltd in Singapore; and China Films Ltd in Shanghai. Under their sway would also fall Ceylon, Peking, Tientsin, 'several towns in Japan' and eventually the Philippine Islands.

The controlling company, Middle East Films Ltd, was to have its headquarters, in the heart of Singapore, in a five-storey building that IW planned to erect on Orchard Road.

When the two men eventually reached California, Smith stayed there 'in connection with some big picture deals' and was soon being taken on a tour of Universal City with the director Henry McRae, while Birch continued east to take charge of Schlesinger's newly launched IVTA office in New York. By the time he got there, IW's brother MA had found an office on Times Square, and they had also opened a movie production company.

IW was about to take on America.

Timing was usually his strong suit, like when he jumped in to buy the Empire, but on this occasion that wasn't the case.

Maybe IW was feeling bullish after all that he had achieved in just a few years, creating a movie industry out of almost nothing. From a blip on the screen, a pinprick, he now had an entertainment organisation that stretched from Cape Town to Cairo to London, and soon would include Java, Bombay and Shanghai.

Harold Shaw was busy with the new spectacle, travelling to Pietermaritzburg and Natal to scout for locations. Besides that, planning was under way not only for *King Solomon's Mines* and its sequel, *Allan Quatermain*, but also for a melodrama called *The Bridge*, during the filming of which an actual old train would be run off a bridge over the Blaauwkrantz River, and *Voice of the Waters*, some of it filmed in a building erected on the very edge of the waterfall at Howick. Joseph Albrecht doubled up as writer and director of *Copper Mask*, a story about the days of stagecoach robberies, and he and Ralph Kimpton travelled to Swaziland to make Bertram Mitford's *The Border Scourge*. The actor Dick Cruickshanks, besides directing several pictures, was filming an all-black comedy series, set in the village at the City of Film, called *Zulutown*.

Around the City of Gold, meanwhile, acting schools were springing up to supply performers for theatre and movies. In Berea and Joubert Park, there were classes offered by Signor Alberto

'The village' at the studio was used for several productions
like the *Zulutown* comedies. Here the character Zulu (in top hat)
opens a skating rink with his friend Daniel.

Terrasi, Professor and Madam Sparnon, Francesco Ferramosca and
Horace Barton. With much fanfare, Norman Lee, who worked for
IW, opened his own acting studio.

And at the Empire and Schlesinger's other theatres, crowds
were coming nightly to see not just movies but his endless stream
of imported acts, such as the magician Horace Goldin and his tiger,
Lily, and Professor Royal Racord, 'the man who tamed electricity'.

Not without reason, IW must have been feeling invincible.

But at the same time that he had been creating his Hollywood
in Africa, the real one in Los Angeles had boomed. Film-making
across Europe, which once led the way, had almost ceased, while
in America, isolated from the war, it got bigger and better and the
movies longer. As the migration from New York to California continued, several bigger studios were now also trying to consolidate.

Early in 1917, *Stage & Cinema* carried the story of one new studio
in particular. Adolph Zukor, the other 'little man', had created a

company that would become Paramount, and he was starting to bring under one roof the means of production, distribution and exhibition, just like IW had done. But it would take Zukor another two years to achieve.

Pitted against Zukor were two exhibitors, Thomas Lincoln Tally and James Dixon Williams, a man who in several years' time would work for IW and clash very publicly with him. They got theatres around the country to come together to buy, distribute and eventually produce their own pictures.

In April 1917, as Birch and Smith were sailing to Java and Bombay and China, First National Exhibitors Circuit held its first meeting in New York. It went well, and out of it came a new consolidated opposition to Zukor.

'Nothing like the storm that arose when First National was first organized had previously been known in the industry.'

A war between the two big players in Hollywood was about to start in earnest, and it was at this very moment that IW chose to enter the belly of the beast.

MAYFAIR

A small mention in the US trade press in March 1917 announced the opening of a distinctly English-sounding movie company, the Mayfair Film Corporation. The chief was MA Schlesinger, 'the American representative of the African Film Trust'.

An office for Mayfair, and for IVTA, was opened in the Putnam Building at 43rd Street and Broadway, the very heart of Times Square. A better, more central place IW couldn't have found.

Down the corridors were a gallimaufry of theatre and movie agents: Feiber & Shea's; the colourful Greek Alexander Stathopoulo, who bought films from America for foreign markets and, in return, sold them titles like *On the Italian Battle Front*; and numerous agents in search of scenarios and actors and chorus girls, or offering the same to anyone in search of them. The most important of them all was Marcus Loew, who would soon own not only a huge chain of theatres across America but the studio with the famous roaring lion logo, Metro-Goldwyn-Mayer (MGM).

The New York offices of other big movie men were all within a few blocks. Adolph Zukor's Paramount was around the corner, and four blocks away, at 1600 Broadway, was Carl Laemmle's Universal. In every direction you looked, there were also the most famous theatres on Broadway: the Liberty, the New Amsterdam, the Lyric, the Lyceum and the Knickerbocker, which now carried all the biggest movies. If Mayfair was looking for success by association – like IW had for his other companies at 10 Wall

Street – the Putnam was the right address.

At the same time, the Schlesingers opened a small studio on West 54th Street, and production was supposed to start almost immediately. On 6 May it was reported in *The Sun* that Mayfair had acquired a British actress named Peggy Hyland, who was making a name for herself in America, to star in a series of movies. The studio was 'determined to spare no expense'.

The Putnam Building, on Times Square, where IW based his doomed American entertainment headquarters. It was torn down in 1925 to make way for Adolph Zukor's 33-storey Paramount Building.

The first movie, *Persuasive Peggy*, was specially written for Hyland, and it premiered in July. Shortly afterwards, an animated MA, who seemed to be less averse to publicity than IW, promised that there would be four more movies starring Hyland, each one made by a different director – to give it a distinct character – although he didn't name any of them.

Curiously enough, while IW was entering the American market, Hollywood was making a more serious play for Africa. That same week, Selznick Pictures announced the release of *Poppy*, 'Cynthia Stockley's famous novel of the love-starved South African girl', who was played by Norma Talmadge, one of Hollywood's rising stars. Its director, Edward José, had lived in South Africa for five years, so 'the Transvaal is as well known to him as Broadway'. William Fox, meanwhile, was releasing his version, the fifth, of Rider Haggard's *She*. Other African-themed movies that had come out were a mix of stories of diamonds, wild animals and women in bad marriages on the veld, including *Prowlers of the Jungle*, *Lord Chumley*, *The Zudora Mystery* and *Avenged by Lions*.

In a less publicised move at the same time as starting Mayfair, IW created a distribution arm to try to sell his own African movies in America. The first title to be offered was *Winning a Continent*, which, in a bid to attract the local market, was given a new title – *The Pioneers*.

A WONDERLAND

Wandering through the new studio below the Parktown ridge, the journalist was entranced, calling it 'more like a visit to Wonderland than anything else'. After three years and a final cost of about $350 000 (about $8.4 million today), the City of Film was being unveiled to the media.

The main building, the headquarters for African Films, was built of cut stone and measured about twenty thousand square feet on each of its two floors. It was 'palatial ... an adornment to any of the principal streets of any city in the world'.

In one wing were offices for IW and at least six movie directors. Harold Shaw was set up in one of them, his assistant Ralph Kimpton in another, and a third was being prepared for Horace Lisle Lucoque. Offices had been set aside for a general manager, a scenario editor, writers, poster artists, publicity and the African Mirror team.

The offices had the latest gadgets that IW had brought from New York, for 'the ingenuity of American men of business ... has admittedly reduced the science of office construction to a fine art, and are far ahead of the English in this respect'.

Beyond that lay a reading room, a library and a dining room, as well as a kitchen that was gearing up to make thousands of meals a day for extras on the new war spectacle. The journalists were taken though film-drying rooms, with their massive turning drums, and film-assembling rooms.

Outside, a large open-air stage measured 6 000 square feet. On the other side of it was a building for the scenery and props – which until now had been stored in buildings around the city – and living quarters and a kitchen for the African workers.

In the costume department, a swarm of people were at work on outfits for the new spectacle, outdoing what they had done for *Winning a Continent*. Once again, the costumes that were needed numbered in the thousands.

For the British soldiers, the journalists were told, there would be 1 600 uniforms and 400 pairs of jackboots; cavalry swords and army helmets; 160 bell tents; and enough imitation flowers to fill six trucks. For the *moochis* worn by the Zulu warriors, 10 000 yards of material was needed; and 350 animal skins were cut up for 5 000 shields, armlets and leg pieces. As for the weapons – thousands of assegais, knobkieries and lances – they had acquired every rubber ball in the city to put on their tips, which were then dabbed with silver paint.

In the carpenter's shop, large enough for 20 people to work at the same time, the main focus was a replica of Windsor Castle. They were making not only an outer façade but a grandiose reception room that, once assembled, would measure 46 feet wide and 90 feet long, with four large Gothic windows and a magnificent fireplace. The grand room for an important scene between Queen Victoria and Empress Eugénie of France would cost £700.

To create the rest of the scenery and props, the workmen were using 25 000 feet of beaverboard, half a million feet of three-ply wood, more than two tons of paint and six tons of paper.

The journalists passed an area that they were told had been set aside for the creation of an artificial river and a lake, which was being excavated; in another area, a zoo would include lions and leopards to be trained for film work. The finest stables in the country were planned, and there would be a garage for all kinds of motor vehicles, as well as a wagon house for anything from a 19th-century coach to rickshas.

Within a year of the first bricks-and-mortar studio going up in Hollywood, at Universal City (below) – until then they were in barns and shacks – IW was building his own at Killarney.

'As for the streets, you will have the kerbed and guttered thoroughfares of a great city, with trams, telephone, and telegraph wires, or the featureless roadway that winds through a quiet village. And the peculiarity of these streets, of course, is that they will be created or removed at the pleasure of the producer. There will also be cottages and residential flats for employees.'

On the edge of the property, two buildings were being constructed out of brick and mortar. One was meant to be the two-storey hospital at Rorke's Drift, the other the adjoining store. To create the laager around the outpost, they would use 600 sacks of sand and 500 boxes.

The journalists were inundated with statistics for the upcoming war movie. The studio would destroy 60 ox-wagons by setting them alight with 400 gallons of paraffin and two carloads of straw. For the battle of Ulundi, workers were building a kraal of almost 300 huts at a cost of £2 750 (almost £250 000 today). In the climactic scene, they would all be burned to the ground.

14 MILES AN HOUR

From the very highs to the very lows. No sooner had the wonders of the City of Film been broadcast to the world than IW was facing accusations in a court of law.

A short newspaper article that seemingly had nothing to do with him, and which most people might have overlooked, appeared in late June 1917. It described a hearing that had taken place at the Rand Police Courts on Government Square.

The courtroom was a place that IW tried his utmost to avoid, but the police courts must have been particularly vexing, as it was reserved for abortionists, bogus doctors, opium smokers and the like. Court A was specially designated for cases of theft, C for illicit liquor, and D for vehicle accidents.

In Court D, a man named Ludwig Japhet testified that he had been driving his two-seater car just west of Joubert Park when, at the corner of Plein and Hoek streets, he was struck by a much bigger car. He estimated he was doing ten miles an hour, the other car 25 to 30. Driving 'recklessly, negligently and dangerously', it hit him with such force, he said, that one of his front wheels landed on the pavement.

Strangely enough, it wasn't Japhet who had laid the charge but a witness to the accident. Making it even stranger, Japhet himself was a lawyer who specialised in defending people charged with this very offence.

In the bigger car were five occupants. Even though the driver was identified as Max Bosman, it was clear as the testimony unfolded that he was Max Zasman, and the man sitting next to him in the car, identified only as 'the owner', was IW. The passengers in the back seat were Harold Shaw, Ralph Kimpton and Charles Herbert Jagger, who also worked for African Films.

'The owner' told the court that he judged 'Bosman', who had been in his employ for about two years, a good driver. He never would have let him drive at 25 miles an hour but estimated they had been going no more than 14.

'Witness (IW) … said he did not drive a car himself but the speedometer was right in front of him and he constantly looked at it.

'Had Mr Japhet sounded his hooter, there would have been no accident. Almost every car in this town was insured with his (IW's) company, and he knew what accidents were.'

Shaw, Kimpton and Jagger all said the same thing as IW – their car was going about 14 miles an hour. Shaw added that he got nervous when cars went fast, and if theirs had been going at a dangerous speed he would have been uneasy. 'Max Bosman' was let off the charge a few days later, and the incident quickly blew over.

As curious as the case was – names left out or misspelled, a lawyer who could have easily won his case but didn't want to lay a charge, a bystander who had recognised IW and couldn't abide seeing him get away without being charged – it gained significance a few months later. A very similar incident, involving three of the passengers and the reckless use of vehicles, found its way to a higher court, although IW was unable to keep his identity hidden and the whole thing turned into a public shouting match.

It would also almost destroy IW's war movie.

A QUATERMAIN COMES TO TOWN

The upcoming movie about the Anglo-Zulu War was just what Johan Colenbrander needed. At the age of 60, his hair was almost white and his moustache broad and a bit unkempt, but his eyes were still lively. For some time now, however, things had not been going well for him.

Once known as an 'adventurer and soldier of fortune', his early exploits read not unlike those of the two famous Fredericks – Selous and Burnham. Some of the exploits even found their way into the adventures of Rider Haggard's hero, Allan Quatermain.

Colenbrander had fought against the great Lobengula, the Matabele chief whom he later befriended and accompanied as a translator on an official visit to Queen Victoria in 1890. After translating for Cecil John Rhodes, he had lived for five years with the Zulu chief Usibepu, who had fought at Isandlwana. In 1902, the same year that Rhodes died, Colenbrander was made a Companion of the Order of the Bath.

Since then, however, things had gone downhill. He tried to organise safari hunting trips, and to sell mining concessions, first in Britain and then America, but with little success. In doing so, he spent so much money that 'he was reduced to absolute penury'.

'It was only with difficulty that English friends In New York who entertained some admiration for his picturesque career in the past could persuade him at length to take advantage of their offers to pay his passage back to England. For he was an incurable

Adventurer, soldier of fortune and friend of Lobengula,
Johan Colenbrander.

optimist, as well as frightfully hot-tempered and peppery; in fact, a very troublesome proposition to handle.'

No sooner had Colenbrander reached England than 'he was arrested on a charge of obtaining money under false pretences … After several hearings in the Bow Street police court in London, the members of the Chartered South African Company came to his rescue and enabled him to make his return to South Africa.'

He was leading 'a sort of hand-to-mouth existence at Bulawayo' when, in early 1916, he met Harold Shaw, during his 'wand of witchery' tour and scouting for locations where they could shoot a movie about Rhodes. When planning for the Anglo-Zulu War movie started, Colenbrander's name came up again.

Even though he was only a teenager in 1879, he had served as a trumpeter with the Stanger Mounted Rifles. He was one of 6 000 who had fought against a Zulu force double their size at the battle of Gingingdlovu – 'the place of he who swallowed the elephant'. For a time, he had even travelled on the same wagon as the commander, Lord Chelmsford.

'We drove them into the Nyezane River,' he later recalled, 'where they drowned by the hundred. After the battle it took our men three days to bury the Zulu dead.'

For IW's war movie, Colenbrander was a godsend. He was military man, translator, historian and advisor all rolled into one. He spoke Zulu and Shangaan fluently and had a rare insight into the history of both sides in the war. Usibepu had 'in his own picturesque language described the engagement to the colonel again and again so that the details of it were as graphically photographed on his mind as if he had actually been there'.

On 4 August 1917, it was announced that Colenbrander was joining the movie not only as an advisor but also to play the pivotal role of General Frederic Augustus Thesiger, Lord Chelmsford. Like Gustav Preller on *Winning a Continent*, Colenbrander was immediately excited about the movie, and quickly became one of its keenest participants. With him on board, it was believed, a repeat of the disaster at Elsburg could never happen.

JOY RIDES

By September, everything seemed to be going surprisingly well, and not just for the war movie.

In London, on the second Monday of the month, the cameras of Pathé Gazette were outside the West End Cinema, between Leicester Square and Piccadilly Circus, for the opening of *Winning a Continent*. Hundreds of people were milling about, a huge banner above them publicising the movie's name, before they went in.

'The huge audience ... vented their enthusiasm by frequent applause.'

Not a mile away, in Wardour Street, Horace Lisle Lucoque was working on the scenario for IW's *King Solomon's Mines*. For some time already, he had been getting the assistance of Rider Haggard, and ambitious plans were discussed for filming all over the subcontinent, including an unprecedented shoot in the Cango Caves, which would be specially lit by powerful electric lamps.

In New York, meanwhile, the first movie made by Mayfair, the six-reel *Persuasive Peggy*, had been completed and was putting a slew of publicity in trade publications. It had a big star, an up-and-coming writer and a director who people were talking about. MA Schlesinger was 'more than pleased with the reception'.

IW hoped to have eight directors at work at the City of Film by the end of the year, including a man named John Winthrop Kelley, whose *The Submarine Eye* had been playing to sold-out houses at the Liberty Theatre near Times Square.

Stage & Cinema was already running stills from the war movie –

they had by now settled on the title *The Symbol of Sacrifice* – even though only a few scenes in Windsor Castle had been filmed so far. Ahead of Shaw and the production team still lay the three big battles – Isandlwana, Rorke's Drift and Ulundi.

But then, in what seemed to be turning into a pattern for IW, he had a falling-out with someone and things suddenly fell apart.

It was about money, at least to start with, and not even a lot of it. But to IW it mattered so much that he was prepared to risk sinking his own super-production.

'Schlesinger would think nothing of giving £10 000 to a good cause,' the journalist Arthur Barlow wrote, 'but would knock the stuffing out of anyone for ten shillings if he believed he had been robbed of it.'

On his movies, IW had shown over and over that he didn't mind excessive outlays, 'never hesitated to spend money' and told his directors that 'no expenses will be spared to make it perfect in every detail'. But he wanted to know where the money went and be sure that it was used sensibly.

During the past year, Harold Shaw and Ralph Kimpton had formed a kind of friendship, which included taking time off from the studio for extended lunches. Shaw was probably also frustrated that IW had made him focus on the spectacles and wouldn't let him film any of the smaller movies, which could have kept him busy and earning more money.

Whenever they left the studio, Shaw and Kimpton would call a taxi, for which they were meant to sign a chit, 'but this Shaw flatly refused to do'.

On 12 September, a taxi driver named Walter John Howes arrived at the studio demanding to be paid for a trip the two men had taken. IW came down and made some serious accusations in front of Howes and employees who were standing around, including Max Zasman.

To Howes he said that Shaw and Kimpton 'get damned well half drunk and bloody well don't know what they are doing. They take bloody whores to Craighall (about four miles away) for joy rides and charge it up to the company's expense. I am bloody well not going to pay for them ... I have lost thousands of pounds through bloody joy riding and I am damned well not going to do it again.'

To another taxi driver, Louis Smith, he allegedly said, 'When Mr Shaw has a few drinks in him he does not know what he is doing and he drives about only looking for a girl to go out for a ride with.'

IW at first denied the allegations, but then said that he had been referring only to Kimpton. Shaw, who was still staying at the Carlton Hotel, bumped into IW in the lobby one day. 'How dare you bring my name in connection with thieves and drunkards?' he said. 'I am a clean-living, decent man, and you have said things about me that I do not permit any man to say. Damn you!'

Shaw and Kimpton sued IW for breach of contract and libel, claiming damages of £10 000, the equivalent of half the budget of *Winning a Continent*.

By October, Shaw had resigned, and at the beginning of December he left Johannesburg for Cape Town. With him went Edna Flugrath, Ralph Kimpton and the cameraman Henry Howse.

Suddenly the war movie was in limbo. There was no director, no leading lady and one fewer experienced cameraman, while all of the big scenes still had to be filmed. Finding someone in New York or London who had the stature and experience of Shaw, and then persuading them to come to South Africa, would take months. But within a matter of days, IW had someone – himself.

'It will be good for my health,' he said, almost flippantly, 'and give me an insight into the business not to be obtained in any other way.'

The task that lay ahead of him was enormous and, for someone who had never directed before, potentially disastrous. The first scenes that he would have to shoot, which were scheduled for the beginning of 1918, were three battles that were meant to be quite unlike anything else ever put on film.

PART FIVE
1918

'The Most Stupendous Spectacular Film of Modern Times'

The Throne Room built for the opening scene of *King Solomon's Mines*, with Lucoque and William Bowden facing the camera.

LEADING LADY

If there was one good thing about the Harold Shaw disaster, at least for IW, it was that he also lost Edna Flugrath.

At the City of Film there was another actress he'd been wanting to make his leading lady for some time already, but while the better-known Flugrath was around, it was unlikely. Now that the American had left, she was going to get her chance.

As soon as Mable May became the studio's leading lady,
numerous photographs of her appeared on the covers
and in the pages of *Stage & Cinema* regularly.

Mabel May had been in most of IW's movies from the very beginning. In her early twenties, and divorced before she came to South Africa with a touring group, she wasn't a natural beauty, more homely. But she was plucky and ready to do stunts and learned how to handle a horse so well that she could snatch a young boy from the ground while she was riding.

In October 1916, she played the lead in *Gloria*, IW's longest movie so far. And, most recently, she had appeared in the serial *Adventures of a Diamond*, which required her to disguise herself as a man so that she could join male prospectors in a rush of new diamond diggings near Christiana in the Orange Free State. If anyone could replace Flugrath, it was Mabel May.

IW had another important reason he wanted to make her a star. She was his girlfriend.

'CAMERAS, GET READY!'

A stranger to Pietermaritzburg early on the morning of Friday 11 January 1918 might easily have been baffled by the scenes playing out in the centre of town. It looked like a cross between a pageant and 'the overflow of a war market', but it was the film crew from *The Symbol of Sacrifice*.

Hordes of young men hung around Church Street and Commercial Road, and after wagons rolled up laden with equipment and piles of newly made clothes, they gathered around them, 'rummaging, sorting, trying on and criticising their uniforms and firing off funny remarks and blank cartridges'. With nowhere else to change, the extras who were playing soldiers stripped in public, and soon were attired in red tunics, Oxford blue trousers, helmets and jackboots. A brass band could be heard practising all the way from Victoria Square, and cavalry trotted up and down the streets.

'It was the first time most of the spectators had had an opportunity of seeing a film in the making and they made the most of their chances.'

The town itself was perfect for capturing an era four decades earlier, its collection of red-brick Victorian buildings lining streets and squares named after English heroes. It was from this very place, in 1879, that Lord Chelmsford had launched the British campaign against the Zulu.

Once the artillery arrived, everyone was put in place, with Colonel Johan Colenbrander, playing the role of Chelmsford, riding up front with the Natal Carbineers' band, followed by the infantry, the drummer boys, the artillery, the lancers and, last of all, two ambulance wagons pulled by oxen. Alongside the road, throngs of cheering people were gathered, ready to toss thousands of the paper flowers that had been made at Killarney at the passing soldiers.

After almost four hours of preparation, the massive parade was ready to begin its march to war. Somewhere in front of the crowd was IW, assisted in his new role of director by Joseph Albrecht and Dick Cruickshanks. With his bullhorn at the ready, he even had his own unique cry for 'Action!'

'Cameras, get ready,' he began. 'Ready. Go!'

The following day, a Saturday, an early-morning drizzle quickly gave way to a picture-perfect sky, and the cameramen shot the arrival in the city of the Prince Imperial.

JB Rowe, a young stage actor from England who had been performing in Johannesburg, was playing the role of the doomed prince. In this scene, he was welcomed by a crowd carrying lilies as they gathered along Longmarket Street.

On Sunday, the crew and extras returned to Church Street, this time for the prince's funeral. The cortege was led through town, and included a scarlet-coated firing party, a band and a gun carriage on which rested a coffin covered in wreaths.

The filming hours were gruelling, which wasn't surprising given IW's attitude to work. The scenes had to be shot in three days, and Albrecht commented years later that IW did not even want to break for lunch. Once edited, however, those same scenes would eventually take up only two minutes of screen time.

By Monday morning, Pietermaritzburg was quiet again, the hordes from African Films gone. 'The operations have been transferred to Isandlwana,' it was reported by Reuters, 'for the purpose of obtaining further pictures in connection with the Zulu war.'

At Isandlwana, hundreds of men stood in the shadow of the 1 400-foot mountain shaped like a cow's stomach.

The previous day, IW had issued 'several columns of instructions' to Albrecht, Cruickshanks and Colenbrander. Several old seven- and nine-pounder guns, which had been transported almost 200 miles from Durban by the navy, stood near the replica of the British military camp that had been recreated at the foot of the mountain.

Early that morning, IW addressed the hundreds of white extras playing British soldiers. He had read up as much as he could about the Anglo-Zulu battles; now here he was, the American transplant, describing to the men, many of them returned soldiers from the war in Europe, the mood that had prevailed in the British camp. It was relaxed, he said, with some of the men playing cricket and other games, before they were caught unawares and attacked.

Two major scenes were to take place at the site: the fight around the flag and the struggle around the guns. Several thousand warriors would storm the camp. After the artillery had been wiped out, the Natal Carbineers would gallop into camp, dismount around the guns and 'fight back to back until every man is killed'.

'Experts tell me the greatest fight ever put up by a few men was that of the handful of carbineers,' IW told the men in front of him. 'So, boys, you must put up a good fight.' Perhaps recalling Elsburg, and even though he had Colenbrander on set, he added, 'Don't hurt the natives. I give you my word they will not hurt you. Remember, they're human beings and know how to play the game.'

Then he moved over to the African crowd, which numbered about 6 000. Watching him was a journalist from the *Sunday Times*, who got a rare view of IW, who comes across as feisty and very blunt, peppering his language with Zulu words. At one stage he saw a warrior in the wrong outfit.

'Look at that nigger with the corsets,' he shouted. 'Does he think I've invited him to a ballet. Take that off. You – *wena!* Why doesn't somebody go and take away those stays.'

Some of the other warriors started chuckling, and he turned to them.

'*Ikona hlega!* (No laughing!) Understand, you mustn't laugh. This is no beer drinking. It must be a real hard fight. You. *Wena!* Take your shoes off. Natives in those days didn't wear shoes. They were men, not silly *umfazis* (women). Stand up straight, you. Take that imbecile coon out of the way, else he'll do something to spoil our scene. Now listen, when the first gun goes off, it's your signal to rush forward.'

Despite his outbursts, IW was always impressed by the Africans' acting, a sentiment that he shared with Albrecht. 'The natives are wonderful actors,' IW told the journalist. 'Explain an idea, and they quickly grasp it. They put their hearts and souls into the business. You might have thought they would be carried away by the excitement and exceed their instructions, but this has not happened in any case.'

Max Zasman, IW's chauffeur, also came in for a tongue-lashing. He had been given the minor role of a bugler trying to save the Union Jack before he is cut down. 'The Zulus were throwing assegais at me and we were supposed to be dropped off our horses,' Zasman later recalled. 'IW stood on the set shouting, "Fall, fall, damn you!" But it was not so easy, but I did it in the end.'

When the article appeared in the *Sunday Times* several weeks later, it added a paragraph of congratulations. Perhaps it had been added by Joseph Langley Levy, the editor, who had been a witness to the disaster at Elsburg. The three battles of *Symbol of Sacrifice*, meanwhile, had gone off without a single serious incident.

'Altogether something like 20 000 whites and blacks have taken part (in the movie) … Throughout there has been not a hitch and no casualties.'

Only one major scene remained to be filmed, but it was on water. After the tragedy at the dam in Elsburg and difficulties on the Vaal River shoot, there was good reason to be anxious.

'These wonderful long shots have been stretched to the very limits of the camera. They represent ... the *ne plus ultra* of mass effects,' wrote *Bioscope* magazine of IW's battle scenes.

DEATH AT THE RIVER

In between the 600 extras gathered on the banks of the river a few weeks later, on 10 February 1918, were Joseph Ralph Levy and William Brown. Like most of the other men, they were soldiers recently returned from the war.

It was a perfect summer's day – a Sunday, once again, which had by now become the traditional day to shoot the biggest scenes – and it felt almost like a holiday, even though they were there to work.

The scene about to be filmed – the very last scene for *The Symbol of Sacrifice* – wasn't complicated, no men clashing, no guns going off. But it was a significant scene, for Colonel Johan Colenbrander in particular: it concerned the one battle of the war that he had actually taken part in, Gingingdlovu.

The re-enactment was to show Lord Chelmsford leading the 17th Lancers and the Natal Carbineers to the Tugela River, only to find it flooded after recent rains, so the troops had to swim across with their horses.

Searching for a suitable place near Johannesburg to film, they selected Henley on Klip near the Vaal River, about 40 miles to the south. Ten days before the shoot, Joseph Albrecht and a man named Petersen went to 'survey' the river.

The manager of the local hotel, Herman Rausch, took them about one and a half miles upriver, where they sounded the water with a ten-foot pole. The riverbed sloped gradually to the middle, until the pole couldn't touch the bottom. Even though the waterway was narrower than the Tugela, at that particular section a dam had been built a while back, making it several hundred yards wide.

Throughout the morning of 10 February, the riverbank was a hive of activity as cameras were set up, hundreds of men put on their uniforms, and the horses were saddled for them to ride across. A medical officer, a Dr Tritsch from Johannesburg, was on hand in case he was needed. Rausch, the hotel manager, put three small boats at their disposal, 'to stand by in case of an emergency', although it became apparent later on that only one of them was 'fit to rescue anyone'.

Colenbrander, 'keen as he was to give the world the true story of a great adventure', insisted that he swim across in the same way Chelmsford had. The colonel had been a good swimmer in his time and had even swum into Table Bay to meet the steamer arriving from Britain with the young woman he was to marry. But he was 60 now, and 'was medically advised that, quite apart from the obvious necessity of an operation, his heart was weak'. IW told him that he needed to go across by raft.

Whether or not they came to an agreement, Colenbrander got on his horse with the extras, and then, in sections of four at a time, they rode into the water. It was about four in the afternoon.

When the first riders reached a depth of about 12 feet and could no longer touch the bottom, one of the horses, which was perhaps 15 feet ahead of the next wave, turned around and crossed in front of some of the others behind it, and then there was chaos.

David Greissell, one of the extras, saw Colenbrander and the returned soldier William Brown close together, 'going up and down' in the water. The horses made for shore, leaving the colonel and the others to swim back on their own. The emergency boats, which were 30 yards away, immediately set out to help.

'One of the boats was overhauling the colonel when he disappeared under the water'. In the turmoil, Colenbrander didn't surface again.

Max Zasman, who was on the riverbank, ran to the nearest phone to call the police. When they arrived, they started dragging the river, but Colenbrander's body was not found. By that stage, they had also learned that two other people, William Brown and Joseph Levy, hadn't returned to shore either. Their bodies were found first, but it took three days to find Colenbrander.

▭▭▭▭

It was Blood River all over again, even the way it played out: a river, an artificial dam, men crossing the water, a lack of preparation, chaos and then drowning. Except now it wasn't one man, but three.

News of the famous Colenbrander's death reached *The New York Times* and the *Washington Post,* while local newspapers immediately started asking questions. It was 'one of the most pathetic incidents in South African history', wrote the *Rand Daily Mail,* and 'a gloom has been cast over the completion of a great film'.

Why was a man of Colenbrander's age, and who was known to have a heart problem, allowed to perform such a strenuous act? Had he been forced to do the river swim, and had the person who forced him been Schlesinger? The subject was even raised in parliament, where the minister of justice was asked if he was going to confiscate the film records and ban 'sensational films depicting native wars'. The minister said he had no intention of interfering.

IW's own magazine *Stage & Cinema* rushed out a story within days, commiserating the deaths but also saying how there had not been 'a single mishap' on the set until then, despite the battle scenes they had filmed using 20 000 extras, including 'the burning and blowing up of Cetshwayo's kraal'.

The district surgeon in nearby Heidelberg examined the bodies of Brown and Colenbrander; he couldn't do Levy's because, in accordance with Jewish rites, the deceased had been buried within 24 hours. Once the surgeon handed in his report, a decision could be made about whether there should be an inquest.

Colenbrander's body was transported back to the city in a hearse provided by African Films. The following day it was taken from the funeral home in a cortege to St Mary's Church and then to the Brixton cemetery. Present at the graveside were IW, Cruickshanks, Albrecht, the cameraman JL Humphrey, and wreaths were received from Harold Shaw and Edna Flugrath.

'Torrents of rain fell while a short service was held at the graveside, where many friends had gathered to pay their last respects to the brave old soldier.'

'HELP, BOATS!'

In the courtroom at Vereeniging, evidence was led of warnings being given on the movie set, poor-quality rescue boats, a dangerous channel in the path of the riders and the possibility that Colenbrander had been coerced into swimming.

The inquest into the deaths of Johan Colenbrander and troopers William Brown and Joseph Levy began before magistrate HE Gill on 5 March and lasted for three days. Like the inquest into the Elsburg disaster, an array of people came to tell their version of events: IW, Albrecht, the hotel manager Rausch, farmers, spectators standing on the riverbank, returned soldiers who had taken part in the fatal scene.

Some of the locals drew a picture of imminent danger and a crew woefully unprepared. A farmer named Andries Potgieter, employed to do 'transport work', said he had warned the men that they were doing a dangerous thing and would die.

'You are going to get drowned here today,' he said in Dutch to the men standing near him. Colenbrander was close by and IW about ten yards away.

Asked by Gill why he had warned them, the farmer said it was dangerous to enter the water with clothes and boots on. When the riders got in trouble, he had been on one of the boats trying to assist, and he saw three men go under, including Colenbrander, 'and these did not come up again'.

Another farmer who took out his own boat, Archibald Alison,

said he picked up several soldiers. If he hadn't, he said, more soldiers would have died because the other boats were useless. A third farmer named Edward Palmer agreed, saying that when he saw the riders getting in trouble, he rushed to put two boats at their disposal.

Rausch, who described the earlier visit to Henley on Klip by Albrecht and Petersen, the reconnaissance of the river, the measuring of the depth and the choosing of the location, said he hadn't thought it would be dangerous to film there.

A series of witnesses described the scene that unfolded after the men entered the water. The first horse was about ten feet ahead and then turned around and swam into another two. 'Then there appeared to be a general mix-up.' Another witness added that 'the horses were plunging about'.

The problem seemed to be the deep channel, where the first few horses went under, then resurfaced, their riders unseated. The rest of the animals, by then in the middle of the river, turned back for the bank, most of them riderless.

David Greissell, the returned soldier, said that at the time he had been employed by African Films, he and the others were told they needed to be able to ride and to swim. Colenbrander, he added, was the only one to have given them orders. When his own horse began to struggle, he started swimming. He saw Levy nearby, unsaddled. Anyone who tried to get back on his horse was repeatedly knocked off. After that, Greissell said, he 'remembered no more except that he was pulled into a boat'.

Albrecht testified that the choice to swim across had definitely been Colenbrander's. Indeed, he insisted, IW 'had made up his mind to change that part of the scenario' and have Lord Chelmsford go across by raft instead of swimming. But the colonel had still wanted to swim across and show the others behind him how it was done.

'No, Colonel Colenbrander,' Albrecht quoted IW as saying, 'you have to go over on a raft with your staff.'

It appeared that while IW was occupied with something else, Colenbrander had entered the water anyway. Seeing that the action had begun, the cameras started rolling.

When the first men got in trouble, Colenbrander tried to remount but was pushed off his horse, then swam for the eastern bank. He and trooper Brown were next to each other. At one point, Albrecht heard Colenbrander shout, 'Help, boats!' When he put his hand up to reach for one that came alongside him, another soldier seemed to swim right over him, 'and he was seen no more.'

IW told the inquest that he had instructed the man organising the extras, whose name was given only as 'Bell', that those selected needed to be able to ride and swim. On the day of the shoot, he had told Frank Fillis, Jr – the son of the famous circus master, who was also in the movie – to test the river for mud.

'Fillis reported it quite safe.'

The magistrate, as had been done five years earlier for *The Great Strike*, decided to see the relevant section of the movie at a local cinema. He was accompanied by IW.

'The portion of the film shown … depicted the "troops" entering the water, and showed Colonel Colenbrander's horse floundering after it was crossed by another horse and the colonel's struggle to regain control.' The film 'provided a unique record of what really happened as could never be furnished by any human witness'.

Even though IW was never accused of wrongdoing, the whispered accusations persisted. The showing of the footage to the magistrate seemed to put rumours to rest, except the one that his spectacles were jinxed.

Every day for two weeks – even during the inquest – the movie was heavily advertised: 'The Most Important Film Produced in South Africa.' It was even being sold as a twin production to *Winning a Continent*.

'What "De Voortrekkers" is to Dutch South Africans, "The

Symbol of Sacrifice" will be to British South Africans,' wrote *Stage & Cinema*. 'This and "Voortrekkers" cannot fail to do the country an incalculable amount of good, both internally and externally.'

On 21 March, a week after the inquest closed, there was a private viewing at the Empire for 'the State, the Army, the Law, the Municipality, the Churches, the professional and trades unions'.

Whether it was because he thought the movie was important or because he wanted to show his face after the inquest, IW made one of his rare appearances for the showing. 'At the conclusion of the picture there were calls for Mr Schlesinger. He did not make a speech but his appearance in the auditorium was greeted with very hearty cheers.'

The next day the *Rand Daily Mail* wrote: 'The Most Stupendous Spectacular Film of Modern Times. Full of Human Interest, Astounding Realism, Perfect Photography, Intense Fighting, Superb Acting. A Feast of Excitement from Start to Finish.'

Another fusillade of advertising began, declaring the film nothing short of the best ever made:

The Super Film (in Eight Stupendous Acts)
Totally Eclipsing in
BARBARIC SPLENDOUR
DRAMATIC INTEREST
PERFECT PHOTOGRAPHY
And SCENIC MAGNIFICENCE
Anything Hitherto Attempted

Less than a week later, on Wednesday 27 March, *The Symbol of Sacrifice* got a true big-city premiere, with all the bells and whistles. It was to be the great opening in the City of Gold that IW had chosen to sacrifice for *Winning a Continent*. The massive main auditorium of the Town Hall was the largest place to show a movie in Africa.

Outside on Market Square, a huge parade was organised, and by 2.30 that afternoon more than 2 000 Boy Scouts, Transvaal Cadets,

The heroine of *Symbol* steps in to protect her manservant from the villain, played by Mabel May, Goba and Holger Petersen.

Girl Guides and Naval Brigade Boys had gathered. Thousands of people came to watch and cheer them on.

Several blocks away, at the Palladium on Commissioner Street, there was a second showing, where so many people gathered that hundreds of them had to be turned away. For those who saw the picture, what struck them most was the magnificence of the battle scenes and the expense of recreating them all. Every review remarked on the scale and cost of the production.

'Cheeseparing has clearly been ruthlessly ruled out from its inception,' wrote *The Star*, 'and money has been spent like water.'

In the first two days, 10 000 people saw the movie in Johannesburg, and by the end of the week *The Symbol of Sacrifice* had established a new box-office record.

A NEW BABYLON

In late April 1918, right after *The Symbol of Sacrifice* finished its successful run at the Palladium, the theatre started advertising a movie that sounded very much the same as IW's, calling it 'the most stupendous spectacle ever presented on the cinema screen'.

If people were confused by the 'Most Stupendous Spectacular Film of Modern Times' being replaced by the 'the most stupendous spectacle ever', that was probably the intention. The new movie at the Palladium was DW Griffith's *Intolerance*.

With great fanfare – saying it was the most money IVTA had ever paid for a movie since *Cabiria* in 1914 – *Intolerance* had been acquired by IW in January, only months after *Winning a Continent* had been compared to that very movie in the British media. Comparisons were also made with Griffith's *The Birth of a Nation*, but *Intolerance* was the one IW noticed, for it was by far the biggest, most expensive movie ever made. And he wanted his next movie – *King Solomon's Mines* – to be the South African version.

Intolerance unfolded in four acts, each one set in a different period over two thousand years, with the common thread being man's inhumanity to man: the crucifixion of Jesus; the massacre of the Huguenots in France in 1572; a contemporary story of a wrongfully condemned man; and the fall of Prince Belshazzar in ancient Babylon.

For the feast of Belshazzar, the most grandiose sets ever had been built in Los Angeles, on the corner of Sunset and Hollywood

The original movie adventurer, Allan Quatermain,
played by the American Albert Lawrence.

boulevards: walls 300 feet high, giant columns topped by elephant idols, with spectators peering from high balconies alongside them, and, in the middle of the scene below, a grand stairway filled with 3 000 lavishly costumed extras and ornate palanquins slowly making their way down its length. Nothing like it had ever been seen on screen before.

Watching the movie at the Palladium, as Wagner's *Ride of the Valkyries* played in the background, no one in the audience could have guessed that the same amazing scenes of mythical pomp and grandeur were about to play out in Johannesburg. For his

Quatermain movie, IW was going to copy Griffith's Babylon.

There was one very big problem, though: the City of Film had no experience with creating big sets. Both of IW's spectacles had been outdoor movies – perhaps the best ever made – but the only set that the studio had built so far for his spectacles was the replica of Windsor Castle, and that had been copied from reality. Now they had to recreate fictitious places conjured by the imagination of Rider Haggard: the Throne Room of King Solomon, the Temple of the Sun, an underground river with a flaming pillar called the Rose of Fire and, the most daunting of them all, the Great Stairway of the Zu-Vendi that towered into the sky.

Making the challenge even greater, it had also been decided to do something that had never been done before. They would shoot the two Rider Haggard movies, *King Solomon's Mines* and *Allan Quatermain*, at the same time.

Horace Lisle Lucoque, the English director who would be leading the back-to-back shoot, arrived in February 1918, in the midst of the Colenbrander tragedy and inquest.

There was no razzmatazz for him. Unlike Harold Shaw and Lorimer Johnston, Lucoque was not given a huge round of publicity or a 'wand of witchery' tour to acquaint him with the South African landscape. Instead, IW immediately sent him off for a few months to film on location for both movies.

'No expense is to be spared,' IW declared before the team set off, 'and Mr Lucoque is confident of being able to turn out two pictures that will become world-famous.'

With him, Lucoque took several cameramen, led by William Bowden, who had worked for him in London, as well as technicians and make-up artists, and the three lead actors, all of whom had been appearing on stage in Johannesburg.

In the role of the hero Allan Quatermain was Albert Lawrence, a handsome actor from Minnesota. As his friend, the jovial, monocle-wearing Captain Good of the Royal Navy, was Raymond Brown from Chicago. And as Sir Henry Curtis, who asks Quatermain to help him find his lost brother, precipitating their adventures, there was a tall English actor and singer, Halford Hamlin.

They set several records during the trip, not only shooting two movies back to back but also the longest distance travelled for a film shoot – 5 000 miles from Park Station to Sabi Reserve, Victoria Falls, Bulawayo, the Skeleton Coast, the Cango Caves and Portuguese East Africa – as well as filming the characters underground and facing a charging elephant in the Maputo Forest.

But the real action was unfolding back at the City of Film. For months already, the wheels of African Films had been turning at an incredible pace. Carpenters, painters, electricians, costume designers making outfits that looked like they were from Roman times, men working for Frank Fillis to create chariots that could be raced, and even dynamite experts – they were all working overtime.

Of the four major scenes for the Quatermain movies, the first to be filmed was the Throne Room of King Solomon. By the time Lucoque and his team returned to Johannesburg from Portuguese East Africa, the set was complete. Using as its model the famous painting by Edward Poynter, *The Visit of the Queen of Sheba to King Solomon*, the studio craftsmen had made an exact life-size replica. Twenty broad pillars, each at least 40 feet high, framed the grand room, at the centre of which was the raised dais where the two rulers would be seated. Leading up to it were five wide steps, a life-sized sculpted lion on each side.

On Friday 20 September 1918, hundreds of extras were on set dressed in the costumes made for them – robes and togas and shields and helmets – while a troupe of female dancers stood ready to perform for the king and the visiting Queen of Sheba.

An eagle and a white dove sat on a perch near the king, while to the left of the throne were a lion cub and a leopard on a leash.

Through this fantastical scene, as the cameras began to roll, wandered a pride of peacocks.

Seated on the bleachers nearby, as if they were watching a tennis match, was an invited crowd that included Sir Thomas and Lady Hyslop, Transvaal administrator Johann Rissik and his wife, Sir William Hoy and his wife, Lady Albu and her daughters, the impresario Leonard Rayne and Joseph Langley Levy of the *Sunday Times*. Over the fence peered dozens more people.

IW had by now copied Carl Laemmle at least four times. Besides the bleachers, there had been the flooding of Elsburg stream, the building of a grand studio headquarters and the creation of an indigenous village. In an upcoming scene in *Allan Quatermain*, Frank Fillis would orchestrate the chariot race. Anything Hollywood could do, IW could match – and the best was yet to come.

Two major world events consumed the last few months of 1918. World War I came to an end with the Armistice of 11 November, while the influenza pandemic known as 'Spanish flu' finally reached South Africa in September. Johannesburg, thanks to precautions it had taken, was spared the high death toll elsewhere.

On 26 December, the day after Christmas, *King Solomon's Mines* had its first showing at the Town Hall, bringing to a close a triumphant year for IW. It had started with him directing *The Symbol of Sacrifice* and was ending with the first public screening of the Rider Haggard story that he had made it his mission to acquire. In London, the movie was eagerly awaited.

'IVTA has created no mean measure of success with "The Symbol of Sacrifice",' wrote *Kinematograph Weekly*, 'and it is anticipated that such a well-known and picturesque subject as King Solomon's Mines will overtop this considerably.'

Much of the sequel, *Allan Quatermain*, had already been filmed, with Zoo Lake doubling as an underground river for the Rose of Fire scene and Rider Haggard's famous warrior character Umslopogaas battling it out in the amphitheatre of the Union Buildings. But the studio still hadn't found a way of creating the most important scene of the novel – the Great Stairway of the Zu-Vendi, a monument leading into the heavens.

'Let the reader imagine, if he can,' Haggard wrote, 'a splendid stairway, sixty-five feet from balustrade to balustrade, consisting of two vast flights, each of one hundred and twenty-five steps of eight inches in height by three feet broad, connected by a flat resting place sixty feet in length, and running from the palace wall on the edge of the precipice down to meet a waterway or canal cut to its foot from the river.'

The stairway, like the one in *Intolerance*, had to be grand enough for 500 people to attend the wedding of the fair-headed princess Nyleptha – who was being played by Mabel May – and wide enough for Umslopogaas, wielding his trusty sword Inkosi-Kaas, to fight his final battle.

At first, IW considered existing structures that could stand in for the Great Stairway, although they were very far away. One was on the island of St Helena, 2 000 miles by sea from Cape Town, and the other in Lourenço Marques.

St Helena, famous only for being the place where Napoleon had been exiled, had perhaps the highest staircase in the world. Built in the early 19th century above the settlement of Jamestown, it was one step short of 700, as high as a 60-storey building.

In Lourenço Marques, on an estate called Polana where IW's friend Solly Joel was building a magnificent hotel, a staircase led down to the beach, a drop so steep that the colonial authorities were considering installing a small funicular railway or motorised lift.

But neither location would work for the movie. One stairway was too narrow, the other not high enough. The only alternative left for IW was to build his own, which meant a structure that would be as high as the walls of Babylon in *Intolerance*.

In early June 1919, after two months of work under an engineer

A rare picture of one of IW's wonder works, the Great Stairway of Milosis in the City of Gold. (Detail from South African Pictorial, 14 June 1919).

named Percy Cazalet, the Great Stairway was completed. It resembled the side of a ziggurat rising hundreds of feet, as tall as a building of 20 or 30 storeys. Broad steps, narrowing as they went up, led to a prominent arch at the top, bordered all the way by balustrades, with a precipitous drop straight down on either side. At the base stood a massive pair of lion statues.

One journalist, upon seeing it, described 'one of the most wonderful achievements of scenic construction in the history of film making'. The most stupefying thing was its location: in the middle of a working Johannesburg gold mine.

'The juxtaposition of the magnificent and imposing Stairway and the picturesque costumes of the Zu-Vendi warriors, priests and maidens, with mine dumps, headgears, slime ponds, and all the busy paraphernalia of a modern and up-to-date gold mine, was a sight which would have made anyone who did not know what was going on rub his eyes in astonishment.'

Like Griffith's Babylon, which had been erected in the middle of Hollywood, the Great Stairway stood almost in the heart of the City of Gold. The colossal set had been carved out of a 300-foot-high mine dump just south of the city centre, Robinson Deep.

In typical IW fashion, little is known about the crazy creation. How they had come upon the location, how they had built the mammoth set and at what cost – those facts remain a mystery. But for as long as it stood there, a colossal golden sculpture depicting something outrageous and fantastic, it was a monument to his industry of dreams. In the most obvious way – and what turned out to be IW's last hurrah – the Great Stairway brought together the City of Gold and the empire of movies that he tried to build there.

EPILOGUE

In 1923, IW embarked on his last major production in South Africa, *The Blue Lagoon*.

Two young actors were brought over from Britain, and a massive shooting schedule was publicised that would take the crew thousands of miles away, into the Indian Ocean. The main filming was to take place, quite amazingly for those days, not only on location but far away from the studio or civilisation – in the Seychelles.

By the time he made his last big movie at Killarney, *The Blue Lagoon*,
IW was getting into his stride as a moviemaker.
Then he moved his studio to London.

But in the end, the budget was cut, closer locations chosen and one of the cameramen doubled as director – all sure signs that IW was giving up on the South African market.

They filmed the island scenes in Porto Amélia (now called Pemba) in Portuguese East Africa. And although they shot a very realistic scene involving an octopus – the film has been lost, so one has to rely on reviews – it took place in Durban harbour.

Perhaps because of the movie's racy subject matter and the poster showing two scantily clad actors embracing under a palm tree, *The Blue Lagoon* was a hit. In Johannesburg, people lined up outside the renovated Bijou, now called the New Bijou Theatre-de-Luxe, waiting to get in, and the movie was shown to great reviews in London and Rome.

Despite public statements at the time about how he was going to make more movies for the international market – no more conditions that it be 'only South Africa' – and offering big prize money to attract scenarios, IW didn't follow through.

And with good reason.

In the decade since he'd bought the Empire, it had become painfully obvious that his movies would never get into the US, the most important market in the world if he was to succeed. Hollywood was systematically shutting out foreign productions, and the big companies were consolidating. It was hard enough for French, German and Italian movies, which had been the most popular before the war, to get distribution there, so what chance did IW have? The American monopoly was exactly the kind he had created in South Africa, but now he was on the receiving end.

There is little doubt that his movies would have done extremely well in America, if only because they were set in exotic locations, especially *King Solomon's Mines* and *The Blue Lagoon*. In a strange way, *Winning a Continent* turned into a blockbuster across the US, except it was an American version.

In 1923, at the same time *The Blue Lagoon* was showing at the Bijou, a movie called *The Covered Wagon* opened at the Rivoli, one

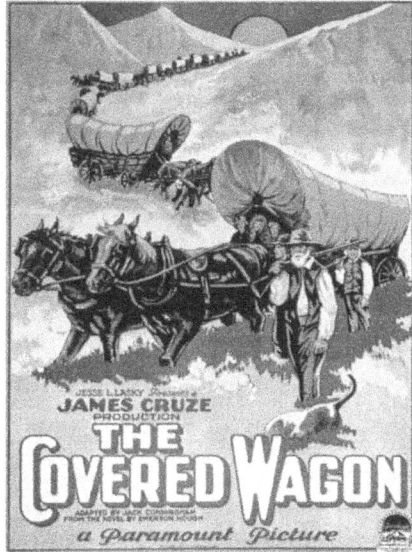

Making the first trek movie, or big-sky Western, long before Hollywood was only one of numerous times IW beat Hollywood to the draw.

of the greatest movie houses on Times Square. It broke box-office records, and then won the Academy Award for best picture.

Staff at the IVTA office on Times Square would have seen the billboards, and they would have noticed something very unusual. The movie looked like an exact copy of *Winning a Continent*. IW the copier was being copied.

Not only was the advertising the same – a train of wagons disappearing over the horizon – but so was the true story of 19th-century settlers heading off into a new wild and alien country. Even the descriptions of the shoot sounded the same. An 'immense number of period costumes' had been specially made and numerous locations thousands of miles apart were found for filming. Hundreds of wagons had been used, many steered by their farmer owners – 'the train of prairie schooners was three miles in length' – and 750 Native Americans took part in the battle sequences.

The Covered Wagon also tapped into US nationalistic pride in the wake of the Great War. It was, said one reviewer, destined to 'stimulate patriotism'. *Movie Weekly* called it 'The Great American Picture', just like *Winning a Continent* was often referred to as 'the national film'.

'Small boys will cheer. Old boys will feel a reawakening of true patriotism – love of the soil of America – as they watch it.' 'It is an enduring record of the greatness of our American heritage,' wrote the *New York Commercial*. 'It should be shown to every citizen of this republic.'

It's impossible to prove that the producer – Adolph Zukor – copied IW, but it's not hard to imagine. *Winning a Continent* had been available in America since 1917 as *The Pioneers*.

The film historian Thelma Gutsche wrote about the similarity in her fascinating 1972 book, *The History and Social Significance of Motion Pictures in South Africa 1895–1940*. More recently, Neil Parsons wrote that IW's movie created a subgenre that came to be known as the 'trek' movie, 'big wide scenes of people and horses and wagons advancing "civilisation" over wild landscapes, intercut with cameos of campfire meals and simple entertainment at which comic relief and romantic triangles between principal characters can blossom'. The modest but popular shoot-em-up cowboy movie had made way for the expensive big-sky Western.

It wasn't the last time IW had pre-empted Hollywood either. His comedy series *The Mealy Kids*, about two naughty African children, came out several years before Hal Roach's hugely popular *Our Gang*.

Then there were his documentaries, a term that didn't exist when IW started making them. In 1915 came Lorimer Johnston's *A Zulu Drama*, followed by pictures about the Mountains of the Moon in East Africa, the Desolation Islands near Antarctica and the attempted extermination of the Addo elephants in 1919. All of them came out well before Robert Flaherty's *Nanook of the North* (1922), which is today regarded as the very first documentary film.

Even the word 'documentary', used for the first time only in 1926, had a link to IW. It was thought up by a Scottish filmmaker named John Grierson. In 1929, Grierson, who had just made a much-praised documentary about the fishing industry in the North Sea, *Drifters*, started working for IW's new studio in London. He was lined up to make his first feature, titled *Smoke and Steel*, 'a drama with the gigantic background of English industrial life'. But it was one of the movies scuppered by a devastating fire at the studio later that year.

African Mirror, IW's newsreel, became the longest-running of its kind in the world. His cameramen obtained some sensational footage, including not only the documentaries but also the Red Revolt of 1922 in Johannesburg and the Bulhoek Massacre a year earlier, when followers of the self-proclaimed prophet Enoch Mgijima clashed with police and the army at his holy village near Queenstown. Almost 200 of Mgijima's followers died. Fearing a backlash if the film was shown publicly, the government of Jan Smuts ensured that IW surrendered all copies. They were destroyed.

Even though IW started building up his entertainment interests in Britain from 1913, when he bought the Empire, these consisted mostly of theatres and movie distribution. But almost as soon as he gave up on movie production in South Africa, he turned his focus to Britain and Europe.

For the first year, however, he dedicated himself to the massive British Empire Exhibition of 1924. Having failed to pull off the Golden City Exhibition in 1916, he became the driving force behind South Africa's contribution to the event.

A 200-acre park at Wembley, once a popular recreation ground, was being transformed into, among other things, a stadium that could hold 125 000 people, several massive exhibition buildings, a new railway station and dozens of pavilions, including one modelled on the Taj Mahal.

The South African pavilion, which had IW's stamp all over it, was called 'the most beautiful piece of architecture in the Exhibition' by *The Illustrated London News*. There were 'diamonds in great profusion', as well as a fifty-ton pile of 'famous blue ground' from a diamond mine, models of gold-extracting machines, stuffed wild animals, a Zulu village, wool products, cheese, a paddock of 23 'ostriches in full plumage', merino sheep, wine and much more. Behind the main pavilion, done in the gabled Cape Dutch style, stood a train with electric engine and coaches, where one could eat a meal in the dining car. Two cinemas – IW's special contribution – showed free movies about ostrich farming and trout fishing, as well as travelogues, all made by African Films.

One of IW's other companies, African Packing and Canning Ltd, displayed its fruits, 'crystallized and glacé', and its jams, which were sold all over the world under the name Gold Reef. To publicise the firm's products, 'a huge pineapple, painted most artistically, attracted the attention of every passerby.' On seeing it, the royal entourage expressed 'special pleasure', and 'to mark their favour the King and Queen of Italy ordered a large supply'.

For the next six years, IW was back in film production, a frenetic period in which he came closest to becoming an internationally recognised movie producer. In 1925, he was the main financier of a new studio, British National Pictures (which would eventually become Elstree Studios, where the first *Star Wars* and *Indiana Jones* movies were filmed). The idea the London Film Company had when IW poached Harold Shaw from them – to make American-type movies in London – was rekindled.

But his main producer, the talented American movie man James Dixon Williams, was soon at odds with IW. After three very expensive productions, whose outrageous budgets IW didn't approve of, he fired Williams and the studio changed its name to British International Pictures. Williams launched a highly publicised lawsuit that IW and his co-accused John Maxwell lost, before IW quietly pulled out of the venture.

In 1928, he started a new studio – this time without partners – on a portion of Wembley Park, site of the British Empire Exhibition. He poured a fortune into acquiring talent from Europe and America, but his biggest ambition was to make 'talkie' pictures, which were going through a painful birth in Hollywood. In preparation, and before his Hollywood counterparts, he bought an American sound company called Phonofilm.

Lee de Forest, the owner of Phonofilm, was 'the father of the talkie movie'. But De Forest, besides being a difficult character, and highly litigious, had made a hash of originally registering his sound patents. He became a liability, and when the big Hollywood studios became interested in movies with sound, they all rejected Phonofilm, going instead with the industrial giants General Electric and Western Electric.

IW made De Forest his chief engineer and was possibly the first to bring out a talkie movie in Great Britain, in 1929. (Film historians can't decide if it was IW's thriller *Dark Red Roses* or Alfred Hitchcock's thriller *Blackmail* that deserves the title.)

On 19 October 1929, with *Dark Red Roses* near completion, a devastating fire broke out at the Wembley Park studio. The inferno quickly got out of control, intensified by the abundance of wood and drapery, growing into a 'terrific blaze', with flames rising up to one hundred feet. Even a strongbox of unexposed film exploded, making things worse. Recording vans were driven away from the blaze. There was only one copy of the film, which was locked away in a storeroom. In a repeat of what happened at the Empire in 1916, it was the prompt action of Joseph Albrecht that saved the day. Arriving on the scene at the height of the fire, he broke down the door to the storeroom and retrieved the film.

In several movies made at that time, IW was listed as the producer, although the production company quite mysteriously bore the name of its main star, the beautiful Russo-German actress Olga Tschechowa – Tschechowa Films. By the early 1930s she would be attracting the amorous attention of Adolf Hitler.

In 1931, one last big movie was made at Wembley Park, a very expensive musical comedy called *City of Song* (its German title was *Der Singende Stadt*). It was a cosmopolitan production of note, directed by an Italian in at least two versions, German and English, with the famous Polish tenor Jan Kiepura in his first movie role, while the well-known German actress Brigitte Helm and an unknown Australian named Betty Stockfeld played the female lead in each version, with filming in Austria, Italy and England.

The production seemed doomed from early on, when the cameraman, a talented Hungarian named Arpad Viragh, died after eating contaminated shellfish on the island of Capri.

IW married his leading actress Mabel May at the end of 1921 in a small chapel in Paddington. He had just turned 48; Mabel was 20 years younger.

The register identified her as Mabel F Ayling, the former wife of Charles Buswell. Just before Christmas, they had a second ceremony, at the New West End Synagogue in Bayswater, where Chaim Weizmann, a future president of Israel, was also a congregant, and whose Zionist cause IW held a fundraising drive for in Johannesburg a few years later.

The Schlesingers' only child, John, was born in 1923, and he was the apple of IW's eye. One of the few photographs of IW has him affectionately holding his young son's hand. Mabel made her last movie in 1920 and afterwards played the role of hostess, presiding over gala events such as the arrival in Johannesburg of the famous ballerina Anna Pavlova in 1926. For someone who had graced the cover and pages of Stage & Cinema so often, now it was only her flamboyant outfits that were written about. She died in November 1957, at the age of 65, while living in the Carlton Hotel.

Of John Schlesinger, much more is known. Educated at Michaelhouse, he served as a bombardier with the US Army Air Force during World War II and studied at Harvard, where he listed film production as his ambition.

During John's 18-month courtship of Ann Lee Iva Willens, the daughter of a New York stockbroker, he sent her daily gifts of orchids or trinkets. In 1944, they married at the Hotel Ambassador on Park Avenue, New York. They lived between South Africa, London, Paris and the Riviera, where they threw lavish parties for as many as 800 guests at a time.

In the 1950s, John showed a flair for turning IW's theatre holdings into a major company by buying 50 per cent of the British Odeon Cinema Holdings, which together with its subsidiaries owned almost 600 cinemas, as well as production and distribution arms.

But it was clear that John did not have IW's talent for running multiple companies and had a taste for enjoying himself. In 1958, and after having two children together, Ann obtained a decree for separation as a result of John's alleged adultery with a Burmese model named Seignon Nystrom. Two more women were later named in the suit.

After disagreements with her lawyers, Ann decided to handle her own case and studied up the law. The case dragged on for years until she was represented by the controversial American lawyer Roy Cohn, whose prosecution of Julius and Ethel Rosenberg for spying for the Soviet Union led to their conviction and execution in 1953. Cohn later became an advisor to Senator Joseph McCarthy in his 1954 witch-hunt investigation of suspected communists.

In 1966, Ann received a settlement of $2.75 million. During the time Cohn worked for her, she had made him a loan of $100 000, and in 1979 Ann sued him for it in State Supreme Court in Manhattan. She won.

In 1966, John married a roller-skating champion, Rita Rosa Pane. They were photographed in celebrity magazines partying or sailing in the Mediterranean on their yacht, *Criniera d'Oro*. They also built a house on Capri. In 1981 'battling a bitter divorce case through three continents', Rita divorced John, and the divorce super-lawyer Marvin Mitchelson won her a $25 million settlement, in a case where John was represented by Cohn.

By this stage, the sprawling Schlesinger empire that IW had

created had been cut up into many pieces and sold off to various buyers. In 1963, John demolished the Carlton Hotel, which IW had finally bought from Solly Joel in the 1920s and to which he had added three floors. The hotel saw many famous guests enter its doors, including the British royal family and the exiled Shah of Persia during World War II. John Schlesinger died in 1994.

That IW could have been the equal of Adolph Zukor, Carl Laemmle or any of the Hollywood titans – had there been a level playing field – is without question. Of the 40 movies he produced in Johannesburg, a surprising number have stood the test of time.

King Solomon's Mines has been filmed repeatedly, as has *Allan Quatermain*, while Rider Haggard's Lost World, the setting for both, features in countless pictures, such as the Indiana Jones and Lara Croft series. *The Symbol of Sacrifice* was remade in 1964 as *Zulu* (by Zukor's Paramount) and in 1979 as *Zulu Dawn*. A year later came *The Blue Lagoon*, starring Brooke Shields, although the first remake of the film had been in 1949.

IW was the first person to envision a large-scale movie not only about the Zulu kings Shaka and Dingaan but about Cecil John Rhodes, which was attempted many times afterwards. *Shaka Zulu* was finally made in 1986 as a ten-episode series by the South African Broadcasting Corporation – a company IW had started in 1926 – and again in 2023 by M-Net.

In 1936 Gaumont-British made the film *Rhodes* starring the American Walter Huston – on which production African Films assisted, as it did on Gaumont's 1937 version of *King Solomon's Mines* with the baritone Paul Robeson – and in 1996 the BBC production of *Rhodes* became the biggest-ever British television series, its eight parts costing £10 million.

South African audiences, for their part, were unstintingly tough on IW. No matter how good his movies were, locals regarded them as second-rate. African Film Productions would always come in last against companies like Metro, Universal, Vitagraph, Selig and even the German company UFA.

'The moment the mystic letters AFP are seen, the picture is condemned, often without even being seen,' a journalist wrote in 1923, at the time of the release of *The Blue Lagoon*. *Swallow*, IW's movie based on another Rider Haggard story about a young girl kidnapped by a band of Zulu, had opened in London a year earlier to great reviews, but 'the South African people considered it a failure'.

Most of the movies made by IW, other than *Winning a Continent* – which continued to draw crowds for many years when it played on 16 December and is still available in an edited version on YouTube – have been lost or destroyed. *The Symbol of Sacrifice* was mercilessly hacked into pieces to be used as stock footage in other pictures, especially its unprecedented battle sequences.

South Africa's National Film, Video and Sound Archives has about five of IW's movies, all on 35 mm film, but no equipment on which to show them. A visit to the poorly funded and almost forgotten archive, in the shadow of the Union Buildings in Pretoria, is a sad epitaph to his incredible achievement.

The only evidence of IW's era that can actually be viewed there is a dated and badly reproduced video that includes random scenes from *Symbol of Sacrifice*. Nevertheless, it is breathtaking – thousands of warriors streaming across the open veld, lines of marching soldiers that stretch to the horizon, magnificent running battles – a small glimpse into the forgotten world that he managed to create.

Every aspect of entertainment in South Africa today can trace its origin back to IW – movie production, theatres, studios, broadcasting, newsreels and even advertising in movie houses.

In 1927, he was already looking into the possibility of investing in television and had talks with the Baird Television Development Company in Britain. In the end, he declared the medium to be in its infancy, and added, unwisely, 'I am doubtful whether it will ever emerge from its present state.'

A year earlier, he had met with John Reith, head of the four-year-old British Broadcasting Corporation. IW had bought three ailing radio stations in South Africa and with them created the African Broadcasting Corporation (ABC). In 1935, he built Broadcast House on Commissioner Street, and then sold the company to the government a year later. It was renamed the South African Broadcasting Corporation.

In the same year that IW started the ABC, 1926, he was drawn into another sphere of the movies business that was spreading like wildfire across America and Britain – huge, expensive and exotic movie houses.

In a bid to attract new audiences, the major studios – who, besides making movies, were now buying up the places where they were shown – began creating 'atmospheric theatres'. The designs and décor were meant to transport audiences to mysterious locations. The new theatres had Moorish and Oriental façades, interiors mimicking courtyards and towns in Spain and Italy, and walls decorated with dragons and lanterns. Arches, trellises and ornate balconies jutted out into the auditoriums, and ceilings became sky-like stretches of cerulean and indigo crossed by wisps of floating cloud or constellations of twinkling stars, or suns that could be mechanically made to rise and set.

With the architect Percy Rogers Cooke, IW visited the most important of these in Britain and America – the Capitol, the Ziegfeld and the Roxy in Manhattan among others – before Cooke was sent to work with Thomas Lamb, a New York-based Scotsman who was the preeminent exponent of the new architecture.

Soon afterwards, IW started a building spree across South Africa. The Alhambra in Cape Town, when it opened in 1929, built at a cost of $1.25 million, was 'Moro-Spanish', 'one of the most lavishly equipped and decorated theaters in the world'. It had 2 000 seats and was not just atmospheric but 'super-atmospheric', with Spanish decorations and a ceiling full of twinkling stars and clouds that shifted across a cobalt sky.

The Colosseum, one of the most splendid movie houses in the world, was demolished in 1985.

The Capitol in Pretoria, built in the Italian Renaissance style, was equally splendid. At its opening in 1931 – presided over by Prime Minister Barry Hertzog – IW showed his last big movie from Britain, the musical comedy *City of Song*. Even though both super-cinemas could compare to the best anywhere in the world, they weren't in IW's hometown, Johannesburg, which, quite astoundingly, was still without an atmospheric theatre.

Not that people hadn't been trying to build one. By 1931, there was a feeding frenzy going on in the City of Gold, with at least two other companies trying to grab control of movies. While Schlesinger's attention was on his new studio in London, his rivals were closing in on what had until now been his monopoly.

A man named Sydney Hyman and his brother David Heydenreich had started a company called Kinemas, which, even though it seemed a bit shady at times – inflating its own statistics, and repeatedly promising to build a super-theatre in Johannesburg that never got further than its foundations – made an impact.

African Films and Kinemas often clashed in the media, and a bizarre game of tit-for-tat played out, where IW kept showing movies that could be mistaken for those being shown by Kinemas.

Finally, the brothers opened their promised super-theatre, the Plaza, on Jeppe Street, around the corner from IW's Orpheum. Then, in 1932, Metro-Goldwyn-Mayer, with whom IW had been in a tense relationship for the past few years and which was also trying to muscle in on his market, opened the Metro, a 3 000-seat cinema as big as anything anywhere in the world.

But then IW outdid them all – with the Colosseum.

One could call it the movie-theatre version *of Winning a Continent*, a spectacle created for a market that didn't really have the numbers to support it. The building took up an entire block of Commissioner Street.

To create the embellishments, statuary and decorations, Art Deco friezes and bas-reliefs, IW brought out an artist from Paris, René Shapshak. For the interiors, he used the architect William Timlin, who had written and illustrated the children's classic *The Ship that Sailed to Mars*.

There was a Golden Foyer, a Wonder Tea Room, Exquisite Cosmetic Room, Mezzanine Promenade and Silver Buffet. Done in an 'old Roman Style', the interiors had touches of Gothic, medieval, Art Deco, Moorish and Egyptian, as if Timlin was putting every possible inspiration into the design.

African Theatres boasted that it had the world's best equipment – lighting, air conditioning, ventilation and sound and projection systems. Thirty-six loudspeaker units behind the screen constituted 'the largest sound horn in the world'.

Lotus-shaped columns, Art Deco lighting and capitals were overlooked by a mezzanine gallery, with the walls lined with Moorish screens. Above it all a stained-glass window had Atlas supporting a map of South Africa. Combining 'luxury and a fairyland illusion', there were sculptures of pharaohs and voluptuous maidens. Straddling one entrance was a copy of *Physical Energy*, George Frederic Watts's horse-and-rider statue from London's Kensington Gardens, and a perfect symbol for IW. The statue, the artist said, was 'a symbol of that restless physical impulse to seek the still unachieved in the domain of material things'.

In the auditorium, the constellations of the southern hemisphere sparkled on the velvet ceiling, while wisps of cloud moved across the dark expanse. Timlin had covered the walls with a three-dimensional townscape made up of steep-roofed houses whose corbelled turrets and leaded windows were illuminated from behind. The audience was to be seated on chairs in the roadway or watched from balconies and windows of the surrounding buildings.

On the opening night, in October 1933, crowds waited for a late-night show while the premiere played on, and 'the façade gleamed and glittered with lights and huge electric signs'. Inside, Jan Smuts – IW's favourite politician, even though he was still the leader of the opposition – was the guest of honour and IW gave him a golden key.

A 50-piece orchestra was mechanically raised so the audience could see them, a choir of 120 sang and Liszt's *Rhapsodie Hongroise No 2* was played. A programme for the premiere – thick, ornate and golden – was embossed with the words 'The Wonder Theatre of the Miracle City'.

A message was sent by the man whom IW had most often tried to copy from his first days at the Empire, Universal's Carl Laemmle, who wrote in his tribute: 'Heartfelt congratulations to my good friend, Schlesinger, on his enterprises giving Johannesburg a theater second to none in the world.'

No story of IW would be complete without a mention of the man who had been guest of honour at the Colosseum, Jan Smuts.

Like most aspects of IW's private life, the depth and complexity of their friendship is largely a thing of guesswork. In Smuts's prolific writings, and those about him, IW is never mentioned. But Smuts made sure to take time out to attend both of IW's big premieres in London during the Great War, and to specially mention *Winning a Continent* in an official speech.

Jan Smuts and IW at the opening of the orphanage for Jewish children saved from Eastern Europe by the philanthropist Isaac Ochberg. One hundred stayed in Cape Town, and 81 came to the Villa Arcadia.

In one of the few photographs that IW allowed to be taken of himself, in 1923, it is Smuts who appears at his side. The prime minister is shown opening a Jewish orphanage at the Villa Arcadia in Parktown that IW had helped finance. It was for more than 80 children brought from Eastern Europe.

Several months earlier, Smuts had also been the guest of honour at a large function at the Town Hall hosted by IW to gather donations for Chaim Weizmann and the Zionist cause. That same year, Smuts also became the godfather of IW and Mabel's son, John. Mabel May and Smuts's wife, Isie, were also good friends, especially during the war years.

IW and Smuts were also afflicted by a similar flaw. They both spent too much time abroad, fostering global interests, probably finding South Africa too small for them. It was to cost both men dearly: Smuts would lose power in 1924 – to Barry Hertzog – and would not be prime minister again until the outbreak of World War II, while IW almost lost his South African entertainment empire while he was distracted by his ambitions in the northern hemisphere

When Hertzog took over from Smuts as prime minister in 1924, IW cosied up to him as much as any businessman needed to. He kept making industrial pictures for the government and, in a bizarre move, made his last few South African movies – his very first talking pictures – in Afrikaans: *Sarie Marais* and *Moedertjie*.

In 1938, with the government still under Hertzog (though by now in coalition with Smuts), the Department of Railways and Harbours financed IW to make a super-production, *Die Bou van 'n Nasie* – an almost direct crib of *The Birth of a Nation* – a retelling of the country's history since the arrival of Jan van Riebeeck.

IW died at the age of seventy-eight on 11 March 1949, at Pinelands on Princess of Wales Terrace, Parktown, after suffering for many years from rheumatoid arthritis. At the time, there were plans to build a new movie studio in one of the Johannesburg suburbs he had created, Parkmore, including a power station with an output large enough to supply a town of 20 000 people. The studio was to have a staff of 400 and accommodation for them. There was no intention to sell off the theatres and film production unit.

But sold they were – by John Schlesinger – to 20th Century Fox.

The extent of IW's other investments was vast.

He had 90 companies in the end, with as many as 20 000 employees spread around the world (almost the exact figure that he had predicted he would have when he addressed a group of his insurance agents more than a quarter of a century earlier, in 1920), and was worth about $140 million ($1.4 billion today).

By comparison, the media tycoon William Randolph Hearst, who died two years later at the age of 88 and to whom Schlesinger was compared, had some 27 000 employees and was said to be worth $200 million.

There was almost no business that IW hadn't been involved in. Under his sway fell the largest advertising agency in the southern hemisphere, a chain of pharmacies (called Publix, which had been the name of Adolph Zukor's theatres), a Sunday newspaper, fruit canneries and investments in the sugar and dairy industries. He planted 1 000 morgen of grass in the eastern Cape and had 1 800 cattle and 70 000 sheep. He also wanted to extend and beautify the foreshore of Cape Town. One of his biggest regrets, he admitted to a friend, was not having bought an area of North London called Golders Green in about 1901: 'If I had done it, I would have made more money than everything else combined.'

In 1915, he began planning and planting an orange estate that would be unlike any other, even in the United States. Located near Potgietersrus, it was called Zebediela, and by the time he died it was 'the largest citrus orchard in the world, with 650 000 trees in bearing', with its own railway line, engines and trucks.

From early on, he supported aviation competitions, including the 1936 Schlesinger Air Race from Portsmouth to Johannesburg, which had a prize of £10 000, to coincide with the Empire Exhibition in Johannesburg, the first such event to be held outside the United Kingdom.

Of IW's almost obsessive desire for privacy, Eric Rosenthal wrote in the introduction to his unpublished biography of Schlesinger: 'Not even his closest collaborators nor the members of his family could gauge the full vastness of his schemes, the variety of his enterprises, and above all, the power of his mind – the staggering capacity for work and the ingenuity and versatility which made it possible for "IW" to achieve so much.

For a man who didn't want to live in a mansion but loved
the apartments of London and New York, Whitehall Court was
IW's solution – a combination of the two.

'It was not merely in the field of insurance, entertainment,
farming, fruit-growing, radio, shopkeeping, diamond cutting,
film-making, town-planning, shipping, advertising, newspapers,
finance and a dozen other subjects that the "Little Man", as he was
affectionately known to his staff, manifested the scale of ambition
and achievement which affected the lives of almost everybody,
black, brown and white, in the Union and in the territories
adjoining. Schlesinger was also a man of importance overseas, in
finance between Britain and the USA and in the development of
trade with Russia, as the holder of basic patents in talkies and
television, and as a personality of the London stage.'

In 1923, IW built Whitehall Court, a mansion block in
Killarney, at a cost of $500 000. Originally, it was to have been
called The Ritz, but in the end, he chose the name of his other
favourite lodgings in London, the magnificent Whitehall Court
on the Thames at Westminster. The building was meant to afford
its well-heeled residents a kind of Manhattan style of living, with

a dry cleaner and a bakery on site. It was also supposed to have exotic birds in its courtyard gardens. IW apparently lived there only for a while before returning to the Carlton Hotel.

In all his years of living abroad, IW never gave up his American passport, but he chose to be buried in South Africa. His grave lies in the middle of the veld, next to Mabel May, on what was once Zebediela. The graves are in the middle of nowhere, and almost impossible to find. Since the 1970s, Zebediela has fallen into ruin, although the original buildings are still standing, mostly empty. People in Zebediela don't know his name, but some of them still refer to a man who lived there long ago, whom they call simply 'the American'.

ACKNOWLEDGEMENTS

The idea to write about the incredible IW Schlesinger has been dogging me for so long – I first started doing research in 2004 – that a number of the people I want to thank have since passed on: Stephen Gray, Percy Tucker, Deirdre Bair, John Ferrone and especially my father, who firmly believed in this story and often gave me leads, including a connection to the Rosenthal manuscript. Thank you to Neil Parsons, who has put together a true labour of love on IW and Harold Shaw that provided me with important insights, and to Kevin Brownlow, who showed a level of enthusiasm about IW's story that was very special. He knew the old movie names and how extraordinary IW's story was in global movie terms. There are people I spoke to so long ago that they have probably forgotten about it already, such as Jacqueline Maingard and Emma Sandon, who have both done wonderful research on the much-overlooked South African movie industry. Incredible assistance was provided, sometimes under difficult circumstances given their budget constraints, by Wits University's Cullen Library Historical Papers, the National Library of South Africa, the Johannesburg Library and the Jewish Archives in Johannesburg (since closed). (As an aside on public resources in general, the abysmal state of the National Film, Video and Sound Archives in Pretoria is matched only by the fast-decaying newspapers in libraries that no one bothers to digitise, both failures contributing to an irretrievable loss of some world-class artefacts and references.) Stellenbosch

University's ESAT was enormously helpful, most notably the contributions by film historian Freddy Ogterop. An especial thanks to those many people – you know who you are – who kept expressing encouragement, when agents and publishers abroad said IW and his African Hollywood wouldn't interest readers outside South Africa. I am always indebted to Marc Latilla for his readiness to offer help on things Johannesburg, especially with maps and minutiae, and anyone who doesn't know his terrific website johannesburg1912.com should check it out. Thank you to Gill Moodie and Jonathan Ball Publishers for taking a chance on the manuscript. And, last but not least, thank you over and over again to Helen Moffett for reading iteration after iteration of the manuscript, which started as an unruly and very thick oak tree and is now a much whittled-down bonsai.

NOTES

iii *ex Africa* This saying from Pliny – 'Always something new out of Africa' – was often used by IW on the cover of his movie magazine, *Stage & Cinema*.

Paris, Monte Carlo Swanson was quoted in *Stage & Cinema* in 1925. It was meant to be a small item on fashion trends in Europe, but IW's agents in London, or IW himself, had obviously convinced the actress to add something about South Africa. Swanson had her own connection to South Africa, having played the wife of a Boer farmer in the 1921 American movie *Under the Lash*, regarded as one of her least successful pictures.

Introduction

2 *Travers* Newly arrived in London from New Zealand in the mid-1920s, Travers handled, among other things, the publicity for the opening of IW's first studio in England, British National Pictures.

3 *The list goes on* In entertainment alone, IW was also acquainted with Alfred Hitchcock's wife, the screenwriter Alma Reville, who wrote the script for Schlesinger's movie *After the Verdict*; German composer Edmund Meisel, who had worked on Sergei Eisenstein's *Battleship Potemkin*; JD Williams, who signed the first-ever million-dollar movie deal, with Charlie Chaplin in 1919 (see notes for 'The Belly of the Beast'); Himanshu Rai, one of the founders of Indian cinema; the future director Jack Clayton (*Room at the Top*); German cinematographer Curt Courant; Brigitte Helm, star of Fritz Lang's *Metropolis*, who starred in IW's *City of Song*; British composer Philip Braham, who wrote the jazz classic 'Limehouse Blues'; Charles Brabin, director of IW's American movie *Persuasive Peggy* (see notes for 'His Double'); documentary film pioneer John Grierson; John Reith, head of the newly created BBC; pioneering Australian movie man Sir Oswald Stoll; African trade unionist AWG Champion, who worked for African Theatres; scriptwriter Frances Marion, called 'the greatest woman creative genius of the screen'; the Gorno family from Italy, who had been in marionettes for three centuries, and whose creations he put in early talkies; Bernard Vorhaus, a director later blacklisted in Hollywood during the McCarthy years; Henrik Galeen (Austrian writer of FW Murnau's classic *Nosferatu* and director of *The Student of Prague*); British director Herbert Wilcox; and Thomas Lamb, the Scottish-born architect who designed many of the massive Art Deco 'picture palaces' across America in the 1920s.

a 'talkie' picture   *The Jazz Singer*, regarded as the first 'talkie', was released in 1927. Sound came slowly after that. It's crazy to think today, but most of Hollywood, which had built its business on the art of silence, balked at the idea of letting their actors be heard.

or JP Morgan   *The New York Times*, 12 March 1949.

prosperity await you   *The Outspan*, 11 March 1927.

4   *out of the spotlight*   In 2008, I approached the British historian Rachael Low, who between 1948 and 1985 published seven volumes of *The History of the British Film*. In this exhaustive work, she made several brief references to IW, and I wondered if there was more that she hadn't disclosed. She said she found my discoveries about him 'intriguing', but 'I very much regret to say I cannot add anything to it. As you say, he apparently did not like publicity and I did not find any other references to his film activities (in Britain) at the time.'

long-lost manuscript   In 1949, Eric Rosenthal, a well-known South African historian, who had long been fascinated by the elusive Schlesinger, was summoned to his bedside in Johannesburg, where, quite to his surprise, he was asked to write the dying man's life story. Two weeks later IW was dead, but Rosenthal spent the next two years writing the book, apparently granted access to Schlesinger's letters and papers. He also interviewed people like Joseph Albrecht and Max Zasman. Publication of the manuscript was eventually killed by IW's son, John Schlesinger, because he felt it would inflame old issues, such as his father's support of Smuts's 1922 plebiscite to make Rhodesia a fifth province of South Africa.

The Fall of the Empire

13   *One wintry Monday*   *Rand Daily Mail*, 20 May 1913.

spectacle of Edwardian luxury   Van de Waal, *From Mining Camp to Metropolis*.

14   *tightrope walker Blondin*   Gutsche, *The History and Social Significance of Motion Pictures in South Africa 1895–1940*.

Theatre Royal   Chilvers, *Out of the Crucible*.

15   *on a leash*   'Pagel's Circus', Ancestors Research South Africa (ancestors.co.za).

his one-man show   Gutsche.

seriously lacked   Chilvers.

16   *Daisy Wood*   Gutsche.

for lodgings until then   *Rand Daily Mail*, 29 May 1913.

17   *Leonard Rayne*   The popular Rayne, whom Jack Stodel calls 'South Africa's leading theatrical manager', was the one person in the theatre world whom IW left alone and respected. He was one of the few people who never seemed to have a falling-out with Schlesinger. See Stodel, *The Audience is Waiting*.

Making Things Hum

18 *hot potatoes in Hell*   Stodel.

on the qui vive   Barlow, *Almost in Confidence*.

19 *jockeys and the horses*   Rosenthal, Unpublished biography of IW Schlesinger.

colourful to a fault   Gutsche.

newspaper production   Rosenthal.

makes things hum   *Motion Picture Weekly*, October 1913.

rubbed many people up the wrong way   On 28 May 1928, Colonel Deneys Reitz MP referred to the impact of Schlesinger's stranglehold on businesses as 'having "octopus claws" on a good many things in the country'.

try his luck   Barlow.

Orange Grove   Tucker, 'IW Schlesinger'.

20 *a man with his soul aflame*   'Waterman', 'Some Memories of the Great IW Schlesinger'. (Some people also used IW's third initial, thus IWS.)

21 *Union Express*   The Union Express (or Union Limited) train service between Pretoria and Cape Town seems to have started only in the early 1920s, but I use the term here by extension to signify the long-established route.

A Conflux of Apparent Miracles

22 *the very word 'movie'*   'When Did "Movie" Replace "Motion Picture"?', pictureshowman.com.

23 *for four hundred yards*   Robinson, *From Peep Show to Palace*.

Cape mail steamer   Murry, *Union-Castle Chronicle*.

24 *standing there alone*   Hertz, *A Modern Mystery Merchant*.

first exposure to motion pictures   David Robinson wrote this of the first public exhibition of a movie in New York City – using a projector called the Vitascope – held on 23 April 1896 at Koster and Bial's Music Hall in Herald Square.

25 *godless thing*   Chilvers.

happy hunting ground   Thelma Gutsche Papers, UCT Libraries.

movie madness   Gutsche, *The History and Social Significance of Motion Pictures in South Africa 1895–1940*.

dainty cup of tea   Chanan, *The Dream that Kicks*.

26 *double-bed sheets*   Prechner, 'How the Cinema First Came to South Africa'.

dog-beater   Ibid.

27 *a passing phase*   Gutsche.

people didn't mind   Gutsche.

lose his arm   The incident involved an early movie pioneer, Victor Sampson, and is recounted by Prechner.

and sporting events   William Guynn (ed), *The Routledge Companion to Film History* (Routledge, 2011).

28 rivaled those of Hollywood   Efraim Katz and Ronald Dean Nolen, *Film Encyclopedia: The Complete Guide to Film and the Film Industry* (HarperCollins, 2012).

About half of that went to Europe   North, 'Our Foreign Trade in Motion Pictures'.

a fraction of one per cent   Ibid.

A Spectacle on Broadway

29 curtain fell on the last scene   *Moving Picture World*, 3 May 1913.

20 000 theatres   Manchal, *Film Study*.

30 without fear of prosecution   Drinkwater, *The Life and Adventures of Carl Laemmle*.

audiences were believed incapable   The Editors of Encyclopaedia Britannica, 'Motion Picture Patents Company', *Encyclopedia Britannica*, 28 April 2023.

31 prolonged applause   *Moving Picture World*, 3 May 1913.

social *indictment, and documentary*   Marilyn Ferdinand, essay on *Traffic in Souls*, Library of Congress (National Film Preservation Board).

Operator Shot Dead

33 and a few others   The identity of most of the cameramen who worked for IW, despite the incredible footage that they would take over the coming years, especially Frederick Ayliff (or Ayliffe), were rarely made known. Along with the African actors in IW's stable of employees, they rank among the forgotten talents of African Films.

34 the theft of a diamond   According to the Encyclopaedia of South African Theatre, Film, Media and Performance (ESAT), *Star of the South* was based on a true story, about the eponymous diamond found by a Khoi worker on the banks of the Vaal River. He sells it to two diggers before 'desperadoes' plot to steal it. 'The colonial mounted police arrive in time to apprehend the would-be robbers.'

Rufe Naylor   It was thanks to Naylor, according to Thelma Gutsche, that South Africa started making movies. Others followed his lead in making newsreels, although they didn't last for long.

race meeting at Turffontein   *Rand Daily Mail*, 5 May 1913.

35 to the scene of operations   *Rand Daily Mail*, 28 May 1913.

the storm broke   Chilvers.

36 Night fell on a horrified town.   Ibid.

trying to protect others   'The 1913 Mineworkers' Strike', South African History Online.

tobogganing down on his back   *Sunday Times*, per Parsons, *Black and White Bioscope*.

a rumbling calm   Mike Alfred, *Johannesburg Portraits: From Lionel Phillips to Sibongile Khumalo* (Jacana, 2003).

37 *one of the African Mirror team*   Gutsche.

   lest they incite to violence   Ibid.

38 *follow details*   *Rand Daily Mail*, 2 August 1913.

39 *the most important person*   Thelma Gutsche, who worked under Joseph Albrecht during World War II, wrote of him as 'the father of South African movies'.

The King's Cameraman

43 *Charles Urban*   Urban was one of the most significant film makers in Britain before World War I, making mostly educational and scientific-type films and pioneering an early colour format.

   Pathé Animated Gazette   The first newsreel, Pathé-Journal, was started in 1908 by the French Pathé brothers, who were already the biggest manufacturers of camera equipment in Europe.

   balloons and dirigibles   *Stage & Cinema*, 28 April 1917.

44 *their source of amusement*   Rosenthal, Unpublished biography of IW Schlesinger.

   First Balkan War   The kingdoms of Serbia, Bulgaria, Greece and Montenegro were facing off against the Ottoman Empire. Rosenthal suggests that Albrecht was the youngest-ever newsman.

45 *tempted to go west*   How Albrecht came to his decision to work for IW is recounted by Rosenthal.

   sanctum sanctorum   Stodel, *The Audience is Waiting*.

46 *you would have to guess*   Ibid.

   smartest pair of shoes   Ibid.

48 *and wooded streams*   Gutsche, *The History and Social Significance of Motion Pictures in South Africa 1895–1940*.

   £60 000   The equivalent of about $300 000 at the time. This, if true, is almost double the price that Carl Laemmle would pay for his Universal City property.

His Double

49 *They came from the ghettos*   Zierold, *The Moguls*.

50 *dominated everyone*   Barlow, *Almost in Confidence*.

51 *Traffic in Souls*   Apparently, Laemmle initially balked at the length of the movie, which was made longer than a reel or two behind his back.

52 *a great chariot race*   Drinkwater, *The Life and Adventures of Carl Laemmle*. Interestingly, and in another of those strange overlaps with IW's movie career, the original director of the great chariot-race film *Ben-Hur*, Charles Brabin, would direct Schlesinger's first movie in America in 1917, six years earlier. *Ben-Hur*, the biggest movie an American studio had filmed overseas, in Italy right after Mussolini

came to power, was famously fraught with problems before Brabin was replaced.

53 *come here after that is over*   Rand Daily Mail, 24 May 1914.

Fitzpatrick saw as his own.   The communication between Fitzpatrick and the Colonial Office is at the National Library of South Africa in Cape Town. From the tone of his letter, Fitzpatrick clearly didn't like IW, whom he called 'IJ Schlesinger, a German-American Jew' – getting his initials and origin wrong. Nothing came of his letters.

Kingdon   HS Kingdon had owned the Vaudette chain of bioscopes, which IW bought. He worked both as a buyer of films in London for IVTA and as manager of African Mirror before becoming one of IW's free agents.

At Sea

54 *coaches led by a four-horsed drag and a band*   Rand Daily Mail, 20 July 1914.

God be with you   Ibid.

telegrams of gratitude   Ibid.

55 *General Jan Smuts*   In January 1914, in a slight thawing of their relationship, Smuts and Gandhi had signed an agreement dealing with Indian immigrant rights in South Africa, and Gandhi gave Smuts a pair of sandals he had made and which the general wore till late in his life.

use the Empire   This Empire was the first one, on the west end of Commissioner Street, which was replaced by the grander version in late 1906. No fan of either theatre or motion pictures, Gandhi later said, 'If I had my way, I would see to it that all cinemas and theatres in India were converted into spinning halls.'

56 *satyagraha*   From the *Collected Works of Mahatma Gandhi*.

zealous activities in Johannesburg   The architect Hermann Kallenbach, Gandhi's companion on the *Kinfauns Castle*, would also have been known to IW. If they hadn't met at Jewish events in the city, IW would have known that Kallenbach had designed the Jewish High School on Wolmarans Street and the Bioscope Theatre on Jeppe Street, one of the theatres he now owned.

beezum in their egos   Rosenthal, Unpublished Biography of IW Schlesinger. The American author Everett McNeil wrote in 1908 that 'beezum' was one of many words that meant money.

1 440 to the best advantage   African Life Jottings.

London and America   Rand Daily Mail, 8 July 1914.

57 *working like a machine*   Rosenthal.

internment camp   Kallenbach returned to Johannesburg after the war.

The Great Search

58 *new entertainment magazines*   The advent of the movies, especially

after 1910, saw the rise of numerous movie and entertainment publications to keep a movie-hungry public informed. These included *Kinematograph Weekly, Bioscope, Moving Picture World* and *The Cinema News and Property Gazette*. The titles kept multiplying, as did the exaggerated claims and statistics in advertisements, and often stories too, in their pages.

59 *the next three decades*   Today, much is made of the fact that by 1919 the producer Adolph Zukor had created the first vertically integrated studio in America – Paramount – which triggered other studios to do likewise, destroying smaller, independent operators in the process. In the end, there were five large studios and three smaller ones. 'Through vertical integration,' wrote *The New York Times*, 'one company would provide a reliable output of films controlled from conception to consumption.' The US Supreme Court ruled in 1948 that the studio system violated anti-trust laws, and movie companies had to divest themselves of their theatre holdings. This did not happen to IW in South Africa, although by that stage the local market was no longer his alone. Hollywood studios had started invading it.

  ones that were set in South Africa   South Africa, despite its remoteness, had already been on the radar of moviemakers since the beginning of the century, especially in America, although the storylines were often of a type. With newspapers still writing about the 'Dark Continent', and 'South Africa' often used interchangeably with 'Africa', it led to movies like *The Leopard's Foundling*, in which a child wanders away from her parents and grows up with wild cats, or *Wiles of a Siren*, in which 'a mission in Africa (is) attacked and burned by savages and then a party of hunters (comes) to the aid of the missionaries'. In 1913, Carl Laemmle released *Won in the Clouds*, the poster of which showed a 'Knabenshue Dirigible Balloon' flying over a charging elephant and promised 'Some wild animal stuff and other genuine thrills'.

60 *Prester John*   Author John Buchan had gone to South Africa in 1901 to work for Sir Alfred Milner and became part of his 'Kindergarten'. South Africa heavily influenced Buchan's adventure novels, as it did Rider Haggard.

61 *tribe of white people*   Andrew Balfour's *The Golden Kingdom* also had the distinction of having the oddest and perhaps longest subtitle ever, 'Being an Account of the Quest for the Same as Described in the Remarkable Narrative of Doctor Henry Mortimer, Contained in the Manuscript found within the Boards of a Boer Bible During the Late War'.

  it was going to be almost impossible   Rider Haggard, coincidentally, stayed at the Carlton Hotel in 1914 during a visit as part of the Dominion Group. The author found Johannesburg 'a marvel and a hell'. He knew the city, as he had worked in South Africa as an official and lawyer, and used the country as a setting for many of his books. But Johannesburg had grown substantially since his last visit. The noise of the traffic and the clanking trams kept him awake at night. 'It is a huge tumultuous city rather more evil and menacing than most and fearfully expensive to live, that is all.' Given that IW was in the penthouse on top of the hotel, and knew everything that was going on within the Carlton's walls, it is clear that the two must have met. It could also have been then, at the very start of his entertainment empire, that IW had set his sights on acquiring the Quatermain books.

Showing on Times Square

62 *ticket in steerage*   Rosenthal, Unpublished biography of IW Schlesinger.

  fastest in the world   IW loved speed in everything: automobiles, ships and eventually planes. Even before commercial air travel started, he did everything in his power to hasten its advent by sponsoring competitions to see who could fly the fastest across Africa. Max Zasman told Rosenthal that his boss 'liked traveling fast, sixty to seventy miles an hour on average', an unusually high speed for early motoring.

  the supernatural   Rosenthal says that Schlesinger, much saddened by the death of his mother in 1924, would in later years try to converse with her spirit.

63 *Over the past decade*   The name 'The Schlesinger Organisation' was sometimes used to cover all of IW's disparate companies, but it seems to have been more of a catch-all than an official title.

64 *sudden death*   Some mystery surrounds Samuel's death, which was most likely in 1910, although the cause was not given and his name appeared in later census figures. However, so did IW's, despite his living in New York for only one or two months a year.

  207 West 110th Street   Unlike the Ritz in London, which was often linked to IW's name, there was no similar hotel in New York. MA and the rest of the Schlesinger family – his parents Lena and Abraham, three sisters and one other brother who was still alive – had recently moved to Harlem from the Lower East Side, where they had lived since immigrating in 1884. MA had an apartment overlooking the north end of Central Park. It is unclear whether Lena and Abraham lived with MA, but IW would have wanted to be close to his mother, to whom he was especially close. Rosenthal wrote that IW never got over the fact that on his arrival in Cape Town, he had pawned the fob his mother had given him, and never got it back. 'No matter how busy he was with his work he always wrote long letters to her, setting out his innermost thoughts. Her passing was a blow to him. He claimed to have regular negotiations with her from the other side, something which he only admitted to a very few.'

65 *Bartolomeo Pagano*   *Moving Picture World*, 6 November 1915. Pagano, who played Maciste, the slave who saves Cabiria, had been working in the harbour of Genoa when he was plucked out of obscurity to be in the movie; the role quickly made him famous and would lead to one of the oldest recurring characters of cinema, the sandalled hero with titanic strength like Goliath, Samson and Hercules.

The Man Who Made Trajan

66 *the studios of Rome*   *Moving Picture World*, 23 August 1913.
side by side   *Billboard*, 18 October 1913.

67 *a very large salary*   *Rand Daily Mail*, 17 February 1915.
absolute power   *Billboard*, 11 March 1916.

War!

68 *staggering £750 000*   *Rand Daily Mail*, 17 February 1915.
a world of danger and adventure   Joseph Albrecht, 'A Continent – in a Camera', *Stage & Cinema*, 27 December 1924.
full of danger   *Moving Picture World*, 11 December 1915.

69 *come from over the water*   *Rand Daily Mail*, 8 December 1914.
the trouble in this country   *Rand Daily Mail*, 12 January 1915.
The Rebellion   *Rand Daily Mail*, 8 December 1914.
mansion of Sir Lionel Phillips   *Rand Daily Mail*, 30 September 1914.
commando on the veld, Van Heerden's   *Rand Daily Mail*, 1 December 1914. Van Heerden was Field-cornet Koos van Heerden. One of the last African Mirror segments to deal with the Rebellion appeared in late 1915, when one of the leaders who had been sentenced to life imprisonment, Christiaan de Wet, was pardoned. Its show, titled 'The Pardon', advertised on 29 December 1915, had the subtitle 'The Elusive De Wet Captured by Camera Man'.

70 *'With our Boys in German East'*   Gutsche, *The History and Social Significance of Motion Pictures in South Africa 1895–1940*.

71 *setting fire to dozens of businesses*   Rosenthal, Unpublished biography of IW Schlesinger.
The rioters left   Ibid.

An African in London

73 *'Supreme Picture of All Time'*   *The Birth of a Nation* opened at the Liberty Theatre on 42nd Street on 3 March 1915. The incredible statistics that were publicised were hugely exaggerated. Later estimates put the number of extras at about 500, the horses at 60, the shoot at six months and the cost at $100 000. An entire town that was supposed to have been burned to the ground turned out to be a model made from packing cases.

74 *predators of white women*   Clark, 'How "The Birth of a Nation" Revived the Ku Klux Klan'.

'*solidified the foundations*'   Kendall Phillips, *Controversial Cinema: The Films that Outraged America* (Bloomsbury, 2008).

no public disturbance   Michael Hammond, '"A Soul Stirring Appeal to Every Briton": The Reception of *The Birth of a Nation* in Britain (1915–1916)', *Film History* 11 (1999): 353–370.

75   *all-black movies*   Some of these movies he had obtained from the Tuskegee Institute, a black college in Alabama.

Through the Colonial & Banking Trust   Limb, 'An African Newspaper in Central Johannesburg'.

demanding that it be withdrawn   Willan, 'Cinematographic Calamity'.

most sympathetic to African interests   Ibid, quoting EA Walker's *WP Schreiner: A South African* (Oxford University Press, 1937).

prevent it from being shown in South Africa   Willan.

76   *until 1931*   A widely held belief was that when *Birth of a Nation* was reissued in 1931, with a soundtrack, and finally shown in South Africa, it was IW who had shown it in his theatres. Even Plaatje thought so, and he wrote a public plea for Schlesinger to reconsider. In fact, the movie was shown – for a very short run – at Kinemas, a new chain of theatres owned by IW's recently established competitors. He would buy out Kinemas within the year.

'The Real Work of My Life'

78   *in the middle of May and sunk*   Within six months of Johnston and Cooke's voyage, the *Llandovery Castle* too would be turned into a hospital ship. It was later sunk by a U-boat, with almost everyone on board lost.

ornamental verbiage   *Stage & Cinema*, November 1915.

written the scenario   Women were carving a sizeable niche for themselves as scenarists in early Hollywood, although Cooke was not a major figure, according to Donna Casella's essay 'Shaping the Craft of Screenwriting: Women Screen Writers in Silent Era Hollywood', Women Film Pioneers Project, https://doi.org/10.7916/d8-jgja-cf13. In 1923, Cooke adapted Dickens's 'The Cricket on the Heath' for Johnston.

79   *movie magazine, Stage & Cinema*   The weekly, a combination of news and entertainment, brought out its first issue in August 1915.

astonish the world   *Rand Daily Mail*, 15 November 1915.

Emerging from the Chrysalis

82   *astonishing testimonies*   Gutsche, *The History and Social Significance of Motion Pictures in South Africa 1895-1940*.

83   *Marmaduke Arundel Wetherell*   Of all the actors at Killarney, Wetherell was the most fascinating. After a good innings at African Films, he fell out with IW. He left in 1921 and went on to some fame in England, where he acted, directed and wrote. He clearly used all the

techniques he had learned from Joseph Albrecht at Killarney to make perhaps the most astounding movie ever shot in Africa, the almost completely unsung *Livingstone*. He and his crew and actors travelled the exact route followed by David Livingstone for an entire year, with hardly an accident along the way. On 22 December 1924, the *Daily Telegraph* began a fascinating series by Wetherell called 'Fifty Years After – In Livingstone's Footsteps', recounting the harrowing adventure. He followed it up with *Robinson Crusoe*, filmed in Tobago, with himself as Crusoe and a local taxi driver as Friday. Wetherell wanted to make a movie of TE Lawrence's *Seven Pillars of Wisdom*, but it never happened. Oddly enough, the cameraman he was working with, Freddie Young, went on to shoot David Lean's *Lawrence of Arabia* almost four decades later. In 1938, Wetherell returned to South Africa with the intention of shooting a movie about President Paul Kruger, with a script written by Gustav Preller, who had written the Blood River epic. Wetherell died before production could start. What he is best remembered for, ironically, is the story, which was carried by the *Daily Mail* on 20 December 1933, that a 'Central African big game hunter', as Wetherell was known, had come upon the spoor of a four-toed, twenty-foot-long creature living in Loch Ness, Scotland: 'It is certainly not a footprint of any land animal known in the British Isles, nor any I have come across in my hunting experience in Central Africa.' A year later, the Loch Ness Monster was proved to have been a fantastic hoax manufactured by the man whose entertainment career had started at the City of Film.

84 *Universal City* Even though Laemmle's masterpiece studio wasn't complete when it officially opened, the two-day event drew some 15 000 people.

our American studios *Billboard*, 11 March 1916.

The Wand of Witchery

87 *never left southern California* Robert S Birchard, 'The Squaw Man'.

seductive and wheedling Schlesinger, *The Outspan*, 11 March 1927.

a strong appeal for me Ibid.

88 *Crusoe, Midshipman Easy* *Stage & Cinema*, December 1915.

trip up the Yangtze Parsons, *Black and White Bioscope*.

feature movies on the continent Besides *The Great Kimberley Diamond Robbery* (1911), there was one other small movie. In 1913, the German explorer, hunter and filmmaker Hans Hermann Schomburgk went to Togoland, in West Africa, to shoot documentaries and 'the first feature movie in Africa'. He chose 22-year-old Meg Gehrts to act in his picture, *The White Goddess of the Wangora*. Caroline Alexander recounts the story in her terrific *New Yorker* article of the same name from 1991.

pictures I am to produce *Moving Picture World*, 18 March 1916.

89 *called 'Dingaan'* Ibid.

great production   Ibid.

cinema art   *Billboard*, 11 March 1916.

Sensation

93 *some mystified*   Parsons, *Black and White Bioscope*.

a mild sensation   *Stage & Cinema*, April 1917.

94 *youngest colonies*   *Moving Picture World*, 8 April 1916.

A Quiet Entrance

96 *The first South African Drama released by African Films*   In 1914, when
IW was still in the early days of organising his entertainment business,
his cameramen had made a one-reeler called *The Trek*. The scenario
was by Joseph Langley Levy, the editor of the *Sunday Times*, who,
according to Neil Parsons, was a friend of IW's. The script was also
apparently submitted to General Christiaan Beyers for approval. If
the film was shown in South Africa, it got little publicity, although in
1915 *The Trek* was briefly distributed in Britain, by a company called
Davison, as 'a Romance of South Africa'.

from their clutches   *Rand Daily Mail*, 29 May 1916.

floor to ceiling   Rosenthal, Unpublished biography of IW Schlesinger.

splendidly   *Rand Daily Mail*, 30 March 1916.

97 *to the audience*   Rosenthal.

Goba   In August 1916, *A Zulu's Devotion* became the first of
Schlesinger's pictures to be released in London, where it was less
the movie itself that one reviewer singled out than the 'remarkably
natural acting' of the title character. WG Faulkner, often referred to
as Britain's first regular film critic, called Goba 'one of the greatest
actors I ever saw'.

How that had happened   As with the African Mirror cameramen, there
are few records available of who the black actors were, where they
came from, how much they were paid or what became of them. This
is particularly glaring in the case of the actor who played Cetshwayo
in *The Symbol of Sacrifice*, whose real name doesn't seem to have been
used in any publication.

a familiar figure on the world bioscope screens   Parsons, *Black and White
Bioscope*. Goba's career was brief, for he died only three years after
he began, in 1919.

Msoga Mwana   Mwana acted under the screen name Masoja as
Reverend John Laputa in 1920's *Prester John. Stage & Screen*,
7 February 1920.

council meeting   Rosenthal.

a fine looking Zulu   Ibid.

98 *by showing his likeness in all parts of the world*   Parsons. According to
an article in *The Outspan* from 27 January 1928, on the widespread
showing of movies on mine and municipal compounds, 'weekly

transformed into a huge open-air bioscope', the bioscope operator was known as 'Goba'. Films for black audiences were censored by the Reverend Ray Phillips, of the American Board of Missions, 'who started this chain of free bioscope performances to stamp out the commercial native bioscope, which specialised in low-grade, suggestive films that seemed to have been gleaned from the gutters of the world, the worst products of the English, French and American studios.'

a practice that would continue   Using white actors in make-up to play black characters was common practice in America. Only in 1914 did a mainstream movie, *Uncle Tom's Cabin*, use an African American in a starring role. All five previous screen versions of the famous novel had used white actors for the main roles. *The Birth of a Nation* did the same, even using whites to portray a black militia. See Stephen Railton's essay 'Uncle Tom's Cabin on Film 1: The Silent Era', https://utc.iath.virginia.edu/interpret/exhibits/utconfilm/utconfilm.html.

99 *became known simply as 'the village'*   Rosenthal.

Men of Speed

100 *a very simple shack*   Rosenthal, Unpublished biography of IW Schlesinger.

He disliked   Stodel, *The Audience is Waiting*.

101 *James Thompson*   A future mayor of the city, Thompson became the contractor for buildings like the Supreme Court on Pritchard Street and the mansion Northwards (artefacts.co.za). The cottage where he lived on Killarney eventually made way for the Beit Emanuel Synagogue.

Solly Joel   Took over the firm of Barnato Brothers, which became Johannesburg Consolidated Investment Co, or JCI, after his brother Woolf was shot dead by the conman Baron Von Veltheim in 1898. The brothers assumed control over the company after their famous uncle Barney Barnato disappeared off the SS *Scot* two years earlier while on a voyage to England. Joel had investments in theatres and hotels, including the Carlton, which for several years he encouraged IW to buy from him. In 1925, IW finally did so, when the price was low enough for his liking.

Sammy Marks   After Marks arrived in Johannesburg in 1870, he became a *smous* (peddler), an industrialist and a friend of Paul Kruger, who presided over the opening of the first synagogue in Johannesburg. In 1912, Marks established the Union Steel Corporation, which eventually became part of Iscor.

Von Veltheim   The sensational circumstances around the trial of Von Veltheim – whose real name was Carl Ludwig Kurtz – are dealt with in my book *Daisy de Melker* (Jonathan Ball Publishers, 2023).

Sir Abe Bailey   Rosenthal. The two men who visited IW the most were Hoy and Bailey. When the diamond magnate stood as a parliamentary candidate for Krugersdorp in 1914, IW 'made one of his few incursions into politics by sending Max (Zasman) to bring voters to the poll'. This was probably the kind of information that IW's son, when he killed Rosenthal's biography, would have liked to keep quiet. IW also liked the company of Count Natale Labia, the Italian consul in Johannesburg who in 1921 married Sir JB Robinson's daughter Ida.

vanity   Steyn, *Louis Botha.*

'Yiddisher' stories   Stodel.

one of his great friends   Rosenthal.

102   *automobilism on the Rand*   *Rand Daily Mail*, 5 March 1914.

     motorcycle was put on display in the foyer   *Rand Daily Mail*, 5 June 1914.

     one thousand cars on the Rand   Prof Alex Duffey, 'Early Motoring in South Africa'.

     'Grand Automobile Night'   *Rand Daily Mail*, 24 September 1913. When the film was shown at the Empire, the theatre was 'almost barricaded by motor cars'. Among the important guests was the Englishman Captain Raleigh Kelsey, who was attempting to become the first person to drive from Cape Town to Cairo, in a specially designed, six-metre-long, five-ton Argyll. Kelsey would fail in his trans-Africa quest, and died en route several months later after being attacked by a leopard.

     three cheers were given   *Rand Daily Mail*, 15 September 1913.

103   *shocked and surprised*   Rosenthal.

     helped her through the crisis   Ibid.

     the great majority of Americans   Barlow, *Almost in Confidence.*

     a sneaking regard   Barlow. One of the most astounding stories recounted by Barlow is that IW had been arrested by the British during the Anglo-Boer War for carrying correspondence from a Boer officer and narrowly missed being executed. A shorter version of the spy story was recounted by Jack Stodel in his memoir.

104   *thanks to his knowledge of German*   Rosenthal.

     last of these pioneers   Ibid.

The Historian

105   *Groot Trek*   Preller also gave Afrikaans the word for 'movies' – *rolprent* (rolling picture).

     Piet Retief   In the index to Preller's thoroughly researched book, interestingly, the greatest number of references (after Retief) are to Dingaan.

     a small town with a big heart   *Rand Daily Mail*, 7 September 1931.

     the better part of the town   *The City of Pretoria and Districts*, 1913.

     began discussions   Rosenthal, Unpublished biography of IW Schlesinger.

106   *In 1838*   IW, who never lost a chance to see South Africa as a new

America, must have noticed an uncanny similarity between the Great Trek and something that happened in his own country. At the same time that the Voortrekkers were setting off, pioneers left Westport Landing in Missouri for the 2 170-mile trek across what would one day become the states of Kansas, Nebraska, Wyoming and Idaho. They faced many of the same challenges and hardships, heading into lands unknown, fording rivers, crossing mountains, sitting around campfires, confronting wild animals and coming into conflict with the indigenous people.

100 elite men   Preller, *Piet Retief.*

Preller became enthusiastic   Rosenthal.

'Come Make Big Movies in Africa'

108 *grandeur and excitement of American pictures*   *The Silent Film Quarterly,* November 2015.

109 *'Traffic in Souls'*   British movies were not held in high regard internationally, and FE Adams of the London Film Company said the importation of the two directors was mostly to thwart a 'patronizing type of American criticism' of British-made movies.

110 *I must forego the pleasure*   Rosenthal, Unpublished biography of IW Schlesinger.

big movies for me in Africa   Ibid.

one of the two men   George Loane Tucker returned to America in late 1916, and made a huge box-office hit in 1919 called *The Miracle Man.* Already unwell, he died two years later.

112 *their mother*   'Edna Flugrath', Wikipedia. The middle sister, Viola Dana, had just appeared in a movie in New York, *The Innocence of Ruth,* in which she was billed as 'The Biggest Little Broadway Star'.

the leading lady   Rosenthal.

The Bloody River

113 *the South African Hannibal*   Bioscope, April 1916 .

'Little Time for Sleep'

116 *their adventurous tracks*   Souvenir programme compiled by Shaw.

117 *a scene without precedent*   The dead at Weenen included 300 Voortrekkers, 185 of them children, and 250 Khoisan and Basuto.

118 *in 1913, he was given*   There seems to be some doubt as to who the director was, but *The Enemy's Baby* was probably shot by Griffith, according to film archivist Paolo Cherchi Usai.

300 authentic pieces   Rosenthal, Unpublished biography of IW Schlesinger.

Magic

121 *slums west of the city*   In *Stage & Cinema,* 6 April 1918, a story captured 'one of the world's worst slums', 'inhabited by all sorts and

nationalities of people', around Vrededorp and what was called the
Malay Location.

mtagati   While Rosenthal gives these as the translations, Albrecht
may have misheard the Zulu words or misheard Albrecht. *I-mhlamena*
means 'spleen', but the correct translation for what he was trying
to say, 'indoda elia emini', would have been pronounced similarly.
I-mtagati means 'sorcerer', which was closer to the meaning that was
given.

reserve called 'The Wilds'   Rosenthal.

Scorpions

123 *nothing incongruous*   Rosenthal.
124 *tragic happenings at Florida*   *Rand Daily Mail*, 27 June 1916.
       belly of a white woman   *Rand Daily Mail*, 22 June 1916. Neil Parsons
       deals with the Smellie murders in relation to IW's *The Illicit Liquor
       Seller*.
126 *almost three hours straight*   *Stage & Cinema*, 28 April 1917.

Finding an Army

127 *more than just scorpions*   A viewing of the river scenes in *Winning a
       Continent* shows how incredibly dangerous and nearly fatal the shoot
       could have been. Some animals clearly didn't make it across.
       daily consumption   *Rand Daily Mail*, 27 October 1916. The board sold
       about 400 million gallons of water a month from several boreholes.
       Daily consumption averaged about 10 million gallons.
129 *telegrams of protest*   *Rand Daily Mail*, 14 March 1918.
130 *Hertzog and the nationalists*   Rosenthal, Unpublished biography of IW
       Schlesinger.
131 *Major Pretorius*   Quite possibly, and fantastically if it is true, this
       was the well-known Philip Pretorius, often referred to in the British
       press as 'the famous Major Pretorius', hunter, adventurer, friend
       of Frederick Courteney Selous and Jan Smuts, and something of
       a war hero. In 1915, when the Royal Navy was struggling to find
       the marauding *Königsberg*, the biggest German warship in the
       Indian Ocean that had already destroyed several of its ships and
       was now hiding out in the Rufiji Delta, south of Zanzibar, Pretorius
       was called in to help find it – which he did, leading to the ship's
       destruction. While being in charge of the weapons on IW's movie
       set seemed an unlikely job for the famous soldier, he would have had
       a profound interest in the project. He was a direct descendant of
       Andries Pretorius, the hero of Blood River, and a friend of Smuts.
       Whether or not it was during the filming that he met Albrecht,
       it was the young cameraman who in 1919 would make a movie
       about Pretorius for African Films. The government had employed
       Pretorius to take on the dangerous and highly controversial job of
       exterminating the last hundred or so elephants from Addo in the

eastern Cape, the southernmost herd on the continent, because they were 'threatening' farmers and locals. 'No decision of a Colonial Government has called forth greater adverse criticism,' Pretorius wrote for a newspaper at the time. Even he had his doubts about whether he could get the job done. 'If ever there was a hunter's hell here it was, a hundred square miles or so of all you would think bad in Central Africa, lifted up as by some Titan and plonked down in the Cape Province.' When Pretorius finally entered Addo Bush for the first time, it was on his own, carrying a Jeffery .475 double-barrelled rifle and accompanied by his dog. He was dressed in a slouch hat and specially made leather outfit – a jacket with ten cartridge holders sewn into the lapels and pants, as well as thigh-high boots – to withstand the thorns. Several people died tragically during the two-year escapade, including a British officer named Brigadier General Hurdis Secundus Ravenshaw. Pretorius finally changed his mind, and persuaded the government to leave a pod of elephants, which make up the herd of today's Addo Elephant National Park. To get some sensational footage for the film, even being charged by an elephant, Albrecht followed Pretorius for several weeks through the almost impenetrable scrub, called 'num-num bush ... a hideous mess of long and diabolical thorns' that grew eighteen feet high and so dense you could barely see five paces any side of you, which had led to many deaths. The film, when it was released, ran only for a few days. The fascinating details of Pretorius's extraordinary life, with an introduction by Jan Smuts, are in his unfinished autobiography, *Jungle Man*. The Addo chapter was called 'Tempting Death for the Films'.

otherwise experienced marksmen   Rosenthal, Unpublished biography of IW Schlesinger.

The Valley of Devils

132   *From early morning*   *Rand Daily Mail*, 16 October 1916.

133   *to witness the proceedings*   Ibid.

warrior finery   The exaggeration of statistics doesn't seem to have been as outrageous as it had been on *Birth of a Nation*, where 500 extras swelled to 18 000 for publicity. For the Elsburg shoot, the number of extras was most likely 3 000 Africans and 350 whites.

134   *Ammunition was given out*   *Rand Daily Mail*, 12 December 1916.

desultory firing   Ibid.

marrow of one's bones   *Rand Daily Mail*, 19 October 1916.

Playing at Murder

139   *Kaffirs Play at Murder*   *The Transvaal Critic*, 20 October 1916.

cretonne and blinds   *The Transvaal Critic*, 27 October 1916.

black savages   Ibid.

140   *the raw footage*   Although a copy of *Winning a Continent* is available, it

has been greatly edited. Many of the scenes the journalist described, if they were in the final version, have been lost.

Realism too Realistic   *Rand Daily Mail*, 19 October 1916.

the raw footage   Although a copy of *Winning a Continent* is available, it has been greatly edited. Many of the scenes the journalist described, if they were in the final version, have been lost.

like a stream of black lava   *Rand Daily Mail*, 19 October 1916.

Sabotage

142   *One hundred thousand feet*   For *The Birth of a Nation*, Griffith shot 150 000 feet and cut it down to 13 000.

inquest into the death   *Rand Daily Mail*, 12–14 December 1916.

143   *Plot to Wreck the Film*   Ibid.

144   *Several of the miners*   The African witnesses were only identified by one name, and these included Fana, Philemon, Alfred and Diamond.

The Premiere

146   *moved him to tears*   Rosenthal.

147   *Forty-four 'special trains'*   *Rand Daily Mail*, 18 December 1916.

148   *When not attending the ceremonies*   Ibid.

The Rise of Quatermain

151   *hero of fiction*   Selous was the father of several children from African women. It was also around him that the myth grew of the great white hunter.

152   *Burnham*   Frederick Russell Burnham had been one of the few to escape the 1893 massacre of a group of British soldiers by Lobengula's warriors that was put on film as *Major Wilson's Last Stand* six years later in London. The movie featured not only Lobengula's son but also the circus master Frank Fillis.

153   *inexhaustible supply of gold*   *The New York Times*, 14 January 1894.

154   *She*   *She, A History of Adventure* was first serialised in *The Graphic* magazine in 1886–1887 before being published as a novel.

titillating story about 'Darkest Africa'   Ayesha was perhaps the first-ever mysterious and beguiling female character of movies, the screen siren, the femme fatale, the vamp. A 1925 version of the movie, initiated by Lucoque, took the titillation to the extreme. The biggest draw of the movie was the lead actress Betty Blythe's scandalous lack of coverage: 'Miss Blythe is so undressed that she must have spent hours getting undressed.' Lucoque committed suicide during filming.

On Top of the World

156   *The Story of an African Farm*   In the end, Olive Schreiner refused to sell the film rights of her book to IW.

nor would he be the last   After Johnston and Shaw, the people who left Killarney either angry or before they were meant to were

Marmaduke Wetherell and then the director Leander de Cordova. IW's biggest confrontation, however, was in 1926, when he forced the producer JD Williams out of British Nati```onal Pictures. That was the only one that led to a heavily publicised trial.

lacked imagination   *Motion Picture News*, 4 November 1916. Clinton made little impact in movies over the next few years. He died in 1919, although the cause is unclear.

157   *got married*   *Stage & Cinema*, 13 January 1917.

brought back again   In Johannesburg, showings of Shaw's movies included: *The Two Roads* at the Carlton, then *The Third Generation*, *The Firm of Girdlestone* and *Me and Me Moke* at the Orpheum; *The Last Challenge* at the Orpheum; and *Mr Lyndon at Liberty* at the Tivoli. IW had done the same for Lorimer Johnston, promoting a number of his American films at some of his theatres.

I hope you will all see it   Jan Smuts, *War-time Speeches: A Compilation of Public Utterances in Great Britain* (George H Doran, 1917).

158   *had cost $100 000*   Figures for *Birth of a Nation* vary widely. While advertising at the time grossly exaggerated the cost, later estimates state that the budget started at $40 000 and ended at 'just a little more than $100 000'. See Richard Schickel, *DW Griffith: An American Life* (Proscenium, 1984).

an even costlier project   The new spectacle would cost $150 000, one and a half times as much as *Winning*.

The War Movie

161   *the other quietly*   Rosenthal, Unpublished biography of IW Schlesinger.

162   *the prince is killed*   This was a fictional twist by Shaw and Horace Rose. In reality, the Prince Imperial was killed in a skirmish while serving with the British Army.

The Belly of the Beast

163   *Middle East Films Ltd*   In *SA Pictorial* (the successor to *Stage & Cinema*), 9 July 1921, IW boasted that he had 'an unbroken chain of (movie) circuits which now extends from the Cape to Rhodesia, and from the Southwest protectorate to Kenya colony, and has even spread itself abroad to Madagascar, Mauritius, the Seychelles islands, Blantyre, India, the Straits Settlements, Java and the Far East, with its own film buying offices in London and New York'. Mideast House, after it was built, was controlled by the Fischer brothers, whose father had been the last major independent holdout against IW at his well-known movie house in Cape Town. Joe and Julius Fischer went on to run the famous Capitol in Singapore. The uninspiring names of IW's companies, African Films, Middle East Films, etc, kept going through British National Pictures and then his own studio, which didn't really have a name, so people called it after

its location, Wembley Park. In New York, besides Mayfair, which was the most uncharacteristic name of them all, there were companies like General Talking Pictures, American Sound Film Productions and International Photoplays Distributors Inc.

164 *Henry McRae*   *Los Angeles Times*, 18 October 1917.

actual old train   While a reference in *Stage & Cinema* says that a real train was used, in photographs it looks like a model.

165 *Film-making across Europe ... had almost ceased*   Manchal, *Film Study*.

166 *James Dixon Williams*   Williams, better known as JD WIlliams, was a legend in early cinema. He would later cross paths with IW, and come off the worse for it. In 1926, Williams became the main producer for British National Pictures, the new studio backed by IW. Williams was used to spending a lot of money to get big stars like Rudolph Valentino, something IW didn't like, so he strategised Williams's removal. Williams – in a repeat of the Harold Shaw incident of November 1917 – sued IW, and won a settlement before the trial got underway. The London press still managed to cover the few days that it lasted, and one can imagine IW trying to duck for cover as the unpleasant details of the clash came out.

Nothing like the storm   Benjamin B Hampton, *A History of the Movies* (Covici Friede Publishers, 1931).

Mayfair

167 *representative of the African Film Trust*   *The New York Times*, 26 February 1953.

Marcus Loew   In the mid-1920s, IW was sucked into the battle of 'block booking' that Zukor had started, whereby exhibitors had to buy a studio's entire output, good and bad. When IW refused to play ball, Loew threatened to open his own business in South Africa. In 1932, Loew opened the largest movie house in Africa, the Metro, in Johannesburg.

168 *studio on West 54th Street*   *Motography*, 9 June 1917.

spare no expense   *Moving Picture World*, 12 May 1917.

169 *as well known to him as Broadway*   Ibid.

Other African-themed movies   The fifth incarnation of *She* was made by Fox Film Corporation and starred Valeska Suratt, one of many actresses who chose exotic screen names – Theda Bara, Nita Naldi and a Danish dancer called Valkyrien. In *Avenged by Lions*, an engineer goes to South Africa to build a railroad. In *A Million a Minute*, the hero 'leaves for South Africa'. Biograph's serial *Lord Chumley*, with Lilian Gish, has one of the characters heading off to South Africa. In December 1916, Jesse Lasky's Feature Play Company released two movies linked to South Africa: *The Plow Girl* (a man who kills a girl's parents and takes her in, turns out to be sought by her rich grandmother in England) and *The Years of the*

Locust (a young woman marries the wrong man, and goes to Africa where he finds her after he is meant to be drowned). *Hidden Valley* was about a 'white goddess who has been captured by savage blacks in South Africa'.

'The Pioneers' *Moving Picture World*, 31 March 1917.

A Wonderland

170 *the City of Film*   *Stage & Cinema*, 1 September 1917.

171 *Empress Eugénie*   On 7 August 1917, a competition to portray the two monarchs was announced in *Stage & Cinema*: 'applicants were asked to send applications and a picture without delay.' 'They will be splendidly coached in their parts, for the chief producer and his assistants are men of patience and experience.' The winners were a 'Mrs D Buxton', a bank manager's wife who, although being too tall, was virtually the exact double of Queen Victoria – the cameramen JL Humphrey and William Bowden had to position the cameras carefully to make up for her height – and 'Mrs Stewart', who played Empress Eugénie. The cost of the set would be about £61 000 today.

173 *As for the streets*   *Stage & Cinema*, 1 September 1917. The fact that this appeared in IW's own magazine means it could be as much truth as conjecture.

14 Miles an Hour

174 *Rand Police Courts*   *Rand Daily Mail*, 30 June 1917.

175 *he got nervous when cars went fast*   In a tragic irony, Harold Shaw, who was again making a name for himself in Hollywood by the mid-1920s, died in a 'spectacular' crash on Rossmore Avenue near Wilshire Boulevard on 30 January 1926. The car, driven by someone else, rolled three times and Shaw's head was crushed. He was 49.

A Quatermain Comes to Town

176 *soldier of fortune*   Obituary in *The New York Times*, 5 March 1918.
     some of their pages   Obituary in the *Washington Post*, 5 March 1918.
     absolute penury   *The New York Times*, 5 March 1918.

177 *his return to South Africa*   Ibid.
     movie about Rhodes   Neil Parsons says the idea of a Rhodes movie was eventually dropped, for fear it could 'injure European prestige'.

Joy Rides

180 *he had been robbed of it*   Barlow, *Almost in Confidence*.
     and earning more money   Parsons, 'Investigating the Origins of *The Rose of Rhodesia*', Part 1.

181 *not going to do it again*   *Rand Daily Mail*, 20 April 1918.
     Damn you   Ibid.

Leading Lady

186 *Adventures of a Diamond*   The serial does not seem to ever have been released.

IW's girlfriend   IW's alleged attraction to showgirls, or 'Gaiety Girls' as Neil Parsons refers to them, probably had some truth to it. The vaudeville artist Ada Reeve, who visited South Africa several times, claimed in her autobiography that IW 'had a remarkable fondness for my society' and would always put his car at her disposal. He would pump her for ideas about theatre and said that if he bought them, it would all be because of her. A report in the *Daily Telegraph* on 22 May 1913 said that a 'Mr Schlesinger in South Africa' was one of the co-respondents in a divorce proceeding instituted by a Mr Cathie against his wife, both of whom were actors who had performed in South Africa. Schlesinger's name was removed during the trial. 'Eventually, on advice, Mr Cathie withdrew the case against Mr Schlesinger, and the latter paid £1 000 towards the case.' Like many of the lawsuits against IW, it was something that he could pay to make go away.

'Cameras, Get Ready!'

187 *blank cartridges*   Unless otherwise noted, the description of the shoot comes from the *Sunday Times*, 27 January 1918.

188 *The operations have been*   *Rand Daily Mail*, 15 January 1918.

189 *At Isandlwana, hundreds*   Excluding Reuters, other reports state that all the battles were filmed not on location but in the Transvaal because of the fear of a real battle breaking out, although not for the same reason as on *Winning a Continent*. It had only been 12 years 'since the bloody Natal (Bambatha) Rebellion of 1906 which had reopened old wounds'. See Coghlan, 'The World's Biggest Battle Picture'.

190 *Despite the outbursts*   The article appeared in the *Sunday Times* several weeks later. It is unclear whether IW vetted the article, but given that it was edited (perhaps written) by his friend Joseph Langley Levy, perhaps not.

shared with Albrecht   Rosenthal, Unpublished biography of IW Schlesinger.

but I did it in the end   Ibid.

Death at the River

192 *a man named Petersen*   *Rand Daily Mail*, 14 March 1918. This was quite possibly the actor Holger Petersen, who was playing the villain Carl Schneider in the movie.

Herman Rausch   Ibid.

194 *no intention of interfering*   Parsons, *Black and White Bioscope*.

Cetshwayo's kraal   *Stage & Cinema*, 16 February 1916.

'Help, Boats!'

198 *any human witness*   Rosenthal, Unpublished biography of IW Schlesinger.

199 *very hearty cheers*   *Rand Daily Mail*, 22 March 1917.

200 *money has been spent like water*   A special musical score was commissioned from David Foote, the man who had once played the organ for Paul Kruger during the showing of Edgar Hyman's footage of him entering the Raadsaal. The score he came up with, quite unusually for the time, included, according to Rosenthal, 'incidental *kraal* music that conveyed Zulu melodies using European instruments.'

A New Babylon

201 *the South African version*   *Rand Daily Mail*, 20 September 1919.

206 *early June 1919*   *Rand Daily Mail*, 4 June 1919.

208 *rub his eyes in astonishment*   *Stage & Cinema*, 14 June 1919.

   how they had built the mammoth set   One of the few news reports about the Great Stairway's construction says it took seven months, but the more likely figure is about ten weeks.

Epilogue

212 *hugely popular 'Our Gang'*   Parsons, *Black and White Bioscope*.

   the very first documentary   *Nanook of the North* also contained staged scenes.

214 *James Dixon Williams*   See notes for 'The Belly of the Beast'.

216 *the island of Capri*   Whether or not IW was jinxed in his movie productions, he had his share of fires and deaths. Two of his directors died unnaturally: Harold Shaw died in 1926 in a car crash in Hollywood; Horace Lisle Lucoque, after running into financial difficulty on a version of *She* in 1925, gassed himself in his flat in West Kensington. JD Williams, who worked with IW in London, died in a Manhattan psychiatric ward in 1934 after a nervous breakdown, said to have been brought on by his worries over his work in the film industry.

   Mabel May   Mabel's last movie was *Madcap of the Veld*, which was released in December 1920.

   holding his young son's hand   *The Outspan*, reprinted in *The African World*, 23 April 1927.

217 *600 cinemas*   *Time*, 27 July 1953.

219 *The moment the mystic letters*   The *Rand Daily Mail* of 27 January 1923 article was titled 'Prejudice Against Local Productions'. The journalist said that even though the attitude was skewered against IW, 'let us hope "The Blue Lagoon" will change all that.' By that stage, it was too late.

advertising in movie houses   Stodel, *The Audience is Waiting*.

221 *The Capitol*   The theatre still exists today, as a parking garage.

222 *made an impact*   The Hyman/Heydenreich brothers (the name difference was speculated on, too, by journalist Stephen Black) were said to be from a family that had made its money in cement in Portuguese East Africa, and their names cropped up occasionally in newspapers, sometimes to do with mining in parts of Africa. IW clearly wanted to paint a bad picture of them, and it was almost certainly he who interested Black in writing a series of scathing articles about the brothers in *The Sjambok*. A legal settlement with the brothers killed Black's publication, mostly because IW suddenly refused to insure it any more. The dubious news reports about the brothers and the way they ran Kinemas left a shadow over them, and within a year IW had bought their company.

223 *the domain of material things*   Commemorative programme for the opening.

224 *were also good friends*   In a rare biography of Isie Smuts, Mabel May comes across as her close friend and is especially praised for her efforts in Hollywood during World War II to help Mrs Smuts – who was affectionately called 'Ouma' (Afrikaans for granny) – raise funds for Allied troops. The two women met often – 'The theatre king's wife loved Mrs Smuts' – and IW put his theatres at the disposal of her fundraising projects. On Isie's 74th birthday, in 1944, Mabel wanted to plan something special, and in America and London she spread word of the modest, little-known wife of the famous general, and of her 'war work'. Artists from all over agreed to take part in 'a tribute such as no man or woman is likely to receive again'. A broadcast was organised that brought together the BBC, the American Office of War Information and the SABC. 'New York and London, Hollywood and Johannesburg forged the links.' On 22 December 1944, 35 stars wished Ouma Smuts happy birthday and hoped that the money would pour in for soldiers. 'Sybil Thorndike spoke,' 'Gracie Fields sang in Afrikaans,' and there was John Gielgud, 'Deanna Durbin singing ... Tauber too, and Nelson Eddy, Joan Crawford and Dorothy Lamour, Bing Crosby crooning, Gary Cooper, Eddie Cantor were there. ... "Happy Birthday" they all said.'

225 *90 companies*   Rosenthal, Unpublished biography of IW Schlesinger.

226 *650 000 trees*   Ibid.

its own railway line   Stodel.

227 *Whitehall Court*   IW's first London apartment was in Grosvenor House, overlooking Hyde Park. In early 1923, with Mabel several months pregnant, they settled into an apartment at 2 Whitehall Court, where other residents included George Bernard Shaw and HG Wells.

228 *exotic birds in its courtyard gardens*   A lengthy description of the
mansion/apartment house featured prominently in the *Sunday Times*
on 13 September 1925. The massive Italianate edifice, with its white
colonnaded exterior and red-tiled roof, looked like it had taken
elements of its design from an Eaton Square townhouse, a Park
Avenue apartment building and Marcus Loew's Long Island mansion,
Pembroke. A journalist who was taken for a tour said it resembled,
from a distance, 'a prince's palace in a wooded setting'. On either
side of three sets of Art Deco brass doors the façade facing the
street presented classical arches, Tuscan-like columns, elegant sash
windows and above them a long decorative balcony. The shining
cream-coloured walls stretched the entire four sides of the property,
about two acres in all. Past the panelled lobby, a series of loggias on
the three floors were decorated with large ornate concrete vases
that overlooked the expansive central gardens. Of the 36 original
apartments, some had been connected to make a 'house' – each with
the latest devices and fittings, and bathrooms the size of a bedroom
– with the Schlesingers in the biggest of them all. Stretching across
much of the second storey, the Schlesinger apartment had floors
of black-and-white marble. In the reception rooms, statues of
Venus and Apollo on marble stands stood near the entrance, with
a large palm in a marble jardinière. Mahogany chairs and settees
were upholstered in gold and mauve silk. Richly embroidered silk
curtains were draped across the full-length windows, and gilded
French doors opened up on to the north-facing exterior verandahs,
the view looking out onto rolling veld and gardens that had turned
green after the early summer thunderstorms. Each room had its
own colour scheme, shades of rose, green, blue. The dining room,
the most ornate, had walnut panels interspersed with carved Ionic
capitals, the mantelpieces decorated with Sienna marble inlay, each
end of the fireplace done with *pietra dura* inlays of birds and flowers,
the chairs around the long table covered in Genoa velvet. The room
'was clearly modelled upon the dining rooms of the old baronial
halls of England'. Even the blue-carpeted breakfast room had three
original oil paintings, and for the day and night nurseries of their
son, John, an artist had painted scenes from a dozen fairytales like
Little Red Riding Hood and Little Jack Horner. On the roof was 'a
typical American roof garden' and below, in the courtyard gardens,
a menagerie was growing. It had been stocked with 150 species of
birds, many of them indigenous, but also parrots, parakeets, macaws,
cockatoos, and several imported from Japan. They were also awaiting
a lion cub, for John.

   his American passport   Rosenthal.

FILMOGRAPHY

Movies, Cartoons and Serials Made by African Films
(A compilation of lists from Neil Parsons and the National Film, Video and
 Sound Archives)

Still in existence:
The Story of the Rand (1916)

The Gun Runner (1916)

Winning a Continent/De Voortrekkers (1916) https://www.youtube.com/
  watch?v=ZQGS_1YHOu8 (edited)

The Symbol of Sacrifice (1917) https://www.youtube.com/
  watch?v=3Vbp1URahrM (edited)

The Mealy Kids (1917)

King Solomon's Mines (1918)

Copper Mask (1919)

Lost:
The Artist's Dream (1916)

The Splendid Waster (1916)

A Zulu's Devotion (1916)

The Silver Wolf (1916)

The Illicit Liquor Seller (1916)

A Kract Affair (1916)

The Water Cure (1916)

£20,000 (1916)

Sonny's Little Bit (1916)

Gloria (1916)

A Tragedy in The Veld (1916)

The Piccanin's Christmas (1917)

Adventures of Ranger Focus (1917)

Second Adventures of Ranger Focus
  (1917)

Don't You Believe It (1917)

The Major's Dilemma (1917)

Crooks & Christmas (1917)

A Border Scourge (1917)

And Then – ? (1917)

Zulutown: The Skating Rink (1917)

The Zulutown Races (1917)

Bond & Word (1918)

Voice of The Waters (1918)

The Bridge (1918)

Allan Quatermain (1919)

The Stolen Favourite (1919)

Fallen Leaves (1919)

With Edged Tools (1919)

Prester John (1920)

The Man Who was Afraid (1920)

Isban Israel, The Buried City (1920)

Madcap of The Veld (1921)

The Vulture's Prey (1921)

Swallow (1921)

The Blue Lagoon (1923)

Reef of Stars (1924)

Sarie Marais (1931)

Moedertjie (1931)

REFERENCES

Books

Acutt, Renault. *Reminiscences of a Rand Pioneer: The Memoirs of Renault Courtney Acutt* (Ravan Press, 1977).

Arvidson, Linda and Mrs DW Griffith. *When the Movies were Young* (Dover Publications, 1969).

Barlow, Arthur G. *Almost in Confidence* (JC Juta, 1952).

Barnes, John. *Filming the Boer War* (Bishopsgate Press, 1992).

Beavon, Keith. *Johannesburg: The Making and Shaping of the City* (Unisa Press, 2004).

Beevor, Antony. *The Mystery of Olga Chekohova: Was Hitler's Favourite Actress a Russian Spy?* (Viking, 2004).

Berger, Nathan. *Jewish Trails through Southern Africa* (Kayor, 1976).

Birchard, Robert. *Early Universal City* (Arcadia, 2009).

Bolitho, Hector. *My Restless Years* (Max Parrish, 1962).

Brooke, Brian. *My Own Personal Star, an Autobiography* (The Limelight Press, 1978).

Brownlow, Kevin. *Hollywood: The Pioneers* (Knopf, 1980).

Bruce, Sir Michael. *Peaks of Hazard* (Bobbs Merrill, 1929).

Busch, Noel. *My Unconsidered Judgment* (Houghton Mifflin, 1944).

Bushnell, Brooks. *Directors and Their Films: A Comprehensive Reference* (McFarland, 2012).

Byron, Lewis. *Recollections of an Octogenarian* (Robinson, 1963).

Cartwright, AP. *The Corner House: The Early History of Johannesburg* (Purnell, 1965).

Chanan, Michael. *The Dream that Kicks* (Routledge, 1995).

Chilvers, Hedley. *Out of the Crucible* (Cassell & Co, 1929).

Chipkin, Clive. *Johannesburg Style: Architecture and Society 1880s–1960s* (David Philip, 1993).

Cohen, Louis. *Reminiscences of Johannesburg and London* (Robert Holden & Co, 1924).

Cohn, Roy and Sidney Zion. *Autobiography of Roy Cohn* (Lyle Stuart, 1988).

Collier, Joy. *The Purple and the Gold: The Story of Pretoria and Johannesburg* (Longmans, 1965).

Crafton, Donald. *The Talkies: American Cinema's Transition to Sound, 1926–1931* (University of California Press, 1999).

Crisp, Ronald. *The Outlanders: The Men Who Made Johannesburg* (Peter Davies, 1964).

De Forest, Lee. *Father of Radio* (Wilcox & Follett, 1950).

Devitt, Napier. *Memoirs of a Magistrate, Including Twenty-Five Years on the South African Bench* (HF & G Witherby, 1934).

Drinkwater, John. *The Life and Adventures of Carl Laemmle* (Putnam, 1931).

Emden, PH. *Randlords* (Hodder & Stoughton, 1935).

Feldberg, Leon. *South African Jewry* (Fieldhill Publishing Company, 1965).

Fitzpatrick, Sir Percy. *South African Memories* (Cassell, 1932).

Flather, Horace. The *Way of an Editor* (Purnell, 1977).

Fraser, Maryna. *Johannesburg Pioneer Journals 1888–1909* (Van Riebeeck Society, 1985).

Gatti, Attilio. *South of the Sahara* (Robert M McBride Company, 1945).

Gleich, Joshua (ed). *Hollywood on Location: An Industry History* (Rutgers University Press, 2019).

Gunther, John. *Inside Africa* (Harper & Brothers, 1955).

Gutsche, Thelma. *The History and Social Significance of Motion Pictures in South Africa 1895–1940* (Howard Timmins, 1972).

Hall, Sheldon. *Zulu With Some Guts Behind It: The Making of the Epic Movie* (Tomahawk, 2006).

Hertz, Carl. *A Modern Mystery Merchant: The Trials, Tricks and Travels of Carl Hertz, the Famous American Illusionist* (Hutchinson & Co, 1924).

Hertz, Joseph. *The Jew in South Africa* (Central News Agency, 1905).

Higson, Andrew (ed). *Young and Innocent? The Cinema in Britain 1896–1930* (University of Exeter Press, 2002).

Jacobsson, D. *Fifty Golden Years of the Rand* (Faber & Faber, 1936).

Jaikumar, Priya. *Cinema at the End of Empire: A Politics of Transition in Britain and India* (Duke University Press, 2006).

Jeppe, Carl. *Kaleidoscope Johannesburg* (JC Juta & Co, 1908).

Kaplan, Mendel and Marian Robertson. *Jewish Roots in the South African Economy* (C Struik Publishers, 1986).

Kindem, Gorham. *The International Movie Industry* (Southern Illinois University Press, 2000).

Knox, Patricia and Thelma Gutsche. *Do You Know Johannesburg?* (Unie-Volkspers, 1947).

Koszarski, Richard. *Hollywood on the Hudson, Film and Television in New York from Griffith to Sarnoff* (Rutgers University Press, 2008).

Leyds, *History of Johannesburg, The Early Years* (Nasionale Boekhandel, 1964).

Low, Rachael. *The History of the British Film*, 7 volumes (Various publishers, 1948–1985).

Macmillan, Allister (ed). *The Golden City: Johannesburg* (WH & L Collingridge, 1933).

Macmillan, Allister and Eric Rosenthal. *Homes of the Golden City* (Hortors Ltd, 1948).

Macmillan, Hugh. *An African Trading Empire: The Story of Susman Brothers & Wulfsohn, 1901–2005* (Bloomsbury Academic, 2017).

Macnab, Geoffrey. *J. Arthur Rank and the British Film Industry* (Routledge, 1993).

Maingard, Jacqueline. *South African National Cinema* (Routledge, 2007).

Maisels, Issie. *A Life at Law* (Jonathan Ball Publishers, 1998).

Manchal, Frank. *Film Study*, 4 volumes (Fairleigh Dickinson University Press, 1990).

May, Henry John. *Red Wine of Youth* (Cassell & Co, 1946).

McDonald, Tom. *Ouma Smuts* (Hurst & Blackett, 1945).

Meiring, Piet. *Inside Information* (Howard Timmins, 1973).

Murry, Marischal. *Union-Castle Chronicle 1853–1953* (Longmans, Green and Co, 1953).

Musiker, Naomi and Reuben. *Historical Dictionary of Greater Johannesburg* (Scarecrow Press, 1999).

Neame, LE. *City Built on Gold* (Central News Agency, 1960).

Parsons, Neil. *Black and White Bioscope: Making Movies Made in Africa 1899–1925* (Intellect/Protea, 2018).

Phillips, Lionel. *Some Reminiscences* (Ad Donker, 1986).

Preller, Gustav. *Piet Retief: Lewensgeskiedenis van die Groot Voortrekkers* (Die Nasionale Pers, 1920).

Pretorius, Major PJ. *Jungle Man* (George G Harrap, 1947).

Reed, Douglas. *Somewhere South of Suez* (Cape, 1950).

Reeve, Ada. *Take it for a Fact: A Record of My Seventy-Five Years on the Stage* (Heinemann, 1954).

Rider Haggard, H. *King Solomon's Mines* (Cassell & Co, 1886).

Rider Haggard, H. *Allan Quatermain* (Longmans, Green & Co, 1888).

Rider Haggard, H. *Diary of an African Journey* (C Hurst & Co, 2000).

Robinson, David. *From Peep Show to Palace: The Birth of American Film* (Columbia University Press, 1995).

Rosenthal, Eric. Unpublished biography of IW Schlesinger (Cambridge University Library).

Rosenthal, Eric. *Gold Bricks and Mortar* (Printing House Ltd, 1946).

Rosenthal, Eric. *The South African Saturday Book* (Hutchinson, 1949).

Rosenthal, Eric. *Other Men's Millions* (Howard Timmins, 1950).

Rosenthal, Eric (compiler). *South African Dictionary of National Biography* (Warne, 1966).

Rosenthal, Eric. *Stars and Stripes in Africa* (National Books Ltd, 1968).

Rosenthal, Eric. *Meet me at the Carlton: The Story of Johannesburg's Old Carlton Hotel* (Howard Timmins, 1972).

Rosenthal, Eric. *The Rand Rush* (Ad Donker, 1974).

Rosenthal, Eric. *Memories and Sketches* (Ad Donker, 1979).

Rotha, Paul. *The Film Till Now: A Survey of the Cinema* (Jonathan Cape & Harrison Smith, 1930).

Sachs, Bernard. *Multitude of Dreams* (Kayor Publishing House, 1949).

Shorten, John. *Johannesburg Saga* (John R Shorten, 1970).

Steyn, Richard. *Louis Botha: A Man Apart* (Jonathan Ball Publishers, 2018).

Stodel, Jack. *The Audience is Waiting* (Howard Timmins, 1962).

Sweet, Matthew. *Shepperton Babylon* (Faber & Faber, 2006).

Symonds, Francis Addington. *The Johannesburg Story* (Frederick Muller Ltd, 1953).

Taylor, CTC. *History of Rhodesian Entertainment, 1890–1930* (MO Collins, 1968).

Taylor, JB. *A Pioneer Looks Back* (Hutchinson & Co, 1939).

Tomaselli, Keyan. *The Cinema of Apartheid: Race and Class in South African Film* (Routledge, 1988).

Van de Waal, GM. *From Mining Camp to Metropolis: The Buildings of Johannesburg 1886–1940* (Chris van Rensburg Publications, 1987).

Van Diggelen, Tromp. *Worthwhile Journey: The Autobiography of Tromp van Diggelen* (Heinemann, 1955).

Walker, Eric Anderson. *A History of South Africa* (Longmans & Co, 1928)

Warren, Patricia. *Elstree: The British Hollywood* (New York Zoetrope, 1983).

Warren, Patricia. *British Film Studios: An Illustrated History* (Batsford, 2003).

Weinthal, Leo. *Memories, Mines and Millions: Being the Life of Sir Joseph B Robinson* (Simpkin Marshall, 1929).

Wentzel, J. *View from the Ridge: Johannesburg Retrospect* (David Philip, 1975).

Wilcox, Herbert. *Twenty-five Thousand Sunsets* (The Bodley Head, 1967).

Zierold, Normal. *The Moguls: Hollywood's Merchants of Myth* (Silman-James Press, 1991).

Periodicals and Newspaper Archives
African Life Jottings
Bioscope 1913–1925
Daily Mail 1900–1949
Exhibitors Herald 1915–1931
The Illustrated London News 1924
Kinematograph Weekly 1912–1930
Moving Picture World 1913–1925
Motion Picture News 1913–1925
The New York Times 1890–1949
The Outspan 1927–1933
Picturegoer 1914–1925
Rand Daily Mail 1899–1925

The Sjambok 1929–1931
South African Jewish Chronicle
South African Jewish Times
Stage & Cinema (*Stage, Cinema & SA Pictorial*, then *SA Pictorial*) 1915–1925
Sunday Times 1913–1925
The Times (London) 1900–1925
Wid's Daily (later *Film Daily*) 1913–1925

Articles and book chapters

Alexander, Caroline. 'The White Goddess of the Wangora'. *The New Yorker*, 31 March 1991.

'Alma in Wonderland'. *Picturegoer*, December 1925.

Arliss, LS. 'Sidakwa, What Our Natives Call Charlie Chaplin'. *The Outspan*, 27 January 1928.

Baneshik, Percy. 'The Early South African Movies'. *Jewish Affairs*, September 1987.

Birchard, Robert S. 'The Squaw Man'. *American Film* vol 23 (September 2014).

Black, Stephen. 'An Unauthorised and Inexact Biography by Posthumorous'. *The Sjambok*, 7 March 1930.

Brewster, Ben. '*Traffic in Souls*: An Experiment in Feature-Length Narrative Construction'. *Cinema Journal* vol 31, no 1 (Autumn 1991).

Burns, James. 'Biopics and Politics: The Making and Unmaking of the Rhodes Movies'. *Biography* vol 23, no 1 (Winter 2000).

'Business Abroad: Yankee Doodle on the Rand'. *Time*, 27 July 1953.

Cartwright, AP. 'The Little Man Set Up a Business Empire'. *Cape Argus*, 16 May 1960.

Clark, Alexis. 'How "The Birth of a Nation" Revived the Ku Klux Klan'. History.com, 24 August 2018.

Coetzee, Martin. 'Cinematographs, Crystal Valves and American Cultural Imperialism: the Role Played by IW Schlesinger's Media Organisations at the Genesis of South Africa's Film and Radio Industries, 1913–1937'. MHCS dissertation, University of Pretoria, 2019.

Coghlan, Mark. 'The World's Biggest Battle Picture'. *Soldiers of the Queen*, The Victorian Military Society (March 1996).

'Diamond Cut Diamond'. *Time*, 29 February 1932.

Duffey, Prof Alex. 'Early Motoring in South Africa'. *The Nongqai* vol 12, no 9B (Part I) (August 2021).

The Editors of Encyclopaedia Britannica. 'Motion Picture Patents Company'. Britannica Money, 19 July 1998.

'Fifty Years After – In Livingstone's Footsteps'. *Daily Telegraph*, series starting 22 December 1924.

Grosvenor, Elsie May Bell. 'Safari Through Changing Africa'. *National Geographic*, August 1953.

Gutsche, Thelma. 'Film Production in South Africa'. Unpublished article, Thelma Gutsche Papers, University of Cape Town Libraries: Special Collections (Manuscripts and Archives).

Gutsche, Thelma. Untitled article on working under Albrecht during World War II, Thelma Gutsche Papers, University of Cape Town Libraries: Special Collections (Manuscripts and Archives).

Hees, Edwin. 'The Voortrekkers on Film: From Preller to Pornography'. *Critical Arts: A Journal of Media Studies* vol 10, no 1 (1996).

Hofmeyr, Isabel. 'Popularizing History: The Case of Gustav Preller'. *The Journal of African History* vol 29, no 3 (1988).

Limb, Peter. 'An African Newspaper in Central Johannesburg: The Journalistic and Associational Context of *Abantu-Batho*'. In *The People's Paper: A Centenary History & Anthology of* Abantu-Batho, edited by Peter Limb, 298–317 (Wits University Press, 2018).

Maingard, Jacqueline. 'Projecting Modernity: Sol Plaatje's Touring Cinema Exhibition in 1920s South Africa'. In *Rural Cinema Exhibition and Audiences in a Global Context*, edited by Daniela Treveri Gennari, Danielle Hipkins and Catherine O'Rawe, 187–202 (Palgrave Macmillan, 2018).

Mandiringana, E and Stapleton, TJ. 'The Literary Legacy of Frederick Courteney Selous'. *History in Africa* vol 25 (1998).

North, CJ. 'Our Foreign Trade in Motion Pictures'. *Annals of the American Academy of Political and Social Science* vol 128 (November 1926), 100–108 (republished by Forgotten Books, 2018).

Parsons, Neil. 'Investigating the Origins of *The Rose of Rhodesia*, Part I: African Film Productions', and 'Part II: Harold Shaw Film Productions Ltd'. Screeningthepast.com, 23 July 2009.

Prechner, Marks. 'How the Cinema First Came to South Africa'. *The Outspan*, 23 June 1933.

Rapp, Dean and Charles Weber. 'British Film, Empire and Society in the Twenties: The "Livingstone" Film, 1923–1925'. *Historical Journal of Film, Radio and Television* vol 9, no 1 (1989).

Roberts, Andrew D. 'Africa on Film to 1940'. *History in Africa* 14 (1987).

Sandon, Emma. 'Preserving a Heritage? South African Archive Documentary, 1910–1940'. *Canadian Journal of Film Studies* vol 16, no 1 (Spring 2007).

Schlesinger, IW. South Africa's Destiny, As I See It'. *The Outspan*, 11 March 1927.

Sklar, Robert and David Cook. 'History of Film'. Britannica.com, updated 28 October 2024. https://www.britannica.com/art/history-of-the-motion-picture/Post-World-War-I-American-cinema.

'South Africa: His Father's Son'. *Time*, 2 August 1963.

Strebel, Elizabeth Grottle. '*The Voortrekkers*: A Cinematographic Reflection of Rising Afrikaner Nationalism'. *Film & History: An Interdisciplinary Journal of Film and Television Studies* vol 9, no 2 (May 1979).

Tucker, Percy. 'IW Schlesinger' (private article provided by author).

'Waterman'. 'Some Memories of the Great IW Schlesinger'. *South African Insurance Magazine*, July 1955.

Willan, Brian. '"Cinematographic Calamity" or "Soul-Stirring Appeal to Every Briton": *Birth of a Nation* in England and South Africa, 1915–1931'. *Journal of Southern African Studies* vol 39, no 3 (September 2013).

Other

The City of Pretoria and Districts: An Official Handbook Describing the Social, Official, Farming, Mining, and General Progress and Possibilities of the Administrative Capital and Surrounding Districts (South African Railways, 1913).

Colosseum Johannesburg: The Wonder Theatre of the Miracle City. Gilded 50-page programme for the opening of the Colosseum, 1933.

Encyclopaedia of South African Theatre, Film, Media and Performance (ESAT).

'Inventing Entertainment: The Early Motion Pictures and Sound Recordings of the Edison Companies'. Library of Congress digital collection, no date.

'London's Silent Cinemas Map'. Londonssilentcinemas.com, no date.

'Music for Silent Film: A Guide to Resources at the Library of Congress'. Library of Congress digital collection, no date.

'A New Era in Electrical Entertainment'. Encyclopedia.com, 2019.

ABOUT THE AUTHOR

Ted Botha has worked for Reuters in New York and has been published in *The New York Times, Esquire, The Telegraph, Condé Nast Traveler* and *Outside*. He has written numerous books, including *Daisy de Melker*, the forensic thriller *The Girl with the Crooked Nose* and *Flat/White*, about living as an immigrant in a chaotic and battered tenement building in Harlem, New York. He has also written the novel *The Animal Lover*. See more at www.tedbotha.com.

www.ingramcontent.com/pod-product-compliance
Lightning Source LLC
Chambersburg PA
CBHW072135090426

42739CB00013B/3200